VCs OF THE FIRST WORLD WAR:

CAMBRAI 1917

VCs of the First World War:

CAMBRAI 1917

GERALD GLIDDON

SUTTON PUBLISHING

First published in the United Kingdom in 2004 by
Sutton Publishing Limited · Phoenix Mill
Thrupp · Stroud · Gloucestershire · GL5 2BU

British Library Cataloguing in Publication Data
A catalogue record for this book is available from the British Library.

ISBN 0-7509-3409-3

Typeset in 10/13pt Sabon.
Typesetting and origination by
Sutton Publishing Limited.
Printed and bound in England by
J.H. Haynes & Co. Ltd, Sparkford.

CONTENTS

Acknowledgements	vii	R.W.L. Wain	121
Prefatory Note	ix	R. McBeath	127
Introduction	xi	C.E. Spackman	132
		J. Sherwood-Kelly	136
E.A. McNair	1	H. Strachan	147
W.R. Cotter	5	J. McAulay	156
E.N. Mellish	14	G.W.B. Clare	162
E.F. Baxter	22	C.E. Gourley	167
R.B.B. Jones	26	S.T.D. Wallace	173
G.W. Chafer	32	N.B. Elliott-Cooper	178
A.H. Procter	36	R. Gee	182
J. Erskine	42	J. Thomas	197
W. Hackett	46	W.N. Stone	200
A.H.H. Batten-Pooll	51	A.M.C. McReady Diarmid	205
W. Jackson	55	G.H.T. Paton	210
J. Hutchinson	59	Gobind Singh	215
N.V. Carter	63	A.M. Lascelles	222
W.B. Butler	68	J.S. Emerson	230
F. Hobson, M.J. O'Rourke,		H.J. Nicholas	237
H. Brown and O.M. Learmonth	72	W. Mills	243
R.H. Hanna and F. Konowal	89		
H.F. Parsons	101	*Sources*	248
S.J. Day	104	*Bibliography*	256
A.E. Shepherd	114	*Index*	258

ACKNOWLEDGEMENTS

I should like to thank the staff of the following institutions for their assistance during the research for this book: the Commonwealth War Graves Commission, the Imperial War Museum, the National Army Museum, and the National Archives. In addition, I should like to thank the archivists and curators of the many county archives, regimental museums and libraries who have replied to my requests for information.

Where recently taken photographs have been used, their owners have been acknowledged in the individual illustration.

As with my previous seven books in the 'VCs of the First World War' series, Donald C. Jennings of Florida has been extremely kind in allowing me to reproduce many of his photographs of both graves or memorials. In addition David Harvey, author of *Monuments to Courage*, has very kindly given permission to use illustrations from his book.

Most of the maps reproduced in this book have been taken from the *Official History of the Great War – Military Operation – France and Belgium*, HMSO.

Other individuals who have been of great help in many ways include first and foremost Peter Batchelor and Dr Graham Keech; John Bolton, Steve Brown, Andrew England, David Fletcher, Winifred Gliddon, Philippe Gorczynski, Peter Harris, Dennis Pillinger and Steve Snelling. Other people whose names are not mentioned here have been acknowledged in the list of sources at the end of the book.

PREFATORY NOTE

The arrangement of this book in the 'VCs of the First World War' series requires a note of explanation. The contents of the previous volumes, which followed either a particular year or main battles, meant there were gaps, and there was always going to be the need of a volume dealing with the men who won the VC on the Western Front at other periods. These gaps were the period in 1916 prior to the Battle of the Somme, i.e. from February to June, and the period from August to December 1917, which dealt with fronts other than those of the Ypres Salient. These periods pertain to the men who gained their VCs during the Battle of Cambrai.

With this book's publication, coverage of the Western Front theatre is concluded, leaving only the thirteenth and final volume in the series, which will cover the lives of the forty-six military men who won the VC in other theatres: this volume will be entitled *The Sideshows*.

INTRODUCTION

1915 had been a year of considerable disappointment for the Allies, culminating with the disastrous of Battle of Loos in September and October and the subsequent replacement of Commander-in-Chief Sir John French by Sir Douglas Haig on 15 December.

The main action on the Western Front in early 1916 was now to take place on the French-held sector at Verdun, where the great battle began with German successes on 21 February. It was the beginning of a battle of attrition that was to last for nearly six months and resulted in bleeding both the French and German Armies to a point of utter exhaustion. Neither side could possibly claim the battle as a victory.

At a conference of Allied commanders held at Chantilly in December 1915 it had been agreed that the Allied powers should act in harness and concentrate their energies in the main theatres, and the suggestion of an Anglo–French offensive north of the River Somme was first mooted by the French at this time. It was not an idea which found favour with Sir Douglas Haig, who was keener on the idea of an offensive to the north, in the Second Army sector. However, Anglo–French cooperation was the most important issue at the time, and the choice of a battlefield astride the River Somme was not one of Haig's choosing.

As the year of 1916 progressed it was obvious that the original contribution in any major offensive of the French Army was to be diminished by their continuing losses at Verdun. Now only six of their divisions were to take part in the planned operations, with two in reserve. The British involvement was to include nineteen divisions; and the date of the battle was fixed for the end of June, and then put back to 1 July.

Although it appeared that the British were doing little more than holding their ground in France and Belgium in the first six months of 1916, a considerable number of raids were carried out, often with the intention of keeping the Germans guessing about where the known Allied offensive was to take place. During the first months of the year operations which led to the awards of no fewer than thirteen Victoria Crosses were carried out at Hooge and St Eloi in Belgium, and in France at the Hohenzollern Redoubt, Blairville, Vimy Ridge, Méaulte, Givenchy, Calonne, Armentières, and Richebourg l'Avoué.

After the Battle of the Somme, in which fifty-one men gained the Victoria Cross (*VCs of the Somme*), came to an end in November 1916, with a total of about one million casualties involving British, French and German troops, the two sides became increasingly bogged down in a war of attrition. In order to try to break this deadlock the enemy planned to build a new line of defence in depth that would be divided up into a series of zones against which they would 'invite' their opponents to attack, thus ensnaring them into a trap that would be difficult to escape from. This line was to be called the 'Siegfried Stellung' and was to be known by the British as the Hindenburg Line. It stretched from the British front at Arras to Laffaux, six miles north-east of Soissons.

The enemy had been preparing this line for several months, when, on 4 February 1917, they retreated to their new defensive positions, at the same time leaving behind them a trail of total destruction involving roads, buildings, the cutting down of trees and the poisoning of water supplies.

Just over two months later, on Easter Monday (9 April), the British First and Third Armies made a surprise attack through showers of sleet and snow on positions around Arras, including the heights of Vimy Ridge. It was a great success, and the Canadians completed their capture of the ridge the following day. The last stages of the Battle of Arras were carried out on 24 May. The men who gained the VC at this period are covered in the volume *Arras & Messines 1917*.

On 15 August the Canadians attacked to the north-west of Lens on a wide front with the intention of capturing the important Hill 70 by assault, together with several villages just outside Lens. Five German counter-attacks were repulsed, and by the time the operations ceased a few days later six VCs had been won by members of the Canadian Expeditionary Force.

As a new tactic, and possibly encouraged by the April success at Vimy Ridge, Sir Douglas Haig was considering an offensive that would avoid the usual necessity of very long artillery preparation and a concomitant lack of surprise. Already as the result of the first outing of tanks at Flers in September 1916 he had expressed his faith in the future of the tank as a battle-winning weapon by placing an order for a thousand more to be produced.

In June 1917 Lt Col J.F.C. Fuller, staff officer to Brig Gen H. Elles, commander of the Tank Corps, drew up a plan for a large tank raid to take place in the Cambrai area that would smash through the much vaunted German defensive positions of the Hindenburg Line. Apart from this considerable challenge the landscape was considered to be ideal as it did not have a low water-table or consist of ground which had been continually churned up and destroyed by artillery fire. Fuller's battle plans were slightly modified in August, and in mid-September Haig discussed the proposal with Sir Julian Byng, commander of the Third Army, who was also keen on the idea and approved Fuller's blueprint.

The town of Cambrai had fallen to the Germans in August 1914, and since then had become a very important centre of enemy communications. The two main obstacles for the British were the Canal du Nord (still not completed but a formidable obstacle in the west) and in the east the St Quentin Canal. It was considered that the wooded area around Havrincourt Wood would be particularly suitable for the concealment of tanks.

Haig informed Byng that he could allow him nineteen infantry divisions, together with the whole of the newly formed Tank Corps. However, there was a catch, as fourteen of the divisions were under strength, having already taken part in the exhausting Third Ypres Battle, which had begun on 31 July and was not going well for the Allies. Operating in the mud of the Passchendaele area was not the ideal place for men to fight, let alone tanks, which could barely make progress at all.

As indicated above, the Flanders battle was not going well and, coupled with the defeat of the Italian Army at Caporetto in late October, Haig was in need of some good news, and was determined not to get into yet another battle of attrition that would simply bleed away the lives of his troops. If a victory was not achieved within forty-eight hours, he reasoned, then the attack would be called off and a new line established. He must have known, too, that he just did not have enough men to exploit a real success even if one was achieved.

In conditions of great secrecy the tanks were ferried up by train from the Somme area near Bray between 15 and 18 November, with some of the carriages giving way under the weight. To maintain security they were brought up at night and then hidden in woods, under camouflage nets, farm buildings or in houses. When they were unloaded from the trains they were driven in bottom gear in order to keep noise levels to the minimum. On the eve of 20 November Brig Gen Hugh Elles issued a special order to his troops of the 'England expects' type message. He told them that the Tank Corps would 'have the chance for which it has been waiting for many months – to operate on good going in the van of the battle'. Furthermore, he told them that he would be leading the attack himself, in the centre of the division, in a tank named *Hilda*.

Each of the tank battalions due to take part consisted of thirty-six machines, with six in support: their task was to break the Hindenburg Line and its supports. The plan was for 378 tanks to play a leading part on a front of four miles. Thirty-two of them were to be used specifically for tearing large chunks in the German wire, to pave the way for the infantry to move forward and, in turn, for the cavalry to then exploit the gaps created. This would lead to the capture of the Bourlon Ridge and Cambrai, with the subsequent advantage of observation towards Valenciennes, together with the creation of bridgeheads over the Sensée River. Haig was particularly aware of the importance of the capturing of Bourlon Ridge, which would include the wood as well as the village of the same name that was to the east.

The much-vaunted Hindenburg Line comprised three sets of double trenches, the first having advanced posts, the second a wide fire trench, and, 200 yards back, a support trench. A mile further on was the Hindenburg support line, another double trench system, and further on again six belts of barbed wire.

On the right of the battlefield the 6th, 20th and 12th Divisions were to break the Hindenburg defences between Crèvecoeur and Bonavis securing the line of the St Quentin Canal. Moving up slightly after the initial advance, the 29th Division, after crossing the canal at Marcoing and Masnières, would form bridgeheads.

On the left the 62nd West Riding Division and 51st Highland Division were going to support the 36th Ulster Division towards the Cambrai–Bapaume road and the village of Moeuvres. Once Havrincourt Village, Flesquières, Graincourt and Cantaing were taken, the British would then be able to bring up their reserves, together with cavalry, and capture the village of Bourlon in the north-east.

Lt Col Fuller suggested a tank advance combined closely with infantry cooperation, a plan which had been practised in training. Fuller provided details of the plan to Brig Gen Hugh Elles and the divisional commanders. However, Maj Gen G.M. Harper, in command of the 51st Highland Division on the left of the battlefield, seemed to think that he knew better. The enemy had conducted raids in which they took prisoners, from whom they had gathered that the British were up to something. Even the use of tanks was hinted at; but probably not the numbers, as this figure would not have been common knowledge. As a result of this information the German 54th Division was put on full alert and reserves were brought into the area. By pure chance, troops from the German 107th Division detrained at Cambrai on 19 November and came under the wing of the German 54th Division: expecting an assault was one thing, but the scale of it was another.

Zero hour on the 6-mile front was to be 6.20 a.m. on 20 November. The artillery began on time and as it accompanied the attack it also fired smoke shells over a two-mile front in order to screen the British advance, in particular in the Flesquières sector.

The tank-led infantry advance began well, with many Germans taken by surprise. Readers may remember that it was still early, and there was also a thick mist as well as the early morning gloom. To see these great monsters appearing to bear down on you must have been a frightening experience. In many places the second line of German trenches, known as the Brown Line, were reached, and on the right the 12th Division had quickly reached the third, or Blue Line.

The main problem in the otherwise successful attack was the village of Flesquières, which although not on particularly high ground was still high enough to look down towards the approaching attackers, and behind it one could see the spires of Cambrai itself. Unfortunately it was also a boundary line between the III and IV Corps, and a considerable toll was taken of British tanks by a concealed German battery.

We have seen that Maj Gen Harper considered that he knew better than Lt Col Fuller, and rather than organising a close cooperation between tanks and infantry his idea was to bunch tanks together or brigade the advance guard so that they could push ahead over the fire trenches, leaving the main body of tanks to support infantry-clearing operations. He also ordered that the infantry should follow at a distance of a hundred yards. Not surprisingly, the infantry had trouble in struggling to negotiate the narrow passages left in the wake of the tanks. They were in extended order rather than in file.

Further to the left of the battlefield the 62nd Division moved along the Canal du Nord and captured Havrincourt village and Graincourt. 86th Brigade reached as far as the Cambrai–Bapaume Road, and the 36th Ulster Division also made progress. By noon the Hindenburg support line had been captured over a wide area. On the right, troops of 12th Division created a defensive flank on the Bonavis Ridge and seventy tanks moved forward to the St Quentin Canal. The 29th Division in particular was doing very well and had reached Marcoing by midday. Almost as a lone gesture, at about 3.30 p.m. B Squadron of the Fort Garry Horse managed to cross the canal at Masnières by a lock bridge and scatter a German battery before they were forced to dismount and return on foot in the dark.

Apart from the problem at Flesquières and the underuse of the cavalry, the British had a very successful opening day: numerous villages had been captured and over 8,000 prisoners taken. When the news of the British progress reached home, church bells rang out for the first time since the start of the war, although nobody knows who gave the instructions. Successful though many of the tanks were, 178 were either knocked out or failed to reach their objectives.

On 21 November the British continued their advance, but were already pretty exhausted. However, Fontaine Notre Dame, two and a half miles to the west of Cambrai, was captured. Flesquières, which had been manned by a 500-strong German garrison, was deserted as the enemy had left with their wounded during the night. Cantaing was taken, together with 300 prisoners, and the Germans made a counter-attack against the 36th Ulster Division, capturing Moeuvres in the process. Overall the momentum of the British advance slowed considerably.

On the 22nd, despite what had been said about victory after 48 hours, Haig decided to continue the battle after calling a halt for rest and reorganisation. Gains were consolidated. But to the west of Cambrai Fontaine was retaken by the enemy, who forced troops from the 51st and 62nd Divisions out of the village. The respite given to the British troops allowed time for the enemy to reinforce, which they were not slow to do.

On the 23rd Haig ordered Byng to bring IV Corps supported by V Corps to try to capture the all-important Bourlon positions; but this was to no avail, resulting in the familiar Western Front slogging match of heavy casualties to both sides in horrendous conditions, which they endured for five days. During this time the British lost another 4,000 men.

On 24 November the British made gains at Moeuvres.

On the 27th the 62nd Division and the Guards were given what was a desperate chance to capture Bourlon, the village as well as Fontaine Notre Dame. The attempt was unsuccessful, as it was rushed and ill conceived. Owing to a shortage of infantrymen dismounted cavalry were brought in, but it didn't alter the situation. In addition, an enemy attack west of Moeuvres was repulsed.

Although on the 29th the British made a slight gain at Bourlon Wood, it was clear that the Germans were preparing for a major counter-attack: the British were desperately caught out by the speed of the onslaught, which almost led to the capture of complete divisions.

On the 30th the enemy, who had reacted so swiftly in arranging for reserves when threatened, launched a massive counter-attack both in the south of the battlefield and in the north. They attacked Vendhuille, Bourlon Wood and Moeuvres and penetrated British positions at La Vacquerie and Gouzeaucourt. It was on this day that Boy Bradford VC was killed. A British counter-attack later regained La Vacquerie.

On 1 December Gonnelieu was retaken, but the British withdrew from the Masnières Salient. By the 7th many of the British troops were back where they had started on 20 November, and some were even back beyond their former line. The enemy casualties in the Cambrai battle had been about 45,000 killed and taken prisoner, with the British suffering equal losses.

The result of the battle was a bitter disappointment to the Allies, and no fewer than four inquiries were conducted in order to find out just how the Germans were so successful in their counter-attack and why the plan had failed. The main reason seemed to be a lack of training of junior officers, NCOs and men. Although this might sound a bit of a whitewash, it may well have been the answer: the novelty of men and tanks working closely together in a landscape that was not only open but also not a mud bath was just too much to be taken on board at this stage of the war.

However, a vision of how to conduct a twentieth-century battle had been glimpsed, and both sides were to learn positively from the experience. For the British the tide began to turn nine months later, in August 1918.

Gerald Gliddon, Brooke, 2004

E.A. MCNAIR

Near Hooge, Belgium, 14 February 1916

(David Harvey)

It is often overlooked that things were pretty quiet on the Western Front in 1916 before the beginning of the Battle of the Somme on 1 July; but, nevertheless, no fewer than thirteen Victoria Crosses were won in Belgium or France within the first six months of the year.

On 14 February Eric Archibald McNair was the first Allied soldier to win a VC on the Western Front since William Young had won his to the east of Foncquevillers just before Christmas in 1915. McNair was a temporary lieutenant with the 9th (Service) Battalion Royal Sussex Regiment (73rd Brigade) 24th Division and won the award close to the Menin Road at Hooge in Belgium.

Prior to the commencement of the German offensive against Verdun the enemy carried out a series of operations against different sections of the Ypres Salient. On the night of 13 February trenches at Hooge and Sanctuary Wood were bombarded, and, according to the 73rd Brigade Diary, on the 14th activity began with British Artillery firing on a section of the German line of trenches that was later reported as being 'knocked in'. The enemy duly retaliated during the early afternoon and heavily shelled Hooge and later carried out a bombardment against an important observation post called the 'The Bluff' close to the Ypres–Comines canal 2 miles south of Ypres. At 5.30 p.m. an order to stand-to was given, and an SOS signal was sent up at Hooge when it was being shelled. An hour later the enemy blew a mine near a map position called H.16, and the inner edge of the crater was soon occupied by members of the 9th Royal Sussex Battalion.

The brigade diary seemed to have played down the story of what really happened that day, failing to tell the full story or even mention that the enemy mine caused a very great deal of damage as well as many casualties. The account even described the enemy as making a 'very feeble effort' after they had blown the mine. However, a later issue of the *Sussex Daily News* described what had really happened to the battalion as a 'terrible ordeal'.

The 24th Divisional War Diary stated that the 'enemy blew 2 mines in front of our trench H.16-H.18', and in an Intelligence Summary it stated that the enemy had been prevented from an attack at Hooge on the 14th 'by one of our Lewis guns' that opened fire on a German machine-gun when it was being brought forward. A company of the 9th Royal Sussex repulsed the enemy at position H.18.

Later, a member of the machine-gun section of the battalion who came from Brighton wrote an account of the events to a friend at the end of February:

> . . . We took over trenches last Thursday week, and on the following two days we suffered one of the worst bombardments of the war. Day and night, continually, our front line trenches and support trenches were shelled with high explosives. On the Monday the bombardment reached its height. The gun team I was in went on duty at 2 o'clock and by 3 o'clock the full fury of the German bombardment commenced.
>
> I cannot describe what it was like in words. At 4 o'clock only myself and another fellow were left with the gun . . . We were thrown to the bottom of the trench five times . . . about 6 o'clock, when the whole trench rocked like a boat. It first seemed to go up at one end, throwing me on my chum, and then throwing us back again. It took me a few minutes to realise that the Germans had exploded a mine . . .

The two men were probably saved from being buried alive by a section of corrugated iron, but they had great trouble with clearing a large quantity of earth that had poured down over their shelter. After they had got over their initial shock they found that what had a few minutes ago been trenches was now 'simply flat ground'. Supports then arrived and they were able to lay their gun, aiming at a gap in the British line 300 yards away, while their colleagues charged for first occupation of the crater.

The above letter gives the background of the winning of three DCMs, together with T/Lt McNair's VC. The official citation of his deed was published in the *London Gazette* of 30 March as follows:

> . . . Eric Archibald McNair, Lieutenant, Royal Sussex Regiment. When the enemy exploded a mine, Lieutenant McNair and many men of two platoons were hoisted into the air, and many were buried. But, though much shaken, he at once organized a party with a machine-gun to man the near edge of the crater, and opened rapid fire on a large party of the enemy who were advancing. The enemy were driven back, leaving many dead. Lieutenant McNair then ran back for reinforcements, and sent to another unit for bombs, ammunition and tools to replace those buried. The communication trench being blocked, he went across the open under heavy fire, and led up the

reinforcements the same way. His prompt and plucky action undoubtedly saved the situation.

McNair received his VC at Buckingham Palace from the King at an investiture on 20 May 1916, and soon returned to the front, being severely wounded on 18 August 1916 by gun-shot wounds to his shoulder and back. He was subsequently invalided home and not passed fit for service until the end of January 1917. At some point he had managed to get home to India for a short leave, but while there he became ill. He was passed fit for service again and put on probation for staff work, attending a special staff course. After being in service at home for several months he was attached to the staff and in 1918 left for the Italian Front, where he was attached to the General Staff, GHQ, Italian Expeditionary Force. It was possible that the Prince of Wales, a friend from college days, assisted in getting him the position.

However, it appears that he was not in fact at all fit for active service at this time: on 27 June his family were alerted that he was seriously ill, and six days later 'dangerously ill'. He was invalided back to 11 General Hospital in Genoa in Northern Italy, where he died of amoebic dysentery on 12 August. He was twenty-four years old.

At this time Genoa was a base for Dominion Forces, and McNair was buried as late as 8 November at Campo Santo Cemetery in the British Portion. The name of the cemetery was later changed to Staglieno Cemetery, and his grave reference, Plot I, B, 32, carried the inscription 'And I Know That His Commandment Is Life Eternal'. The CWG Register describes the cemetery as 'steeply terraced with numerous steps'.

After his death McNair's VC remained in his family and at one point was the property of Sir George Douglas McNair, one of Eric's brothers, who died in Torquay in 1967. The medal was bequeathed to the Royal Sussex Regimental Museum. Eric McNair's name is commemorated in the Regimental Memorial in Chichester Cathedral and as part of the VC display at the Regimental Museum. His deeds of February 1916 were written up twice in comic form, in *The Victor* on 1 May 1965 and 25 June 1977.

Eric Archibald McNair was born in Calcutta on 16 June 1894, second son of George McNair, a senior partner in Morgan & Co., solicitors, and his wife Isabella Frederica, née Gow. The family lived at 5 Harrington Street, Calcutta.

Eric left for England to attend Branksome College in Godalming, Surrey, where he was a pupil in Mr Sylvester's House. He moved on to Charterhouse in

Staglient Cemetery (*Commonwealth War Graves Commission*)

Horsham for three and a half years, where he joined the OTC and became Head of School. He was a classical scholar and head monitor at the school, a good athlete and an excellent disciplinarian. In midsummer 1913 he went up to Magdalen College, Oxford, where he had a Demyship (scholarship). It is possible that at this time he met the Prince of Wales, who was at the same college for a brief time, just before the outbreak of war. Their friendship was renewed five years later in 1918 on the Italian Front.

As a student in residence McNair was working for the Indian Civil Service examinations and was considered to be 'very clever', but the outbreak of the war in August 1914 put paid to his ambitions. He decided to join the Army and enlisted on 14 October as a second lieutenant in the 10th Royal Sussex Regiment. He was made a full lieutenant on 22 December and in August 1915 was transferred to the 9th Battalion and left for the front the following month. In October he was promoted to captain and company commander.

W.R. COTTER

Near Hohenzollern Redoubt, France, 6 March 1916

(*David Harvey*)

The 6th (Service) Battalion The Buffs (East Kent Regiment) was formed at Canterbury in August 1914 and became part of the 37th Brigade of the 12th Division. The division arrived in the area of the Hohenzollern Redoubt, near Bethune, in mid-February 1916, where they had been three months before. They took over from the Cavalry Corps, who, according to the official history, '. . . were holding the Quarries and Hohenzollern sectors from opposite Cité St Elie to opposite the dump of Fosse 8'.

Near the end of February the 170th Tunnelling Company Royal Engineers had completed three mines under the enemy's shallow system. It was decided that these mines should be blown as soon as possible, which would allow the British to recover a position close to the Triangle Crater called the Chord, which had once been the front line but was now in enemy hands.

The Chord ran along the front of the German line between the sites of the first two mines, A and B, and at mine C it changed its name to Little Willie. The three mines were duly fired on 2 March and most of the objectives were captured, except for a northern portion of the Chord. Over the next few days the enemy made strenuous efforts to retake the lost ground and in particular Mine A, which allowed the British to have good observation over their lines.

On 5 March the 36th Brigade was relieved by the 37th, whose HQ was based at Vermelles, and the 6th Buffs became the right battalion. According to the 37th Brigade Diary, their orders were to capture Triangle Trench and consolidate on the line the Chord–Big Willie, 50 yards south-east of its junction with the German trench running to the south of Triangle Crater:

> . . . We exploded a mine at midnight just south of Sap 6, close to the German front line to blow in hostile gallery; no attempt made to occupy crater by either side. Hostile Trench Mortars and artillery fire did some damage to Sticky Trench, Northampton Trench & Vigo Street. 5.10 a.m. enemy blew a small mine near Sap 2. No damage done. Neither side occupied crater. . . .

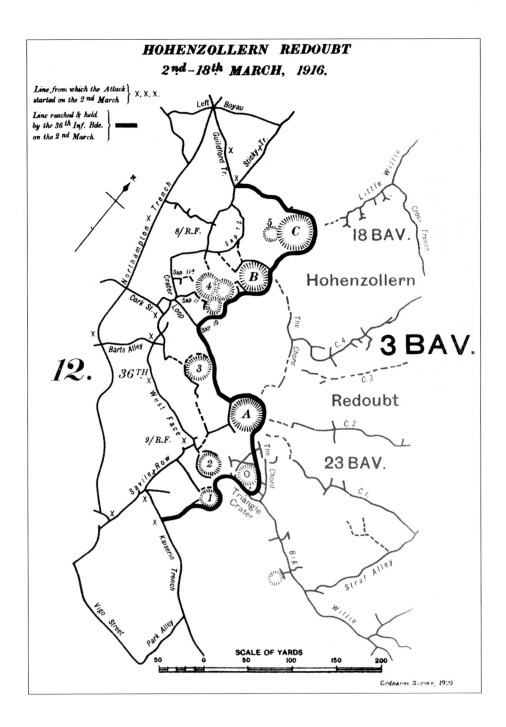

HOHENZOLLERN REDOUBT
2ⁿᵈ–18ᵗʰ MARCH, 1916.

At 9 a.m. the enemy blew a mine of their own, this time near Sap 6, only 20 yards from the parapet. No damage was done but Saps 5 and 6 were partly filled. Seven hours later, and preceded by heavy bombardment, another German mine was exploded, this time in front of Alexander Trench close to Sap 6. Sixteen men suffered badly from shock and there was slight damage to the trenches. An hour later, at 6.00 p.m., C Coy of the 6th Buffs attacked the Triangle Crater and the Chord in three parties. Two of the parties were held up within ten minutes by accurate bombing, and the third by the nature of the heavy ground conditions, with water and mud being knee-deep. Only one party made any real progress reaching their objective, but without the assistance of the other two parties the situation was hopeless. Reinforcements were requested and a company from the 6th Royal West Kents was ordered up to try to assist.

The attack turned out to be entirely unsuccessful, and the battalion diary recorded casualties of twenty-nine killed and 233 missing or wounded, including those men who had suffered from shock. The battalion diary considered that the attack failed because of a preponderance of the enemy (it was later discovered that a hundred German bombers with unlimited supplies of grenades were on the point of making an attack of their own launched from deep trenches intersecting the Triangle), muddy conditions and the short notice given for the attack. In addition, no allowance was made for the ground to be reconnoitred. Finally, the process of bomb supply was severely interrupted by a very active enemy.

On 7 March mining and counter-mining continued and the 6th Buffs were relieved by the 6th Royal West Kents.

The fighting at the Hohenzollern Redoubt, which had begun on the 2nd with the British firing five mines and occupying forward lips of the craters, continued with fluctuating intensity through deteriorating weather conditions of cold and heavy snowstorms. However, these conditions did not deter the enemy from making active preparations for regaining their former positions, which they eventually achieved on the 18th, when the 37th Brigade had been in the line for fourteen days.

There were many acts of heroism during the crater fighting, but one that stands out is that of Cpl William Cotter, who despite his shattered legs continued to direct a bombing attack and even managed to continue to throw bombs himself. There is no shortage of information in the records about his gallant deed, and it would seem sensible to quote in full from Appendix L from the 37th War Diary signed by Capt R.O.C. Ward under recommendation of Cpl W. Cotter for the Victoria Cross.

In the attack made by the 6th Battalion The Buffs, along the Northern Trench of TRIANGLE CRATER, on the night of the 6th March, the party led by

The Leas, Folkestone, 1956 (*Anon*)

Corpl. Cotter was cut off owing to casualties in the centre. He returned under heavy bomb fire, reported the matter and then took back bombs to his party, so enabling them to fight their way back to No 2 CRATER.

While directing this latter operation his right leg was blown off close to the knee and he was also wounded in both arms.

He made his way unaided along 50 yds of trench in order to reach No 2 CRATER.

While doing so he came upon a junior N.C.O. (Lance/Corporal Newman) who with his section was bombing towards the right. Corpl. Cotter appreciating where help was most needed directed him to bomb towards the left.

He reached No 2 CRATER and by this time the Germans had developed a violent and rapid counter-attack.

Matters became somewhat disorganized as the garrison of the Crater was throwing bombs and firing wildly, whilst they were suffering heavy casualties from the enemy's bombs.

Corpl. Cotter then from a position on the side of the Crater although suffering great pain, steadied the men, issued orders, controlled their fire and then altered their dispositions to meet the attack on his side of the Crater. He also directed and controlled the supply of bombs and S.A.A.

He remained in this position for about two hours and only after the attack had been repelled and matters had quietened down a little would he permit his wounds to be roughly dressed.

It was not possible to evacuate him until 14 hours later and during this time he had a cheery word for all who passed by the entrance of the 'dug-out' where he was placed.

Undoubtedly the fine example he showed to all by his endurance under suffering, coolness under fire, and keen sense of duty, helped greatly to save what might have become a very critical situation.

During the time he has been with the 6th Battalion The Buffs he has always proved himself a fine soldier. In the trenches his activities lay chiefly in Sniping and Scouting, and in this connection he has rendered very valuable service.

He was always ready to volunteer for such work as patrols, wiring etc, and never considered a task too dangerous or disagreeable for him.

Cotter was taken to a casualty clearing station (CCS) at Lillers, where his right leg was amputated below the knee. Both of his arms were also wounded. In *Unknown Warriors*, a book of extracts from the letters of Nursing Sister K.E. Luard, RRC, who was a sister-in-charge of a CCS, is a letter written from Lillers on 15 March 1916:

There is a story to tell you about the quiet, determined-looking little man in the 'Surgical,' with the glass eye – Corporal Cotter of The Buffs – who came in with his leg bombed off.

Yesterday morning he was so much better he was able to talk a little more.

He told me (only when asked how he got it) that he was leading a bombing attack at the Hohenzollern Redoubt, and took his men up a wrong turning and came on 'thousands of Germans'.

He somehow got his men away again, minus his leg. 'It was dark, and I didn't know me leg was gone – so I kep' on throwing the bombs, and Little Wood he kep' by me and took the pins out for me.' (His hand was badly wounded as well.)

At last 'Little Wood' got him into a dugout in a crater and stayed with him all night.

Yesterday morning, General Gough, Corps Commander, and two other Generals turned up and asked to see Corporal Cotter of The Buffs, to tell him that he was recommended for the V.C.

General Gough told me he was a marvellous man, known throughout the Division as the 'Corporal of The Buffs with One Eye,' famed for bravery and scouting at night for snipers by himself.

They were awfully nice to him, and Capt. R. told them all about the leg and the drip treatment, etc.

Later that day the Corporal had a severe haemorrhage and so nearly died that they daren't give him an anaesthetic, but Capt. R. took his gangrenous leg off through the knee as he was, without his feeling it as he was unconscious.

We slaved at him all the evening, but he died at 8 p.m.

Wasn't it horribly tragic? But he did know about his V.C.

Cotter died on 14 March. A priest who attended him wrote the following to his mother soon after:

Dear Mrs. Cotter, – Your son William, I regret to say, has just collapsed after a serious operation for amputation. He seemed so strong and in such good spirits when he came in that I felt assured and full of hopes of his recovery. However, Almighty God has disposed otherwise. He will be missed from the Army, he was a great favourite, and so full of bravery. The General came to tell him that he was going to be recommended for the Victoria Cross. This no doubt will console you somewhat, but I am sure you will be more pleased to know that he received devoutedly Holy Communion, and shortly before he expired extreme unction and the last blessing.

His last words were 'Good-bye, God bless you all'. RIP. I am now going to lay him to rest.

Cotter's body was taken to Lillers Communal Cemetery, north-west of Bethune, and buried in Plot IV, E, 45.

The general who visited Cotter in hospital, pinning a VC ribbon on his breast, was General Hubert Gough. There was to be no delay with approving Cotter's deeds as being worthy of the VC, and the citation was published in the *London Gazette* on 30 March, only sixteen days after his death.

William Richard (*sic*, Reginald) Cotter, No. 6707. Lance/Corporal. (Acting Corporal.) 6th Battalion. East Kent Regiment. For most conspicuous bravery and devotion to duty. When his right leg had been blown off at the knee, and he had also been wounded in both arms, he made his way unaided for 50 yards to a crater, steadied the men who were holding it, controlled their fire, issued orders, and altered the dispositions of his men to meet a fresh counter-attack by the enemy. For two hours he held his position, and only allowed his wounds to be roughly dressed when the attack had quieted down. He could not be moved back for 14 hours, and during all this time had a cheery word for all who passed him. There is no doubt that his magnificent courage helped greatly to save a critical situation.

The regimental history says of Cotter:

> His letters home were always of a cheery type, and in the trenches he was one of the happiest and best of men. He kept his comrades in good spirits, and he was always ready to help the wounded or dying. Corporal distinguished himself on several occasions in bayonet fighting, and in December last (1915) he was recommended by his officers for conspicuous bravery. He was then, it appeared, recommended for the D.C.M.

Cotter's parents were invited to an investiture at Buckingham Palace on 29 November. They were given railway warrants from Folkestone to Charing Cross and took with them a nephew who had also served in the trenches. From Charing Cross they left for Buckingham Palace, where they were to spend about three and a half hours. It was Mr Cotter's first visit to the capital for thirty years, and the King expressed interest in the elderly man's campaign medals before presenting the VC to Mrs Cotter.

In July 1916 Cotter's effects were returned to his family, and in May 1917 at Sandgate a memorial plaque was erected, fixed to a wall at the entrance to the Chichester Memorial Hall in the High Street, at a time when the building housed the offices of the Sandgate Urban District Council. The marble tablet was surmounted by a dragon scroll and paid for by public subscription. It was unveiled on 5 May 1917 by Col F.G.A. Wiehe at a ceremony in the presence of the mayor of Folkestone, a group of local dignitaries and a large crowd. A detachment of the Buffs took part, together with a bugler who sounded the general salute after the sheet covering the memorial was pulled away. In addition many of Cotter's former Army colleagues attended, as did a group of local Boy Scouts. The Sandgate War Memorial was unveiled at the foot of Military Road on 11 May 1921 by the Countess of Rocksavage, and among the forty-five names on the memorial were those of Bernard and William Cotter.

In 1956 a brief service of commemoration was held at the Chichester Hall Memorial and in the same year another memorial to William Cotter was set up on the seafront at Folkestone, which took the form of a floral tribute in the Leas, the mile-and-a-half promenade adjacent to the sea.

However, by the early 1960s usage of the hall in Sandgate had changed it into a social centre, and the memorial now found itself adjacent to a ladies' public lavatory, with direction notices outside. This was felt by some to be unseemly and there was a considerable local controversy about the suitability of the site for the local VC hero. Some people wanted the memorial to be moved to the local parish church; one of his brothers argued that as William had been a Roman Catholic this decision would be quite wrong.

In July 2000 eleven members of the Cotter family, together with more than thirty members of the Sandgate Society, decided to make a pilgrimage to France in order to visit the places associated with William Cotter. Led by the Revd John Botting, the group visited the spot near Bethune on the site of the former Hohenzollern Redoubt where Cotter won his VC. They also commemorated his memory at his grave at Lillers Communal Cemetery, where a short service was held and a wreath of poppies was laid on the grave. At one point a framed commemorative scroll together with a badge of the Buffs and a replica VC was presented to the Sandgate Society as a memento of the visit.

Of William's brothers, three served in the Army and two in the Navy. William and Bernard (died 19 October 1914) both of the Buffs, were listed on the Sandgate War Memorial. A roll of honour in St Paul's, the parish church, was later erected; carved in stone or slate panels it forms part of the entrance porch. Another Cotter brother, Fred, had died in South Africa, when also serving with the Buffs.

❖❖❖

Lillers Communal Cemetery
(*Donald C. Jennings*)

William Reginald Cotter was the eldest of six sons of Richard and Amy Cotter of 2 Barton Cottages, Wilberforce Road, Sandgate. These cottages are now no more. William was born in Young's Road, Folkestone, in March 1883, although there is conflicting evidence of his date of birth, and even his family seemed unsure as to which year he was born in. Richard, his father, was a former soldier who had served with the South Wales Borderers and taken part in the South African Wars in the late 1870s. He later worked in the building trade for various firms and was recognised as a hard worker. He was well known in Folkestone and, being an Irishman, was inevitably known as 'Mickey'. Owing to rheumatism he had to give up building work and later took up selling papers instead.

From about the age of five William attended a Roman Catholic school behind the church in Guildhall Street, Folkestone, and after leaving he worked at various labouring jobs in the building trade. He then decided he was in need of some adventure and ran away to sea, working with the crew of a liner for a short time before returning home because he knew that his mother would be anxious about him. He then decided to try to get into the Army and enlisted in the East Kent Regiment (The Buffs) on 8 October 1901. He was slightly under 5 ft 8 in in height. A year later he joined the 1st Battalion, and during his early years in the Army he served in Dublin, India and Aden. Only six weeks after joining he was involved in a fight in the Lion public house in Folkestone. During the fracas he was badly injured in the face by a glass that was thrown at him by a rowdy customer – possibly the assailant was 'taking the micky' out of Cotter and his friends. But, tragically, Cotter's injuries led to the loss of sight in one of his eyes. Inevitably, a court of enquiry was set up, which was convened on 13 December. Cotter's injuries were still too bad to allow him to sign an account of what had happened in the pub. His left eye (according to the records) was subsequently replaced by a glass one, which had obvious repercussions on his good eye, which then had to compensate for the extra work it had to do.

It is tempting to write off this incident as a fight or scuffle which for Cotter went disastrously wrong. However, it was not to be the only 'black mark' against him on his Army record in the thirteen years of service prior to March 1914: his service record shows six misdemeanours of drunkenness, being absent from duty and irregular with the hours that he kept! He was sometimes warned or admonished but on two occasions was confined to barracks for five days. His misdeeds were spread over his Army career from 1901 to 1913; not surprisingly he remained a private.

After thirteen years in the Army, where he had become one of the best bayonet fighters in the regiment, he was discharged in mid-March 1914 to join the Reserves. He then took a job with Sandgate Council. When war broke out he promptly rejoined the Army from Reserve on 5 August 1914, returning to the 1st Battalion of the Buffs, and proceeded to Canterbury before going on active service in France for six months from 7 September until 29 May 1915. He was then invalided home sick, as with only one eye the strain on his sight had become too much, and he took up garrison duties at Dover instead. An operation was carried out on his good eye and his sight slowly improved. On 20 October he joined the 6th Battalion (37th Brigade) 12th Division and left again for France. He was promoted for the first time to paid lance-corporal on 14 November and paid corporal on 12 February 1916. He won his VC on 6 March and died of wounds eight days later.

E.N. MELLISH

St Eloi, Belgium, 27/29 March 1916

(David Harvey)

During an attack in March 1915 at St Eloi in an area south of Wytschaete, the enemy had created a salient some 600 yards wide with a depth of about 100 yards, which intruded into the British line. For a year this area was to witness much mining and counter-mining. In March 1916 General Plumer decided to 'straighten out the line at St Eloi' and thus cut off the small German salient. This sector included a position named 'The Mound', an artificial bank of earth which, although reduced in size, still provided the enemy with a valuable observation post.

The two battalions chosen to carry out this dangerous task were from the 9th Brigade (3rd Division), the 1st Northumberland Fusiliers and the 4th Royal Fusiliers. The operation commenced on 27 March with the blowing of five mines at 4.15 a.m. Artillery put down an accompanying barrage, and when debris from the explosions had settled, four companies of the Royal Fusiliers rapidly moved forward. However, the enemy were more than prepared for this assault and retaliated with machine-gun and intense rifle fire, accompanied by artillery fire. Four mines had gone off under the enemy front line and a fifth destroyed a bombers' post, and although the Fusiliers entered the German front line, despite the wire being uncut, they became so weakened that they were unable to make further progress and had to make do with consolidating the ground they had covered.

The 1st Northumberland Fusiliers on the right, on the other hand, had a very different experience, encountering very little opposition in their section as they found that the enemy had been caught by surprise. They also managed to capture several German prisoners.

Since the Royal Fusiliers had not reached their objectives, a gap opened up between the two assaulting battalions. Later, when other battalions proceeded to consolidate the ground, they found the mining had disturbed the deep drainage system, resulting in trenches filling with water. It was also freezing cold, with showers of sleet and snow.

For the rest of the day an artillery duel was fought and it was impossible for any of the by now very heavy casualties to be brought in, certainly not until dusk at the earliest. At midnight small groups of men from the 2nd Royal Scots did manage to carry out a relief of the Royal Fusiliers, but it took six hours to complete.

On the following night other battalions took over the captured trenches, including the 2nd Suffolks and 10th Royal Welch Fusiliers. On the third night it was reported that the enemy were in occupation of two of the craters and had wire and machine-guns in front of them.

Having been informed of the heavy casualties of the Royal Fusiliers, many of whom he would have known personally, Capt the Revd Edward Mellish, who was attached to the 4th Royal Fusiliers as their chaplain, came up from transport lines. He even ventured out into No Man's Land on the first night when the ground was already thick with casualties. Accompanied by his servant and groom, Pte Robins (Worcestershire Regiment), he attended to his colleagues in the most dangerous of conditions and managed to bring some back to safety. In his unpublished memoirs he described the scene:

> Along the edge of the mine craters and that which had once been a trench, but was now a sea of churned up mud, our men were subjected to a continuous volume of fire. In the dark it was a hell of white flares, red flashes and screaming shells, while dead and dying men lay with those who still kept their sanity. . . .

At one point Mellish's own life was probably saved by Private Robins: '. . . I think that on one occasion I should never have extricated myself from the unthinkably clinging mud of a crater's edge, if he had not come back and hauled me out by his great strength. . . .'

On the first day Mellish, single-handed, brought in ten men, followed by twelve the following day. To indicate how close he was to being killed, at least three casualties were killed while he was attending to their wounds. On the third night a call went out to the 2nd Suffolks for stretcher-bearers to work with Mellish in No Man's Land, and six stretcher-bearers promptly volunteered. The last man to be brought in was a very tall man '. . . who was lying with a broken leg in an exposed position. As daylight dawned they got him out and then the German gunners saw and opened fire, but just as they had 'bracketed' them a fall of snow came and hid them from their views and they were protected. . . .'. Later, when the totally exhausted padre got back to Capt Carpenter's dugout (named after Capt G.G. Carpenter, Mellish's company commander) he was given a well-earned mug of cocoa! The casualties of the Royal Fusiliers were 265, including ten officers.

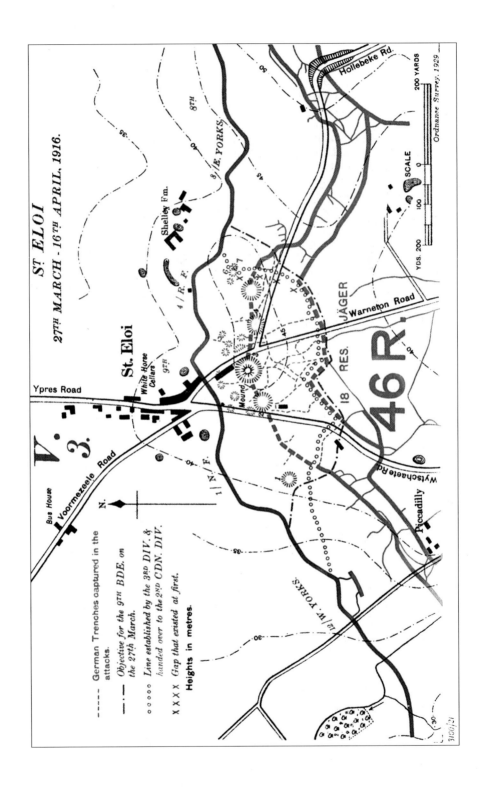

ST ELOI
27TH MARCH - 16TH APRIL, 1916.

German Trenches captured in the attacks.

Objective for the 9TH BDE. on the 27th March.

Line established by the 3RD DIV. & handed over to the 2ND CDN. DIV.

Gap that existed at first.

Heights in metres.

Flêtre (*Peter Batchelor*)

Mellish was the first padre to win a VC in the First World War. All six members of the Suffolk Regiment who assisted him on the third night received the MM. Mellish's VC citation was published in the *London Gazette* of 20 April, and four days later a 3rd Divisional parade was held at Flêtre, close to Hazebrouck, by Maj Gen J.A.L. Haldane, GOC 3rd Division, in 'a soggy meadow beneath the red-brick church with thatched and limewashed cottages about it'. While other men received their decorations Mellish was obliged to stand embarrassingly to attention for the duration of the parade in the dank conditions of the low-lying marshy field. He was the last man to be decorated and was presented with a VC ribbon and then given three cheers. (The low-lying field still exists, and the red-brick church, which has the date of 1901 on its tower, also survives. As for some of the mine craters at St Eloi, they have become large innocent-looking ponds within a farm complex.)

Mellish's citation read as follows:

Edward Noel Mellish, Capt. The Reverend, Temporary Chaplain to the Forces. During heavy fighting on three consecutive days he repeatedly went backwards and forwards under continuous heavy shell and machine-gun fire, between our trenches and those captured from the enemy, in order to tend and rescue wounded men. He brought in ten badly-wounded men on the on the

17

first day from ground swept by machine-gun fire. The battalion to which he was attached was relieved on the second day, but he went back and brought in twelve more wounded men. On the night of the third day he took charge of a party of volunteers, and once more returned to the trenches to rescue the remaining wounded. This splendid work was quite voluntary, and outside the scope of his ordinary duties.

As a registered reader of the *Daily Mail*, Mellish was fortunate in becoming the first recipient of its £100 award set up to encourage men to win a VC. On 10 June he was given a civic reception at Deptford Town Hall, South London. He was a curate at St Paul's, Deptford, and his parents lived nearby in Lewisham. In the municipal reception room in the Town Hall, where the ceremony took place, Mellish was invited to sign his name in the Borough roll of honour. He was presented with an illuminated address together with a sum of money. Two days later he was presented with his VC by the King at Buckingham Palace.

After the St Eloi incident Mellish was with the 4th Royal Fusiliers in the Kemmel area before they were ordered down to the Somme in early July 1916. They camped at Happy Valley near Bray before taking part in the fighting at Bazentin le Petit in the middle of the month. In his memoir Mellish mentions Carnoy, Bernafay Wood, Delville Wood and Ville-sous-Corbie, and in some of these places he would have worked closely with the 142nd Field Ambulance, which was part of the 3rd Division.

It was soon after his service on the Somme that Mellish had a bad accident: in early August he fell down some cellar steps in the dark and was concussed. A short time later he was in hospital, where he met up with Maj V.E. Cotton, when the two men were in adjacent beds at No. 45 CCS at Daours on 7 August 1916. Both were suffering from a sort of trench fever, with a fluctuating temperature. Cotton described his companion in the following way:

> My next door companion is the redoubtable 'parson VC' Mellish, who has the same trouble as I have and is a singularly cheery, charming and modest individual who looks like the mildest of the mild in gold rimmed spectacles but has knocked about the world a good deal before he entered the Church and has been in the S. A. Police and also a number of years diamond mining.

The two men left Daours by ambulance train, arriving at No. 2 Red Cross Hospital, Rouen, on 10 August.

In 1916 a medical board noted that Mellish had suffered from concussion of the brain as well as trench fever, and in September the latter caused him to black out and fall down some stairs; this notwithstanding, on 4 December he was declared fit for general service. He was then transferred to the XIII Corps Heavy Artillery. In early 1917 he was back in the Somme battlefield, this time at Hébuterne. He noted that the wire at Gommecourt was still not cut and that several hundred bodies from 1 July 1916 had still not been brought in.

In June his health let him down once more, and as he was no longer fit for active service he left the Gunners. This was followed by a brief leave in Scotland, but in September 1917 he was back with the 3rd Division, this time joining them at Vlamertinghe while the Battle of Passchendaele was being fought. In the following month he moved to Bullecourt, which was part of the Hindenburg Line, and was close to Moeuvres during the German retaliation at Cambrai at the end of November. In December he returned to the Bullecourt trenches.

In early 1918 Mellish mentioned that the battalion boasted an excellent concert troupe called 'Elegant Extracts'. In May he was stationed in the Hinges Section and at Havrincourt near Cambrai in mid-September. During the autumn advance to victory he visited Nimy Bridge near Mons, the scene of the winning of two VCs by members of the 4th Royal Fusiliers, Lt Maurice Dease and Pte Sidney Godley. Afterwards the 3rd Division moved forward into Germany as the leading division; Mellish was at home on leave at this time, but was later demobilised there. In addition to winning the VC in 1916 he won the MC in 1918.

From Mellish's memoirs it is quite clear that some officers regarded padres as an embarrassment or even a downright nuisance. Being a padre was not an easy role to play on the battlefield, but Mellish certainly proved to the men at least that he was of use. He not only gave much-needed spiritual comfort but in practical terms helped to save their lives when working among the wounded, either on his own in No Man's Land or in tandem with the divisional field ambulance. At one point he was actually offered command of a company – and with his experience it is likely that he would have been an excellent company commander. However, he declined the offer as he considered his work as a padre to be more important.

Edward Noel Mellish was the second of five children of Edward Mellish and Mary (née Coppin) and he was born at Oakleigh Park, Barnet, on Christmas Eve 1880, hence his middle name. His father moved the family to Cornwall for a brief period before returning to Hertfordshire where from the age of thirteen Noel attended King Edward VI Grammar School.

After leaving school and working briefly in his father's firm he fell out with his father's business partner and for a brief time worked in the wine trade. He joined the Artists' Rifles Volunteer Rifle Corps in 1899 and served as a trooper in the

South African War with Baden-Powell's South African Police, from December 1900 to 1902. After the war was over he returned briefly to England and then later went back to South Africa, where he worked in a diamond mine at Jagersfontein. Having learnt the local patois while helping out with sick or dying natives, he decided to make the Church his vocation. In all he was in South Africa for ten years. After returning to England he studied theology at King's College, London, and was ordained in 1912. He was curate of St Paul's Church, Deptford, London, a poor parish, until 1915.

In May 1915 he felt that he could be of use to men in the trenches and was temporarily commissioned as a chaplain to the forces in the same month. He served for most of the war as acting army chaplain 4th class, attached to the 4th RF (City of London Regiment) 9th Infantry Brigade, 3rd Division, until February 1919. He began his service in the British base town of Rouen and spent some of his time rescuing young soldiers from the 'women and men who fattened on the British soldier and robbed him of his money, health and honour'. In September he received orders to join the 9th Brigade. Before the Battle of Loos he was invited to join the 4th Royal Fusiliers HQ mess and was with them when the plans for destroying a position at St Eloi were drawn up.

When he returned home to Deptford after the war he converted a former public house into a boys' club; the club came to be known as the Noel Club, and the award from the *Daily Mail* was used to defray some of the running costs. The building was at the back of the Empire Music Hall.

Mellish became commander of the St Paul's Lads' Brigade, and on 3 December 1918 got married at St Paul's to Elizabeth Wallace Molesworth. They were to have five children who survived, including Paul, Patrick, Robin and Claire. Patrick was to serve with the 2nd Royal Fusiliers in North Africa, where he lost a leg, and Robin, a member of the same battalion, served in Greece and later with the 1st Battalion with BAOR. In 1919 Mellish's home address was 8 Lewisham Hill, south-east London. In the same year he officiated at the wedding of Private Sidney Godley VC of the 4th Royal Fusiliers, who had won the second VC of the war, which took place at St Mark's, Harlesden, north-west London.

On 26 June 1920 Mellish was one of several hundred guests at a garden party in the grounds of Buckingham Palace given by the King and Queen for holders of the Victoria Cross, together with members of their families. In October 1922 Mellish was sent by his bishop as a member of a Mission to India and returned in March the following year.

Mellish held the position of vicar of St Mark's, Lewisham, until September 1925, when he was appointed vicar of Wangford-cum-Henham and Reydon in Suffolk, until 1928. In the following year, on 9 November 1929, he attended the Prince of Wales's dinner at the House of Lords.

Like so many ex-service personnel, Mellish became a firm believer in preventing another world war, and was a keen supporter of the League of Nations rather than the alternative – to arm to ensure peace.

Moving from Suffolk, he became vicar of St Mary's, Great Dunmow, Essex, from 1928 to 1947; his name is listed there on the list of incumbents. In 1932 he was involved in an incident that caught the attention of the press: when dressed in his pyjamas he appeared on the floor of a local dance held at St Mary's room adjacent to the church and ordered the dance to cease at midnight, although it was licensed to continue to one o'clock.

In 1933 Mellish was left £500 by an admirer, 'in grateful remembrance of his share in the Great War'. During the Second World War he became an air raid warden.

When he had reached retirement age in 1948 Mellish moved again and worked as curate at Baltonsbury near Glastonbury in Somerset until 1953. The parish had a population of 500 and 180 houses.

Mellish had always kept close contact with the Royal Fusiliers, and in June 1950 officiated at the re-dedication of the regimental chapel. He also took part in the 250th regimental birthday celebrations. In June 1956 he attended the Victoria Cross centenary celebrations in London and was a guest at a dinner given by the Royal Army Chaplains, which was also attended by Geoffrey Woolley VC and Arthur Procter VC.

The Mellish family moved to a farmhouse in 1953 near Castle Cary in Somerset, where, although retired, he took the occasional service. In 1959 they left South Cary and moved to South Petherton, also in Somerset. In September 1959, alongside other surviving holders of the VC, he was awarded a life pension of £100 by the Ministry of Defence to be paid once a year beginning that month.

Mellish died at his home, the Court House in South Petherton, on 8 July 1962 in his eighty-second year, and after the funeral his body was cremated in Weymouth and his ashes scattered in the grounds of St Mary's, Great Dunmow, Essex. He was also commemorated in the Lewisham Civic Centre, along with Sidney Godley and six other VC holders who had local links.

Mellish's family presented his medals to the Royal Fusiliers Museum in 1966. They include the VC, MC, Queen's South African Medal and Clasps 'Orange Free State' and 'Cape Colony'. He was mentioned in Despatches on 3 June 1919. Some of his papers are housed in the Liddle Collection at the University of Leeds, including a typescript of his war memoirs, entitled *The Gallant Comradeship*. Although Elizabeth Mellish remained in South Petherton after Noel's death she moved to a smaller house in the village where her daughter Claire cared for her until her death on 27 December 1982. As with her later and very much loved husband, she was a truly Christian person, devoted to family and friends alike.

E.F. BAXTER

At Ransart near Blairville, France, 17/18 April 1916

(*David Harvey*)

Nearly three weeks after Edward Mellish won his VC at St Eloi, Belgium, a fourth Western Front VC of 1916 was gained approximately 5 miles to the south of Arras on 17/18 April by 2/Lt Edward Baxter of the 1/8th (Liverpool Irish) Battalion.

As it was deemed necessary to obtain regular information about the dispositions of the enemy, raids, or incursions, were regularly carried out and it was always a bonus to take a prisoner or two. At the beginning of April 1916 the 55th Division were in the area west of Blairville and Ficheux, occupying front-line trenches with three brigades in the line. A large-scale raid was planned to take place on the night of the 17th/18th, and the 8th Irish under the command of Lt Col E.A. Fagan was the battalion chosen for the task.

When Baxter arrived in France in January 1916 his duties were mostly those of bombing officer, and during his first few weeks he took part in several raids and sorties against the German lines. The group of men he worked with became known as 'The Forty Thieves'.

On 16 April three officers, including Baxter, and forty-three other ranks went out into No Man's Land in order to cut the wire in preparation for the raid. However, despite cutting three rows of wire, they had not finished their work by the time dawn had begun to break. The following night a patrol went out to check on the state of the cut wire and found it untouched. At midnight two officers and two NCOs went out and at 12.30 a.m. began to cut the remaining wire. The job was virtually finished by 2.10 a.m., and one of the NCOs was sent back to bring up the storming party of one officer and twenty-three men. It was at this stage of the raid that one of the group tripped on the wire and fell forward, knocking a grenade that Baxter was holding out of his hand. Reacting quickly, he picked it up, removed the detonator and smothered it in the ground. In doing this he saved his colleagues from being injured and prevented the alarm being given. The raiders then entered the enemy trench at 2.25 and, immediately cutting a cable, they moved down the trench, bombing dugouts as they went and killing seven Germans.

Cries and groans were heard from all the dugouts.

However, no prisoners had been taken at that point. When regaining their own trench it was found that 2nd Lieutenant Baxter was missing. A patrol that went out to look for him failed to find any trace but did bring back some German helmets as trophies. The battalion was relieved at 6.30 a.m. and marched the three miles to Monchiet. Baxter was found to be the only officer casualty.

The above account of the raid was based on information found in the battalion war diary, but the regimental history includes the following additional information: although several of the enemy were killed when their trench was entered, it was found that the trenches were from twelve to fifteen feet deep, and so without long ladders it was difficult to take prisoners. (Those ladders that were taken were only six feet in length.) Baxter had given orders to return, and after assisting the last man out he was later found to be missing. The regimental history concluded that he 're-entered enemy trench for some purpose and did not inform his party', and in a footnote quoted a German prisoner as stating that the raid had resulted in fifty-seven German casualties.

From an appendix included in the war diary it is quite clear that the bombing raid carried out on the night of 17/18 April was a great success, and the battalion, 164th Brigade and 55th (West Lancashire) Division were all congratulated. Baxter, who was still officially missing, was one of those singled out for a decoration: his VC was published in the *London Gazette* of 26 September 1916, which contains an account of how he saved the lives of some of his colleagues:

Edward Felix Baxter, Second Lieutenant, 1/8th Battalion. King's Liverpool Regiment (Territorial Force). For most conspicuous bravery. Prior to a raid on the hostile line he was engaged during two nights in cutting wire close to the enemy's trenches. The enemy could be heard on the other side of the parapet. Second Lieutenant Baxter, while assisting in the wire-cutting, held a bomb in his hand with the pin withdrawn ready to throw. On one occasion the bomb slipped and fell to the ground, but he instantly picked it up, unscrewed the base plug, and took out the detonator, which he smothered in the ground, thereby preventing the alarm being given and undoubtedly saving many casualties. Later he led the left storming party with the greatest gallantry, and was the first man into the trench, shooting the sentry with his revolver. He then assisted to bomb dug-outs, and finally climbed out of the trench and assisted the last man over the parapet. After this he was not seen again, though search parties went out at once to look for him. There seems no doubt that he lost his life in his great devotion to duty.

Baxter's body, which was found in a position to the north of Blairville, was first buried by the Germans two or three miles to the south-east in Boiry-Ste-Rictrude churchyard. During their occupation of this village and of Boiry-St-Martin to the south, the Germans had included an inscription on the gravestone giving Baxter's rank, name and date of death. The discovery of this grave was noted by Arthur Kidd, a sapper, when he visited the shelled parish cemetery in 1917.

Mrs Baxter was presented with her late husband's award at Buckingham Palace by the King on 29 November 1916, and, as Baxter had been a reader of the *Daily Mail*, she also received a cheque for £100 in connection with her late husband's award. In his will her husband left effects to the value of £212 8s 5d.

When Baxter was buried by the Germans they must have put his effects to one side, as a note in his National Archives file indicates that they were returned by the German government to his widow in 1920.

Mrs Baxter moved back to Kidderminster after the war to be near to her family, and lived at 3 Roden Avenue with her daughter. She later remarried.

In 1925 Baxter's remains were exhumed and reburied 25 miles westwards in Row A, Grave 10 of Fillèvres British Cemetery.

His VC is held in the Imperial War Museum, London.

Fillèvres British Cemetery (*Donald C. Jennings*)

Edward Felix Baxter was born on 18 September 1885 at Thornleigh, 35 Hagley Road, Old Swinford, Stourbridge, in Worcestershire. His home later became a YMCA Centre. He was the second son of Charles Baxter, a corn merchant who worked in Lower High Street, Stourbridge. His mother's name was Beatrice, née Sparrow.

When Edward was about six the family moved to a house called Ivy Crest, Inn Lane, Hartlebury, and later to Mostyn, Shrubbery Street, Kidderminster. Later he attended Hartlebury Grammar School in Worcestershire and Christ's Hospital. He grew to be six feet tall. His first job on leaving school was as a bank clerk, but in his early twenties he moved north to Liverpool and lived at 5 Blantyre Road, Sefton Park, to became a tutor at Skerry's College in Rodney Street.

Baxter married Leonora Cornish, who also came from Kidderminster, and was a daughter of Mr H.W. Cornish of Roden Avenue. The couple had married in Liverpool on 24 February 1906 and were to have one daughter, born in June 1907. Both he and his wife were keen motorcyclists, and Baxter was well known for his successes in track racing and road trials in northern England, and particularly in Liverpool. He and Leonora were both members of the Liverpool Auto Cycle Club, and Baxter took part in the 1910 Isle of Man TT Race but didn't finish the course. The couple usually rode motorcycles manufactured by Rex Motor Manufacturers in Coventry, a firm which survived until 1930.

Baxter was at the college when war broke out. He became a despatch rider with the Mersey Defence Corps and was attached to the HQ Staff in Rodney Street, Liverpool, under Brig Gen Edwards. He enlisted in September and became a sergeant, and about nine months later was recommended for a commission by Edwards and later awarded a commission in the 1/8th (Irish) The King's (Liverpool) Regiment TF in mid-September 1915. After four months' further training he left for France in January 1916. His battalion now belonged to 165th Brigade of the 55th (West Lancashire) Division.

R.B.B. JONES

Broadmarsh Crater, France, 21 May 1916

(*David Harvey*)

Just over a month after 2/Lt Edward Baxter gained a posthumous VC near Blairville to the south of Arras, a fifth Western Front VC of 1916 was won on the heights of Vimy Ridge by another young officer.

The enemy was keen to recover territory on the ridge lost in September 1915, and in particular to rob the British of access to mine shafts that had allowed them to carry on a programme of mining and counter-mining on the ridge. This activity had created a very high state of nervousness on both sides over the previous eight months.

Unbeknown to the 25th Division, which occupied positions close to the top of the ridge, the enemy were planning a strong attack for 21 May, in order to secure the lost territory.

However, two days before the planned attack, the enemy captured Broadmarsh Crater, an awkward advanced position to the south of the British line, which the 1/10th Cheshires (7th Brigade) 25th Division had been holding. After this enemy success, a company of the 1/8th Loyal North Lancashires was given the task of making a counter-attack in order to recover the lost ground. The battalion provided three parties totalling 100 men, and the artillery shelled the position until 9.15 p.m. on 19 May when the counter-attack began. At a cost of thirty-three casualties it was deemed to be a great success.

Two days later, on 21 May, the enemy bombarded the crater without success, though later managing to cut off the front line from the battalion using a 'curtain of gas shells'. It would now be impossible for a Lewis gun to be brought up. Lt R.B.B. Jones was in command of a platoon within the crater itself and told his men that he expected the enemy to attack from the left. Arrangements were therefore made for covering the left flank of each bomb post, of which there were four. One of the posts was on the lip, two on the way down and one at the bottom, halfway to the bridge traverse.

At about 7.30 p.m. the enemy blew a mine some 35 yards to the south of the crater, and immediately after lifting their artillery from the front-line trenches

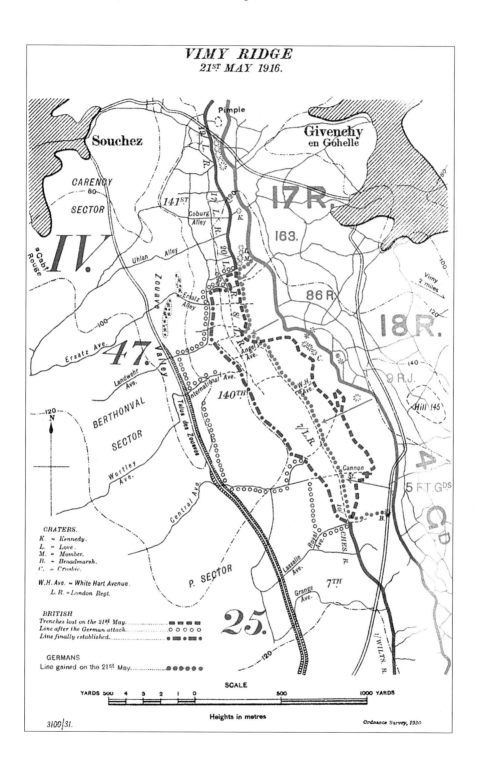

VIMY RIDGE
21ST MAY 1916.

CRATERS.
K. = Kennedy.
L. = Love.
M. = Momber.
B. = Broadmarsh.
C. = Crosbie.

W.H. Ave. = White Hart Avenue.
L.R. = London Regt.

BRITISH
Trenches lost on the 21st May. ▬ ▬ ▬ ▬
Line after the German attack. ○ ○ ○ ○ ○
Line finally established. ●▬●▬●▬

GERMANS
Line gained on the 21st May. ●●●●●

SCALE

YARDS 500 4 3 2 1 0   500   1000 YARDS

Heights in metres

3100/31.

Ordnance Survey, 1930

27

they attacked in successive lines of infantry at only 3-yard intervals. The second and third waves were carrying timber and barbed wire for use when consolidating the position. Lt Jones had in his platoon several very skilled bombers, one of whom, Pte Regan, threw the contents of no fewer than fifteen boxes of bombs. The Germans attempted to set up a machine-gun position, but it was soon knocked out by a bomb. The lip of the crater was kept clear of Germans for at least half an hour by the actions of both bombers and snipers. The platoon proceeded to do 'great execution', and managed to hold its ground. The battalion war diary entry for 21 May described what happened next:

> Finally when all the bombs were gone (and no further supplies were available) the men used their rifles. Lieutenant Jones lay near No. 2 post calling out the hits as he made them on Germans coming along between the two craters. He got to 15 when the supply of ammunition ran out. By his side in the mud were 3 bombs. He picked up one and jumped up to throw when he was shot through the head & fell back dead. His Sergeant (Sergeant Grayson) had been killed sometime before and the command of this section fell on Corpl. Coates who had been wounded some time previously in 4 places . . . .

Coates strongly encouraged the men by cheering them on with the prospect of an early relief. All the ammunition, including that found on the dead and scattered, had now been used up, so finally the men were reduced to throwing lumps of chalk and flint and even empty bomb boxes. As has been seen, the crater was defended without the assistance of a Lewis gun; the survivors considered that had it been possible to have one they would have been able to hold out much longer. However, the original party became totally split up and began to fall back, and several men were suffering from the effects of the gas shells. By 10 p.m. the advanced position was evacuated. The 3rd Worcesters then took over while members of the 1/8th LNL withdrew to dugout billets in the rear. Nine men got back unwounded and twenty-four were brought in later in the day.

The attack against the crater was part of a larger enemy assault on the whole front of the brigade to the left, and although the 1/8th LNL were ready to make another attempt to regain the position there was insufficient support from the left and the attack was called off.

Lt Jones was one of the two officers killed on the night of 20/21 May, while during the operations in the period 19/21 May the battalion suffered 154 casualties. Later in the month the battalion was withdrawn to rest at Monchy Breton. The war diary noted that 'all ranks worked extremely well' and 'the battalion may well be proud of the whole operation'. The very important part that Lt Jones played in defending his occupation of the crater during these operations was recognised by the publication of a VC in the *London Gazette* of 5 August:

Richard Basil Brandram Jones, Temporary Lieutenant, 8th Battalion. North Lancashire Regiment. Lieutenant Jones was in charge of a platoon which was holding a crater recently captured from the enemy. Forty yards away the enemy exploded a mine, and isolated the British platoon by a heavy barrage fire. Attacking in overwhelming numbers, the platoon was in great danger; but, organizing his men, Lieutenant Jones set an example by shooting no fewer than 15 of the enemy as they advanced, and counting off his victims as they fell. When all his ammunition was used, he was about to throw a bomb, and was shot through the head. The platoon continued to resist the enemy attack until they had used all their ammunition, and then resorted to throwing stones and ammunition boxes. When only nine of the platoon were left the men retired.

A Special Order of the Day published by the second army commander congratulated the battalion for their work against Broadmarsh Crater on the night of 19/20 May.

Jones's commanding officer wrote to his father as follows:

It is with very great regret that I have to write to you of the death of your son. He was killed instantaneously by a bullet on the night of the 21 and 22 May, when defending a crater against an attack by the Germans. He behaved in the most gallant manner, holding on with a few men till the last moment, and himself shot 15 Germans before he was killed. . . . Your son's death is a great loss to the regiment. He was my sniping officer, and a very gallant fellow.

A lieutenant colleague wrote:

Nothing could have been finer than the fight he and his men put up against the Germans. . . . He was always cheerful, always ready to do daring deeds, and a good comrade. . . . Jonesie hung on to the last with his men, and as the Huns attacked he shot them down one by one. . . . Hero he was alive and hero he remained till death. We are all intensely sorrowful.

. . . Jonesie kept his men in the crater, which was well in advance of our line. . . . He was a first-class shot, and coolly showed himself above the parapet and fought to the last. . . . Once wounded in the head he picked himself up and carried on – fine fellow that he was. He died a hero's death. Ever since I have been in the regiment we have been together in the same company. He was a topping pal.

A sergeant in the same regiment wrote:

Broadmarsh Crater (*Peter Batchelor*)

It was a very strong attack, and the men under his command were out-numbered, but they stuck to their post and fought to the last, for they knew that they had a great leader with them, one who could cheer and give them courage. His name will live for ever with the men of the Regiment. Before he was shot he accounted for no less than 15 of the enemy, which was a very brave act, for the position he held was sure death. He died a hero. No one in the battalion will miss him more that the men of his platoon and battalion snipers, for he was a gentleman, and was loved by everyone. . . . The men would have gone anywhere with him. Many a time have I heard his cheerful voice while passing through the trenches, joking and cheering the men when they were a little downhearted.

Jones's body was not recovered from where he fell, but his name is commemorated on Bay 7 of the Arras Memorial. His name is also listed on the Dulwich College Memorial, and a silver cup for rifle shooting was named after him and Cecil Howard, the Jones and Howard Memorial Cup. Howard, a member of A Company of the 8th Loyal North Lancashires, died of wounds two days after Jones (a member of B Company) and was buried in Aubigny Community Cemetery Extension.

On 20 December Jones's father received his son's VC at Buckingham Palace, and the *Daily Mail* duly presented him with the £100 award, which was divided between the Dulwich College Mission and the RN Division Mixed Club at Anerley. The college later acquired the VC.

At Vimy Ridge the pockmarked Broadmarsh Crater where Lt Jones died still exists, adjacent to the road leading to the tunnel's entrance and near Canadian Cemetery No. 2 and Givenchy Road Canadian.

Richard Basil Brandram Jones was born in Honor Oak Rise S.E. 23 on 30 April 1897, the son of H. Thomas Brandram and Caroline Emma, of 2 Thicket Road, Anerley. He was educated at Dulwich College Preparatory School before moving on to the upper school in 1909. He became an excellent shot and gymnast. In 1913–14 he was a captain of the Gymnastic VI and a member of the Shooting VIII. He won the Lady Hamilton's Challenge Cup in both years and Mrs Grey's Cup in 1913. He also won the Lane Challenge Cup at Bisley. He was a member of the College OTC and probably the finest shot in the school. He left Dulwich in 1914, having already passed the London Matriculation, and enlisted in the Army in September. He was gazetted in October and promoted to lieutenant in December, and soon and unsurprisingly was appointed sniping officer.

Jones left for France in September 1915 as a lieutenant in the 8th Loyal North Lancashires (7th Brigade) 25th Division, served in trenches in the Ploegsteert Wood sector and was slightly wounded on 12 December. In early March the Division was transferred to XVII Corps and served in corps reserve. The brigade was billeted in Maizières. On 11 April the battalion relieved a battalion of the 46th Division in trenches in front of Mont St Eloi. The regimental history noted that at this time 'the enemy began to show considerable activity, his bombardment being at times exceptionally heavy. . .'. Then on the night of 18/19 May the enemy in a surprise attack seized a section of Allied posts in the area known as 'Broadmarsh Crater', close to point 145 on Vimy Ridge where Jones was to win a posthumous VC two days later.

G.W. CHAFER

3/4 June 1916, East of Méaulte

(*David Harvey*)

On 3/4 June 1916, four weeks before the start of the Battle of the Somme, the 1st East Yorkshires (64th Brigade), 21st Division were in positions to the east of the village of Méaulte, south-west of Albert. Although recent German activity had been minimal, according to the regimental history 'he suddenly became aggressive' and late on the morning of 3 June a heavy bombardment began which mainly fell on C Coy. At 11.00 p.m. the enemy began a further 20-minute heavy bombardment on the left of the battalion and in the C Coy area again. There were no casualties but there was much damage to trenches.

Early on 4 June at 12.45 a.m. the bombardment began once more in the same area, and at 1.15 a.m. the enemy followed up with an attack on the trenches of the 21st Northumberland Fusiliers Battalion to the left, and entered their trenches as well as those of the East Yorkshires. The enemy captured a listening post, although the men forming the garrison got away. The enemy were driven out, but not without fifty-nine casualties, including two officers killed. It was in this action that Pte George Chafer, when seriously wounded, gained the first regimental VC of the war.

The regimental history told the story of Chafer's gallant deed as follows:

The scene was terrible. Our trench had almost been levelled by enfilade shell fire and enemy trench mortars. It was being swept by deadly machine-gun fire, and the air was poisoned by gas fumes. Chafer was lying seriously wounded in hand and leg, bruised and dazed by the concussion, choking and blinded by gas, when he saw a man coming along with a written message. Another shell burst and partially buried this orderly, who shouted: 'Someone take this message for the Captain.' There was no one within hearing but Chafer: only dead and mortally wounded in sight. 999 men out of a thousand would have said, 'I can't do anything. I have done my bit. Now I lie low in what cover I've got. The message can't be delivered.' 'Not so', said Chafer. . . . He took the message from the soldier, and, as the trench had been knocked in so badly, crawled on to the parapet in spite of excruciating pain. There were big shells, small shells, bullets from machine-guns and rifles were raining round, and how he came through without further injury is a miracle. The first living occupant of our trench whom Chafer reached was a corporal. The latter could hardly believe his eyes when he saw someone, wearing a gas helmet, his left hand shot through and bleeding profusely, yet clutching his rifle, he dragged himself painfully along the parapet, with one leg torn by shell wounds, crying all the time 'A message for the Captain.' After handing it over Chafer collapsed.

C Coy was relieved by D Coy later on 4 June and was held in reserve. The enemy once more bombarded the same area as before.

The *London Gazette* published the citation for Chafer's bravery on 5 August 1916 as follows:

George William Chafer, Private, No.19384, East Yorkshire Regiment. For most conspicuous bravery. During a very heavy hostile bombardment and attack on our trenches a man carrying an important written message to his company commander was half buried and rendered unconscious by a shell. Private Chafer, at once grasping the situation, on his own initiative took the message from the man's pocket, and, although severely wounded in three places, ran along the ruined parapet under heavy shell and machine-gun fire, and just succeeded in delivering it before he collapsed from the effect of his wounds. He displayed great initiative and splendid devotion to duty at a critical moment.

Later in the month the 21st Division prepared itself to take part in the early part of the Battle of the Somme, and on 1 July it employed the 63rd and 64th Brigades, as well as the 50th, which was attached from the 17th Division. The plan had been to cut off the very-well-defended village of Fricourt by using two divisions in an attempt to pinch out the village by joining hands to the north of it. However, the plan failed and the 21st Division was held up in front of German trenches in front of Lozenge Wood on the Fricourt–Contalmaison road. Nevertheless, the enemy soon decided to vacate the village as they considered it untenable and retreated towards Contalmaison and their second line. The 1st East Yorkshires had suffered grievously, with casualties of twenty-one officers and 478 other ranks.

A fortnight later the 1st East Yorkshires were back in action again when the battalion took part in the attacks towards the Flat Iron Trenches on 14 July, when their role was to protect the flank from Pearl Wood along the west side of Bazentin le Petit Wood.

As Chafer's file did not survive the blitz, details of his service career after he won his VC are scant, but an article published in *The Sapper* had this to say about this modest hero:

> During his training he [Chafer] did not distinguish himself specially with rifle or bayonet. His whole appearance and career in the Army are a valuable reminder that the great thing in a soldier is not physique, and not even skill with his weapons, but the spirit that is in him. In a moment of crisis, forced to choose between ordinary and extraordinary action, Chafer chose the highest and the best course open to him, and achieved the seemingly impossible.
>
> The story of Chafer's gallant deed will be ever enshrined in the records of the East Yorkshire Regiment. It is a splendid instance of that indomitable courage which constantly shines forth in our Army, and is our best guarantee of final triumph.

When Chafer returned home to Rotherham later in the year he was given a rousing welcome home and shared an open car with the Lord Mayor, Alderman Joseph Heminsley, together with the town clerk. He was presented with his VC by the King at Buckingham Palace on 4 November 1916. In 1918 he was demobilised and settled in Bramley, a village where he was to remain for forty-eight years.

George William Chafer was born an orphan in Epworth, near Doncaster Gate, Rotherham. Known as Bill, he was brought up by Mrs Brooks, an aunt, in Ravenfield Common, Rotherham. He went to school in Rotherham before working as a weigh clerk in Silverwood colliery and lodging at 15 Silverwood Cottages with a Mr and Mrs Reed.

Although slightly built he was enlisted in the East Yorkshire Regiment on 2 June 1915, and after six months training left for the front to join the 1st Battalion, which was part of the 64th Brigade (21st Division). As a member of C Coy he was given bombing duties and won his VC six months later on 3/4 June 1916, east of Méaulte.

On 11 November 1920 he attended the services in connection with the burial of the Unknown Warrior in Westminster Abbey.

In the 1920s Chafer appears to have tried his hand at running a dairy business, which failed, and he then switched to a small-scale poultry business. In 1928 he took a job with the Ministry of Labour and National Service and remained with them for thirty years before retiring in 1958. He worked in various branches in the South Yorkshire and Lincolnshire areas.

His home address was 2, The Villas, Bramley, near Rotherham, and on 9 November 1929 he attended the dinner hosted by the Prince of Wales in the House of Lords for all current winners of the VC. He was very impressed with the special nature of the event and his account of it was published in an issue of *The Sapper*. Three hundred and twenty men attended and Chafer stated 'the Band of the Brigade of Guards played a selection of suitable melodies'.

Chafer's war wounds, including the loss of his left leg, still troubled him, and his application to rejoin the Army in 1939 was rejected; instead he served as a sergeant in a platoon of the Home Guard. He attended the Victory Parade in London on 8 June 1946, which was followed by a dinner at the Dorchester Hotel.

Chafer was an active member of the local British Legion and at one time branch chairman. In June 1956, the centenary of the presentation of the first VC, a fund was opened locally in order to allow him to go to London for the Hyde Park Parade and other functions. On the 23rd he was given a cheque for £189 in the Mayor's Parlour and was escorted to the railway station by the Mayor at the beginning of his journey to London. At the station he was invited to inspect a Guard of Honour drawn from the ATA Signal Squadron, and was given three cheers by the crowd that had gathered. Chafer was a regular attender of gatherings of the VC/GC Association until 1964, when he found it too difficult to make the journey to London.

As well as his Legion activities he was also a member of the parish council, and in particular worked for youth in his home village of Bramley and was a key player in creating a local youth centre.

Chafer had moved from The Villas to 11 Flanderwell Lane, Sunnyside, in Bramley by the time he became ill at the end of 1965. He died at Rotherham General Hospital on 1 March 1966. On receiving notice of his death members of Rotherham Town Council stood in tribute to his memory and flags on public buildings in Rotherham and District flew at half-mast. He was given a full military funeral at a service at Bramley parish church two days later, before being cremated in Rotherham. 'The Last Post' was played in the church by a bugler from the Prince of Wales's Regiment. His ashes were buried in the area in front of the Community Youth Civic Centre.

In his will Chafer left £3,062 (£2,786 net) and his medals to his regiment. Apart from the VC these included the War Medal, the 1914/15 Star, the BWM, Coronation Medals of King George VI and Queen Elizabeth II and the 3rd Class Russian Order of St George awarded to him before the fall of the Tsar. His VC is with the Prince of Wales's Regimental Museum.

A.H. PROCTER

Near Ficheux, France, 4 June 1916

(*David Harvey*)

Towards the end of May 1916 a group of nearly a hundred men from the 1/5th King's (Liverpool) Regiment were training at Beaumetz, south-west of Arras, over a period of six days in preparation for an important raid. Exact replicas of German trenches had been dug, and the raiding party of two officers and eighty-seven other ranks arrived in their positions near Ficheux on 3 June. With blackened faces and all other marks of identification removed, they set off for the enemy lines close to midnight. However, despite the elaborate training and preparation, the raid turned out to be a disaster.

The support of preliminary artillery and trench mortars took place as cover to the raiding party, which had been divided into sections and had set off at 12.15 a.m. extending along a ridge 75 yards from the British line. At 12.35 a.m. the artillery was signalled to start their attack; however, the bombardment, including the trench mortars, fell short over the heads of the raiders, as an insufficient margin had been allowed. The TMs were ordered to cease fire and the raid was abandoned at about 12.55 a.m., and those who survived returned to their lines. This 'friendly fire' resulted in fifty-seven out of the eighty-nine men who took part in becoming casualties.

At 10 p.m. the following day a party of the 5th Kings went out to the ridge between the two trench lines and managed to rescue two men, six bodies and a quantity of arms and accoutrements. The dead were later buried at Wailly. The battalion remained in the village of Wailly until they were relieved and marched westwards to billets at Beaumetz.

The above account is based on the war diary kept by the battalion and brigade diaries. The commander of the 55th Division was so incensed over what had happened that he instituted an inquiry with a view to establishing responsibility for the disastrous artillery shortfall.

During the day Pte Arthur Procter, a stretcher-bearer, peered over the parapet and saw two wounded men move. A note in the battalion diary states:

T. Veale, Arthur Procter, A.C.T. White and R.E. Ryder (*Sunday Times, 1966*)

On June 4th . . . an act of extraordinary daring was performed by 3156 RFN Proctor [*sic*], A, a stretcher-bearer. This man crawled out of our trench in broad daylight, made his way to where the two wounded men were lying & tended them. He also lent his cardigan jacket to one who was cold. He crawled back across the 75 yards of open ground which separated him from our trench, and regained our lines unhurt in spite of hostile fire.

Procter's heroic actions were rewarded by a VC, which was published two months later in the *London Gazette* on 5 August as follows:

Arthur Herbert Proctor [*sic*], No. 3156, Private, King's (Liverpool) Regiment. (Territorial Force). For most conspicuous bravery. Private Proctor, noticing some movement on the part of two wounded men who were lying in the open in full view of the enemy at about 75 yards in front of our trenches, went out on his own initiative, and, though heavily fired at, ran and crawled to the two men, got them under cover of a small bank, dressed their wounds, and, after

37

cheering them up with a promise of rescue after dark, and leaving them with some of his clothing for warmth, regained our trenches, again being heavily fired at. At dusk both men were brought out alive. . . .

The Blairville/Ficheux area was where a few weeks earlier another VC had been won, this time posthumously by a member of the King's Liverpool, 2/Lt Edward Baxter of the 8th Battalion, in a raid that took place on the night of 17/18 April.

Arthur Procter received his Victoria Cross from the King at Fourth Army Headquarters near Amiens on 9 August 1916 at 'a great gathering of British and French Officers'. It was the first time that the King had presented the VC in the field, and the investiture was attended by Sir Douglas Haig and General Joffre.

When Procter arrived home later in August he received an enthusiastic welcome and was taken to meet the Mayor of Bootle, together with members of the Borough Council. He was also introduced to Mrs Jones, whose son he had rescued, only for him to die later. He was also welcomed at the Territorial Headquarters Depot in St Anne's Street, Liverpool, and congratulated by the Lord Mayor; Cpl Joseph Tombs VC was invited to the reception.

Procter was then carried shoulder high through the streets by his comrades to the Produce Exchange, where he had been employed on the outbreak of war. Here he was presented with a gold watch and chain, a cheque for a hundred guineas and £100 War Loan, 4½ per cent scrip subscribed to by members of the Exchange. In his speech of thanks Procter stated that others deserved similar recognition, but were not equally fortunate in coming under the eyes of the powers that be.

In the following year he married Hilda May, daughter of Mr and Mrs Codd, with whom he had lodged. They were married at St Paul's Presbyterian Church, Tranmere.

In 1918 Procter was discharged with the rank of corporal. At one point he had been recommended for a commission but as he had been 'knocked about' by his experiences his physical condition was too poor for him to be passed sufficiently fit.

Arthur Herbert Procter was born at 55 Church Street, Bootle, Liverpool, on 11 August 1890, eldest son of Davenport Procter and Ellen Procter, née Cumpsty. His father worked at Parr's Bank as a clerk and the family lived over the premises on the corner of the street with Derby Road. After the First World War the bank was acquired by the Westminster Bank.

Procter began his education locally at the nearby St Mary's Church of England School, which was in Church Street. Owing to his father's poor state of health and the early death of his mother, Arthur, his two brothers and a sister were packed off to Exeter, where one of their uncles brought them up. Arthur continued his education at Exeter Training College, but appears to have returned to a Dr Barnardo's Home in Merseyside. The home was at Marford, Dibbinsdale Road, Bromborough, and from there he completed his schooling at Port Sunlight School, which he left in 1904 to become a clerk in the firm of Wilson & Co. of Temple Street, Liverpool, a provisions wholesaler in the grocery trade.

Before joining the Army in 1914 Procter had become a Sunday school teacher in Tranmere and was a member of the St Luke's Church Lads' Brigade. He lodged with a Mr and Mrs Charles Codd and became a member of the voluntary aid detachment of the local Red Cross and also gained St John's Ambulance first-aid proficiency certificates. With his involvement in the Church and in first aid it can be seen what sort of career he might later follow.

At the age of twenty-four he enlisted on 30 November 1914 in the 5th Battalion King's (Liverpool) Regiment (TF) as a rifleman. The regiment had a depot in St Anne's Street. After initial training he served in France from February 1915 and took part in the battles of Neuve Chapelle, Festubert, Givenchy, the Somme and Arras. While in the Bethune area in May 1916 he was wounded in the arm by shrapnel and was sent to 2nd Canadian Field Hospital at Le Touquet in mid-May. A few weeks later he returned to his battalion and won the VC on 4 June near Ficheux.

After the war he returned to employment in his former trade and became a grocery salesman, moving from Wilson's to George Wall & Co. Ltd until he gave the job up in 1926, having decided on a career in the Church. He then became a student at St Aidan's College in Birkenhead in 1926, where he trained for a year before being ordained in Liverpool Cathedral.

On 26 June 1920 he attended the royal garden party for VC holders in the grounds of Buckingham Palace and in November the services for the Unknown Warrior.

On 19 July 1924 the King and Queen visited Liverpool to attend the consecration of the cathedral. During the afternoon the King reviewed members of the 55th West Lancashire Territorial Division at the Wavertree Playground. Procter was one of nine VC holders presented to the King, who told him that he remembered decorating him in France in August 1916. Procter was present at the House of Lords' dinner in November 1929.

His first parish job was the curacy of the parish of St Mary the Virgin, the parish church at Prescot, from 1927 to 1931. He was then given his own parish and became vicar of the village of Bosley near Macclesfield in Cheshire, before moving to St Stephen's, Flowery Field, Newton, near Hyde in the diocese of Chester, where he remained until 1944.

Procter held strong beliefs and was not afraid of expressing them in public. While at Newton he was involved in a dispute as to how the church was to be used. He would not allow entertainment events 'which did not fit in with God' to be performed. Also, because he was of a nervous and highly strung temperament, he quickly bridled when he failed to get his own way. Lummis noted that at a parish council meeting, for example, he would even take his jacket off and square up for a fight with someone expressing a different viewpoint from his own. In addition he probably 'ruffled some feathers' when at a regimental service in 1936, addressing members of the 5th King's at a service in St Luke's Church in Liverpool, he said of Parsons: 'We clergymen are not recruiting sergeants.'

During the Second World War Procter served as an RAF chaplain for five years, from 1941 to 1945, with the rank of squadron leader. During the war he lost Peter, one of his three sons, in a bombing raid when he was serving with the RAF.

After the war he was able to attend most VC gatherings, including the Victory celebrations of 1946 and the VC centenary of June 1956. He was also invited to a dinner given at the Royal Army Chaplain's Department, to which Geoffrey Woolley and Edward Mellish, both VC holders, were also invited. Having been one of the founder members of the VC & GC Association he attended his last such function in 1972.

In 1946 he changed parishes again and became rector of St Mary's, Droylsden, Manchester, a post he occupied from 1946 to 1951 before moving to be vicar of St Peter's, Claybrooke with Wibtoft, Rugby, Leicestershire, until 1963, when he was in his early seventies. He finally retired in 1965 when he was vicar of St John the Baptist, Bradworthy with Pancras-Wyke, near Holsworthy, North Devon.

In 1966 Procter was one of a small party of VC guests of the Ministry of Defence who were invited to attend the services for the 50th anniversary of the Battle of the Somme at Thiepval on 1 July 1966. They left Victoria Station on 30 June and were photographed by the press before beginning their journey. When interviewed by a *Sunday Times* reporter Procter stated:

Getting decorated was often a matter of luck as much as anything. You just happened to be seen doing something by someone who remained alive long enough to mention it to a superior officer until it was eventually sorted out at HQ.

In 1967 he took part in a service of remembrance at Liverpool Cathedral for the 7th and 5th King's (Liverpool) Regiment.

His next move was to Shrewsbury, where possibly he had family connections, and in 1970 he made what was to be his last home in a bungalow for retired clergymen at 1 Cherry Tree Close, Netheredge, Sheffield. In the same year he had a stroke, but was well enough two years later to travel to London for a VC/GC function. He died at home on 26 January 1973 and his funeral was held in the

Chapel of St George, Sheffield Cathedral, five days later. He was cremated at Sheffield City Road Crematorium and his ashes were later interred in the crypt chapel of the cathedral and a tablet erected to his memory, which reads:

Arthur Herbert Procter VC
11 August 1890 – 26 January 1973

Mrs Procter outlived her husband by ten years, dying in 1983, having returned to Shrewsbury. On 18 September 1990 Procter's medals were put on the market and sold by Glendinings. The sale estimate was £12,000 to £15,000, and Liverpool Museum secured them for £18,700. In addition to the VC the sale lot included the 1914/15 Star, BWM, VM, and from the Second World War the DM and WM. In addition there were Coronation Medals of 1937 and 1953 as well as the collar badge that Procter was wearing when he won the VC. Also included in the lot were a collection of letters, together with telegrams of congratulation. His VC is held by the King's Regiment.

On 20 April 1995 Procter's name was one of eight Tameside Metropolitan VC winners commemorated on a plaque outside the entrance to the Manchester Regiment Museum in Ashton Town Hall, Ashton-under-Lyne.

J. ERSKINE

Givenchy, France, 22 June 1916

(*David Harvey*)

Two and a half weeks after Pte Arthur Procter saved the lives of two men in the lines south of Arras between Blairville and Ficheux, another similar deed was carried out in the Duck's Bill position at Givenchy by L/Cpl Acting Sgt John Erskine.

On 22 June 1916, while the 33rd Division was holding a line astride the La Bassée Canal, the 2nd Royal Welch Fusiliers (19th Brigade) 33rd Division were occupying the Givenchy trenches. Their front projected on to a ridge known as the Duck's Bill, an area pitted with craters. Beyond it the ground then fell away, and the enemy had taken the opportunity to carry out frequent mining and counter-mining in the ground between the two opposing front lines.

The 2nd Royal Welch Fusiliers, who had only recently taken over the line, occupied the Duck's Bill craters and were assured on their arrival that things were very quiet. As often happened on the Western Front, this was the time to worry, and sure enough at 1.55 a.m. the enemy exploded a mine in front of Duck's Bill that turned out to be the largest they had ever exploded on the Western Front. The new crater 'dominated the landscape'. Some 80 yards of the RWF line had been totally destroyed and their support line was damaged as well. Not only was the front line destroyed but an area of about a hundred yards was covered with earth, resulting in over a hundred casualties, many from B Coy A heavy enemy bombardment swiftly followed the explosion, which lasted for about an hour. It firstly concentrated on the front-line trenches and then on the support lines. The waiting and suffering 5/6th Cameronians' (19th Brigade) 33rd Division relieving company expected an enemy attack, which duly came with 150 men pouring through on each side of the crater, about 120 feet across. Many men of the 2nd RWF were buried alive or half buried, but a few of those who had survived the explosion quickly manned the parapet and opened fire on the attackers, some of whom stormed the front-line trenches. However, they were bombed and forced to fall back. As the Allied flanks had held, the enemy advantage in blowing the mine was minimised.

Work on consolidating the damage to the front line and saps, and in particular the near lip, which was about 15 feet high, was then carried out – work in which Lt David Stevenson, the Cameronians' platoon sapping officer, took an active part before being wounded by a sniper. Under continuous fire L/Cpl John Erskine, a member of the sapping platoon, without regard to any danger, dashed out twice in order to bring in a wounded sergeant and then a private. He then saw that his officer Stevenson had become a casualty, and on seeing him make some movement decided to try to bring him back to safety as well. Stevenson was totally exposed and when Erskine reached him he firstly bandaged his head and then scooped out some cover for him, staying with him a whole hour. He was continuously fired at and a shallow trench was being dug towards him. Shielding his officer with his own body he brought the mortally wounded man in.

In *Old Soldiers Never Die* Frank Richards, a signaller with the Royal Welch Fusiliers, told the story in the following slightly incorrect way:

> . . . During the day one of the men of the 5th Scottish Rifles to our right noticed a wounded man of ours lying out in front who was trying to crawl back to the trench. He jumped over the parapet and ran towards him and under a heavy fire of rifle-bullets safely brought him back to his trench. He was awarded the Victoria Cross for this.

The 5th Cameronians' War Diary described what happened as follows:

> In the early morning, one of the largest mines ever put up on the Western Front was blown at the Duck's Bill, by the Germans, and followed by one hour's intense bombardment of the front and support lines. The enemy attacked with about 200 men and got into our trenches, but were gallantly counter-attacked and driven out by the 2nd Royal Welch Fusiliers. A Company of the Royal Welch Fusiliers who had had most of the fighting was relieved by a company of the Cameronians which in turn was relieved by A Company of ours. Lieut Stevenson, the Sapping Officer, was killed by a sniper while assisting in the consolidation of the crater. Lance-Corporal Erskine was successful in bringing in two wounded men, and very gallantly went out over the open and attended to Lieutenant Stevenson, lying beside him until a shallow trench had been dug to the spot where he lay, whereby he was brought into the trenches.

Sadly, despite Erskine's very gallant efforts to save the life of Lt Stevenson, the officer died of his wounds the same day and was buried at Gorre British Cemetery, Beuvry. The crater created by the German mine was later christened the Red Dragon Crater after one of the badges of the Royal Welch Fusiliers.

In the following month Erskine, now promoted to sergeant, was himself wounded in the right leg, for which he needed treatment. His citation for the VC was published in the *London Gazette* of 5 August:

John Erskine, Acting Sergeant, Scottish Rifles, Territorial Force. For most conspicuous bravery whilst the lip of a crater, caused by the explosion of a large enemy mine, was being consolidated. Acting Sergeant Erskine rushed out under continuous fire with utter disregard of danger, and rescued a wounded sergeant and a private. Later, seeing an officer, who was believed to be dead, show signs of movement, he ran to him, bandaged his head, and remained with him for fully an hour, though repeatedly fired, whilst a shallow trench was being dug to them. He then assisted in bringing in his officer, shielding him with his own body in order to lessen the chance of his being hit again.

On 7 July the 33rd Division left the Givenchy sector to join the Fourth Army on the Somme. A few days later the 5/6th Cameronians were heavily involved in the failed attempts to capture and hold High Wood in the Somme battlefield.

Erskine was unable to collect his VC from the King, as he was killed at the end of the first phase of the Battle of Arras, near Fontaine-les-Croisilles, on 14 April 1917, the day of a British attack on the German defensive positions at Monchy le Preux. In operations close to the Hindenburg Line the 5/6th Battalion advanced about half a mile from Hénin Hill on high ground to the east of St Martin-sur-Cojeul. Their left flank was meant to have been covered by the 56th Division, but it wasn't, and a barrage was of little assistance in curbing unchecked machine-gun fire. This made progress well-nigh impossible, and they were ordered to dig in. The barrage should have concentrated on the enemy positions, but it was of the 'creeping variety': the lack of coordination led to the battalion suffering 200 casualties; those of D Coy were exceptionally heavy, and included Sgt Erskine VC.

On 2 June 1919 Erskine's mother, accompanied by her daughter Bessie, received the posthumous medal from the King at a ceremony at Hyde Park. Erskine's body was never found, and his name is commemorated in Bay 6 of the Arras Memorial. At the time of his death Dunfermline Town Council were preparing an illuminated address, together with a gold watch and chain, to give to their local hero.

His VC is in the collection of the Cameronians (Scottish Rifles).

John Erskine was born to William and Elizabeth Erskine in Park Avenue, Dunfermline, Fifeshire, Scotland, on 13 January 1894, the eldest of six brothers

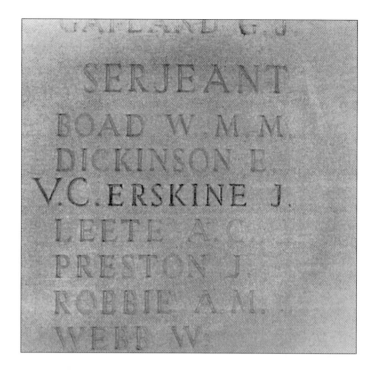

Arras Memorial
(*Donald C. Jennings*)

and one sister. William was a partner in the old-established draper's firm of W. & J. MacLaren & Co., of Bridge Street, Dunfermline. John was educated at Dunfermline High School, and on leaving he became an apprentice draper in Princes Street, Edinburgh, before moving to Glasgow to work with the firm Pettigrew & Stephen.

Six days after the war began he enlisted, joining the 5th Battalion, The Cameronians (Scottish Rifles) (TF). His service number was 200476. When a lance corporal he became a member of the battalion sapping platoon (June 1916) and acting sergeant. His battalion had fought in the Battle of Loos in the autumn of 1915 and in June 1916 was in the area of Givenchy.

After the war Mrs Erskine bequeathed her son's VC to her only daughter, Miss Bessie Erskine of 1 East Saville Road, Edinburgh, which was also Mrs Erskine's address. In May 1965 Bessie presented it to the Cameronians' Regimental Museum in Hamilton. Bessie is buried in the family grave, which also commemorates John Erskine VC and William Mclaren Erskine who fell at Beaumont Hamel on 18 November 1916 aged twenty-one. Acting lance corporal with B Coy of the 17th HLI, William was buried at New Munich trench, Beaumont Hamel, F3. John Erskine is also commemorated on the Dysart War Memorial and the Dunfermline High School roll of honour.

W. HACKETT

Shaftesbury Avenue Mine, near Givenchy, France, 22/23 June 1916

(David Harvey)

Close to where L/Cpl John Erskine won his VC for attempting to save the life of a wounded officer in the Red Dragon Crater, Givenchy, another deed of self-sacrifice was being performed by William Hackett, a sapper of the 254th Tunnelling Company. The deed took place underground on 22/23 June at the Shaftesbury Avenue Mine.

The mine, which the enemy had exploded at 1.55 a.m., caused a great deal of damage underground. An account published in *The Tunnellers* by Grieve and Newman tells the story.

Red Dragon is also connected with one of the most poignant incidents in tunnelling warfare. Considerable damage was done below ground when the enemy mine was fired. The main drive from Shaftesbury Shaft had not proceeded very far, and five men were in it at the time of the blow. The shock broke some of the timbers near the shaft, causing a fall of roof and cutting off the men. Relays of workers set to work at top speed to release the trapped men. After twenty-four hours a small opening was made through the soft fallen ground and broken timber. Three men scrambled through it to safety.

It was then discovered that a smaller fall of roof had occurred near the face. Of the two men remaining in the gallery one, a big man, was badly injured by the fall near the face; the other was Sapper William Hackett. The opening which the rescue party had driven through the outby fall was too small to permit the injured man to be passed through, and as there was immediate danger of further falls, Hackett was ordered to come out. Well knowing his fate, he steadfastly refused to leave the injured man, saying 'I am a tunneller. I must look after my mate.' Scarcely had he finished speaking when both men were overwhelmed by a fall of clay which filled the gallery completely. All efforts to re-open it failed. For this calculated act of courageous self-sacrifice Sapper Hackett was awarded the Victoria Cross posthumously.

. . . Shaftesbury Shaft received such a buffeting that finally it collapsed, and new shafts were started. These were equipped with electrical pumps and were therefore able to overcome the water trouble. Such rapid progress was made that we were able to make the new line built behind the 'Red Dragon' crater, secure underground before the enemy could strike again and drive home his advantage.

Hackett's VC was published in the *London Gazette* of 5 August 1916:

William Hackett, Sapper, late Royal Engineers. For most conspicuous bravery when entombed with four others in a gallery owing to an explosion of an enemy mine. After working for twenty hours a hole was made through fallen earth and broken timber, and the outside party was met. Sapper Hackett helped three of the men through the hole, and could easily have followed, but refused to leave the fourth, who had been seriously injured, saying 'I am a tunneller, and must look after the others first.' Meantime the hole was getting smaller, yet he still refused to leave his injured comrade. Finally the gallery collapsed, and though the rescue party worked desperately for four days, the attempt to reach the two men failed. Sapper Hackett, well knowing the nature of the sliding earth and the chances against him, deliberately gave his life for his comrade.

The history of the corps of engineers noted of the tunnelling companies: 'The success of these RE mining units was outstanding and largely attributed to by the excellence of the personnel. Many of course would be experienced miners who were quite used to the rigours and dangers of life in the pit.' They could also more easily withstand the hardships of trench life.

The *Mexborough & Swinton Times* reported on 12 August 1916 that Hackett had gone out three weeks after enlisting and had been out for eight months, and his home had been at 47 Cross Hallgate. After her husband died Captain G.M. Edwardes of Hackett's company wrote to her in the following terms in a letter first published on 22 July (so the announcement of the award of the VC did not come as a surprise to Hackett's home town):

I find it very difficult to express to you adequately the admiration I and all the officers had for the heroic manner in which your husband met his death. Sad as his loss may be to his own people, yet his fearless conduct and wonderful self-sacrifice must always be a source of pride and comfort to you all. Your husband deliberately sacrificed his own life to save his comrades, and even when three or four were saved he refused to save himself because the remaining man was too injured to help himself. He has been recommended for the V. C. – that simple medal which represents all that is brave and noble. In token of our esteem, the officers and men of this unit are sending you a small gift in the near future, which we trust will be acceptable.

Sapper W.H. Vernon from Rotherham, who was in the same company as Hackett, wrote in a letter the following account:

We succeeded in getting three out alive after being entombed for thirty hours. Hackett being the tallest and knowing his chum was hurt, gave the other three preference to get out of the small hole – the way to liberty and to God's sunshine – well knowing that if he had gone first the passage would have been blocked. The heroic rescue party (officers as well as men) worked like Trojans, but after the third man got out the Fates were unkind. The gallery collapsed and poor Hackett and his chum were entombed a second time. We kept them alive for some time, feeding them through pipes, but the Fates were again cruel. Another fall came, smashing the pipes, and that was the end. Having done our best and knowing they had given their lives for their country, we retired to avenge their deaths.

In an interview with a reporter Mrs Hackett, on hearing the news about her husband, said:

I knew he was no coward. I could never understand the doctors rejecting him on account of his heart. There wasn't much wrong with that was there? He was always after joining the Army, and I know he tried hard to get into the York and Lancaster Regiment. Only a few weeks before he enlisted, he got cut across the back by a fall of roof in Manvers Main Mine, and had a very narrow escape from death so the deputy afterwards told me. The deputy wanted him to be taken home at once, but he refused, saying he would work the shift out, because his missus would be upset if she thought he had been hurt so badly that he had had to give up work before the shift was up. That's the sort of man he was. I can just imagine what he would think when he was down in the mine where he met his death. He would think when he heard that another poor fellow was fastened up in there. What would my feelings be if I was lying helpless and nobody would stay with me? I must go to him, even if we both go under.

As early as August a memorial fund was opened for Mexborough's first winner of a Victoria Cross, with the aim to raise enough funds to provide generously for the family. The War Office awarded his widow a small pension. She was presented with her husband's medal at Buckingham Palace on 29 November 1916, and fifty years later his daughter Mrs Mary Hopkins presented it to the

Royal Engineers Institution, Chatham. In September 1917 Alice Hackett was invited by Manvers Main Colliery to a ceremony where she was presented with a gold watch in commemoration of her husband, which is now in the ownership of his granddaughter Freda.

Hackett's name is further commemorated on Panel 1 of the Ploegsteert Memorial, and with a special memorial in Mexborough bearing the following inscription:

To the Memory of our Townsman
SAPPER WILLIAM HACKETT, V.C.,
Killed on June 22nd–23rd 1916 in France,
While rescuing his Comrades,
'Greater love hath no man than this, that
a man lay down his life for his friends.'

William Hackett, son of John and Harriet Hackett, was born in Nottingham on 11 June 1873. He received scant, if any, formal education while attending a local board school. His father was a travelling brewer whose main customers were rural inns; he probably died in 1899 and his wife in 1913.

By the time he was eighteen William had already worked at various factory jobs before going to Denaby Main coal-mine, where he worked for the next twenty-three years, leaving in about November 1913. While working in the Nottinghamshire pit he had the habit of addressing his younger colleagues as 'Youth', and after he won his VC he was to become known as 'Youthy, VC'. When his job in Nottinghamshire ended he had to move to Yorkshire to find similar

Ploegsteert Memorial (*Donald C. Jennings*)

work, which he found at the end of 1913 at Manvers Main Colliery, Wath upon Dearne, near Rotherham, as a detailer – a sort of maintenance man – paid at a daily rate, as opposed to being a miner. He was a quiet and unassuming man and not one to talk much.

On 16 April 1900, when he was twenty-six, he married Alice Tooby from Morley, near Leeds, at Conisborough parish church. The couple had two children, Arthur and Mary. Tragically, in January 1916 Arthur, the fourteen-year-old boy, had to have his right leg amputated above the knee as the result of a serious accident in the Manvers Main mine when he was hit 'by a train of 'tubs' which had run off the road'. He had only been working there for four weeks. As his father was now in France Arthur had become the main breadwinner in the family, and after his accident he took up shorthand and typing.

William had tried to join up four times with the York and Lancaster Regiment but had been rejected owing to suspected heart trouble; he was also above military age. However, he persevered and enlisted at Doncaster in early November and attested in Chatham on 5 November 1915 with the Royal Engineers Tunnelling Corps. His experience as a skilled miner meant that his training only lasted a fortnight. He then returned home to 47 Cross Hallgate, Mexborough, Rotherham, for a few days to see his family in the house where his parents-in-law also lived. Towards the end of November he left for France with the 254th Tunnelling Company and was to be involved in 'much heavy fighting'. Communication with home was not easy as Hackett was unable to read or write and had to ask another sapper to write home on his behalf. Some of this correspondence is in the archive of the Royal Engineers in Chatham: it was presented to the museum by Hackett's granddaughter in 1996.

In the 1990s, when the Market Hall carrying a tablet to Hackett's memory became a bingo hall, the local branch of the Royal British Legion considered that the site was no longer appropriate, although they used to lay a wreath there annually. So in early 1997 it was decided to move the tablet to a position close to the town's war memorial, and when it was taken down it was put into storage for a few months while the necessary funds for costs were raised and site preparation carried out.

The Doncaster Council and the Dearne Valley Partnership joined in the funding, and the tablet was erected in its new position in Castle Hills Park in May 1997. A dedication service was planned which had to be delayed until August 1997 when the memorial was unveiled by the Mayor of Doncaster. A Lancaster and Spitfire from the Battle of Britain Flight flew overhead during the ceremonies and a march past of veterans also took place. Prior to a recent Remembrance Day service the memorial was vandalised but was cleaned up in time for the service. For some reason Hackett's name was not included on the original list of names on the adjacent war memorial, but this omission was rectified in 1976.

Manvers Colliery has long been closed and in its grounds a sandstone memorial has been erected to the memory of 204 miners, including William Hackett VC.

A.H.H. BATTEN-POOLL

Near Cité Calonne, France, 25 June 1916

(David Harvey)

Before the Battle of the Somme, which was due to begin on 29 June but was postponed because of rain, many raids were organised in various sectors of the Western Front in order to confound the enemy's suspicions about preparation for a large battle in the Somme area. As a consequence of these raids four VCs were gained, and one of these raids was carried out by members of the 2nd Royal Munster Fusiliers (3rd Brigade) 1st Division, near Lens in the mining area of Cité Calonne, a mile north of Lievin.

Volunteers were called for from the 2nd Royal Munster Fusiliers for the raid which was due to take place on the 25th, and intense preparation was carried out at nearby Grenay to the north-west of Lens, where a replica of the ground to be covered was created. The raid was to be carried out by two parties, the southern and northern, to be led respectively by Maj L.R. Shildrick and Lt A.H. Batten-Pooll. The distance to the enemy saps was 330 yards, and the two parties would move off together before acting independently. The objectives were to capture prisoners, establish their regimental identification and capture arms and equipment. The enemy system of defences was to be reconnoitred and loss was to be inflicted.

Men blackened their faces and hands and removed all signs of identification. Helmets with sacking covers were worn and each participant had a knot of white material on both of his shoulders. In addition, every man except for the bayonet men carried four bombs as well as a bludgeon.

After a preliminary bombardment at 11.10 p.m. the two parties moved forward to raid the hostile trenches, their progress being greatly assisted by a railway cutting to their left that led diagonally towards the enemy lines – it had been used by previous raiding parties. After the box barrage lifted on to the enemy support trenches the raiding parties moved into a dip in No Man's Land. Maj Shildrick's southern party went straight for the enemy trench and, encountering little resistance, managed to block the exits and proceeded to clear the trench.

Batten-Pooll's northern party on the other flank had a very different experience. After passing through the German wire they reached the enemy trench, which they found full of troops who proceeded to open rapid fire, causing the raiders many casualties. Batten-Pooll, cheering on his men, immediately dashed forward and climbed onto the German parapet, where he was severely wounded in his left hand and arm. This did not deter him, and with fingers dangling he then proceeded to walk along the parapet shouting, 'Tally-ho! Tally-ho, lads! Have at 'em, lads!' Clearly this hunting rallying call had its effect, and the Munsters' blood was up for they quickly got down into the German trenches and conducted an extremely savage and bitter hand-to-hand fight with an enemy that had already been 'softened' by the British barrage and was now simply unable to stand the Irish battalion's onslaught. The raid had already lasted forty minutes when it became prudent for the Munsters to withdraw. When Shildrick and Batten-Pooll returned, the latter collapsed and was taken to hospital with the other Munster casualties. The regimental history commented: 'Dirty. Dishevelled, blood-stained, and breathless, the raiders staggered back over the open, the officers being the last to leave.' Of the several prisoners taken none reached the British lines alive, but when identification marks were removed from the German prisoners and returned for later examination it was discovered that their adversaries had been members of the 27th Infantry Regiment of the German 7th Division.

The 1st Division war diary has this to say of when the Munsters reached the enemy trenches:

> They were met with stout opposition and were subjected to bombing attacks on the flanks and rifle grenade attacks from the hostile support line. Fierce hand to hand fighting took place in which most of the Munster leaders became casualties; it is believed that the enemy suffered heavy casualties. After remaining in the enemy's trench the Munsters withdrew without very great opposition, bringing back most of the wounded. There were 45 casualties. On the following day fire was directed on the enemy's front line and his retaliation was 'feeble'.

Batten-Pooll's extraordinary heroic personal leadership was rewarded with the VC, which was gazetted on 5 August 1916. Other awards later presented to members of the Munsters included two MCs, four DCMs and nine MMs. Batten-Pooll's VC citation was published as follows:

> Arthur Hugh Henry Batten-Pooll, Lieutenant, 3rd Royal Munster Fusiliers. For most conspicuous bravery whilst in command of a raiding party. At the moment of entry into the enemy's lines he was severely wounded by a bomb, which broke and mutilated all the fingers of his right hand. In spite of this he continued to direct operations with unflinching courage, his voice being clearly heard cheering on and directing his men. He was urged, but refused, to retire. Half an hour later, during the withdrawal, whilst personally assisting in

the rescue of other wounded men, he received two further wounds. Still refusing assistance, he walked unaided to within one hundred yards of our lines, when he fainted, and was carried in by a covering party.

Batten-Pooll was presented with his VC by the King at Buckingham Palace on 4 November 1916.

In November 1917, now a captain in charge of C Coy, he won another medal, this time the MC 'for inflicting heavy loss on the enemy'. On 10 November 1917 the Canadian 1st Division was hoping to finally capture Passchendaele Ridge. On their left were troops of the British 1st Division aiming to reach the crest of the main ridge to the north of Goudberg. The two British battalions directly concerned in the action were the 1st South Wales Borderers and the 2nd Royal Munster Fusiliers. After a barrage which began at 5.55 a.m. the attack began at 6.00 a.m. with men from four companies from the Munsters trying to move through a terrain waist-deep in mud and water. On top of this it was very difficult to keep the mud from clogging up their rifles and putting Lewis guns out of action. Not surprisingly, progress was very slow, with enemy machine-guns to the left adding to the hazardous conditions.

Nevertheless, a position called Tournant Farm was occupied, and Captain Batten-Pooll's C Company reached and partially occupied some buildings called Vat Cottages, and those Germans present were ordered to the rear. Parts of D Coy, and men from other companies then pressed further onto Veal Cottages, where they were met with heavy machine-gun fire from the right. Fortunately B Coy, arrived very soon after and rushed the building with the bayonet.

Despite the well-nigh impossible conditions the battalion objectives were met and the order to consolidate was given; but in the circumstances consolidating was not an option. No fresh orders arrived and the men who were left from the Munsters decided to have a go at capturing the main Passchendaele Ridge, visible half a mile away. The battalion history says that 'they pressed forward in mud bespattered, bloodstained and sodden groups'. Their right-hand battalion, the 1st South Wales Borderers, was of little help as it had wandered too far off to the right, but the Canadian 1st Division could be seen moving forward towards the prize of the Ridge. At 7.30 a.m. the Munsters' advance came to a halt and gunfire cut off any communication with Battalion HQ. Two of the surviving captains, Batten-Pooll and Frizell, put in a group of posts and the enemy were seen gathering for a counter-attack from the direction of Mallet Copse. Part of the rear of C Coy was now in the air, and pigeons were sent back with requests for artillery support. A message must have got through as a barrage did finally start, but unfortunately fell on ground that had been captured and held by the battalion, not on the advancing enemy.

During a counter-attack the enemy returned to recapture Vat Cottages, and by now revolvers, rifles and Lewis guns were almost ceasing to function as they were so clogged with mud. Despite this setback Batten-Pooll set about forming a defence, and the Munsters proceeded to fight for every yard of the enemy advance. They came to the point when they had no bombs left, but even this did not deter them since when the Germans came within bombing range the Munsters continued to throw 'bombs', which were in fact actually clods of mud shaped to look like a bomb.

Realising just how isolated the Munsters were, the enemy pressed harder for possession of Veal Cottages, and by 8 a.m. the German regiment, which turned out to be the 'Cockchafers', was in a position to push the Munsters back from the north and north-west, and it was only a matter of time before the few men who survived round Vat and Veal Cottages were mopped up and the Irish battalion was almost back at its starting point. In casualties the day had cost thirteen officers and 374 other ranks. During the final stages of the fighting Capt Batten-Pooll had been taken prisoner and was later posted as missing. He spent the final months of the war in German, and later Swiss, POW camps, from which he was later released.

St Lawrence's Parish Church, Woolverton
(*Donald C. Jennings*)

Arthur Henry Batten-Pooll was born in Knightsbridge, south-west London, on 25 October 1891, son of R.P.H. Batten-Pooll of Rode Manor, Somerset. His father was Lord of the Manor of Rode and Woolverton and Deputy Lieutenant of Somerset. Arthur was educated at Eton and was especially interested in science, as well as being passionate about fox-hunting. On 1 June 1911 he was commissioned into the 3rd Somerset Light Infantry, where he remained until June 1914, when he resigned. He later joined the Royal Munster Fusiliers from the 5th Royal Irish Lancers.

He attended the 1929 House of Lords' dinner and 1956 Centenary Review and various other functions until July 1964. In 1961 he became Vice-President of the Royal Humane Society.

He died at Ugborough House, Ivybridge, Devon, on 21 January 1971 in his eightieth year. Six days later he was buried at St Lawrence's parish church, Woolverton, near Bath. In his will he left £105,400 and his medals are with the National Army Museum.

W. JACKSON

Near Armentières, France, 25/26 June 1916

(David Harvey)

Soon after the 17th Battalion (New South Wales) (5th Brigade) 2nd Division arrived in France from Egypt in April 1916 it was given the task of taking part in a number of harassing raids against enemy positions in the eastern Armentières sector, where it arrived on the 10th. With the planned Battle of the Somme due to commence at the end of June it was decided to mislead the enemy as much as possible in order to detract their attention from finding out too much about the battle preparations further south.

At the beginning of June volunteers were called for from the 5th Brigade for a large raid, and the men selected were given a three-week intensive training course for a raid due to commence on 25 June south-east of Bois Grenier. The training included a full-size replica of a sector of German trench, which was to be the Australian objective.

Eighty-two men from all ranks and from four battalions were chosen to take part, and after darkness fell on 25 June the scout party moved out first and on its return indicated that the enemy were working on their wire. The raiders then crawled out to their allotted positions. At 11 p.m. the Allied artillery opened up a bombardment on the enemy front lines, and as it grew heavier the Germans sent up coloured alarm rockets for artillery assistance. At 11.30 p.m. the Allied artillery lifted off the front lines and onto the support lines, and in addition shells were also directed across each side of the objective. The enemy listening posts were quickly dealt with by the scout party but the raiders found themselves faced by a deep ditch with barbed wire. Although the enemy were ready with machine-gun fire, the raiding party, by keeping low, managed to cross the ditch either by foot or by way of a foot-bridge that led to a German listening post. The men cleared a strip of trench 60 yards wide before storming forward, and only remained in the German trenches for five minutes, most of the garrison having taken shelter in dugouts and therefore offering little in the way of resistance. The engineers blew up two bomb stores. The enemy counter-attack was too late, and most of the Australian casualties were in fact caused by the German artillery. The raid was deemed successful as thirty Germans were killed and four taken prisoner. The bomb stores, a mineshaft and pump were destroyed as well. The Germans turned out to be members of the 50th Reserve Division (231st RIR).

Pte William Jackson, who had acted as one of the scouts and had also captured one of the four German prisoners, returned through 400 yards in No Man's Land to the Australian lines despite enemy shell and machine-gun fire. Knowing full well that there were injured men lying out in No Man's Land, and despite the considerable risks, Jackson returned to rescue the wounded. On his second mission an exploding shell, which made one man unconscious and mortally wounded another, took Jackson's right arm off above the elbow. Seemingly oblivious of his injury he returned to his lines to have his stump bound up, knowing that there were still wounded men needing assistance: he therefore went out yet again to search the battlefield before he was satisfied. After he returned the final time he was taken to a casualty clearing station and a few days later left Boulogne on board a hospital ship. On 30 June he was operated on at the 3rd London General Hospital where the rest of his right arm was amputated. Nearly three weeks later he was moved to Harefield Hospital in Middlesex and in October to an auxiliary hospital in Southall before being transferred to Queen Mary's General Hospital.

It appears that Jackson was first awarded the DCM, but this was later changed to the VC, which was announced in the *London Gazette* of 9 September 1916:

William Jackson, No. 588, Private, 17th Battalion. Australian Infantry. For most conspicuous bravery. On the return from a successful raid, several members of the raiding party were seriously wounded in 'No Man's Land' by shell fire. Private Jackson got back safely, and after handing over a prisoner whom he had brought in, immediately went out again under heavy shellfire and assisted in bringing in a wounded man. He then went out again, and with a sergeant was bringing in another wounded man, whose arm was blown off by a shell, and the sergeant was rendered unconscious. He then returned to our trenches, obtained assistance, and went out again to look for his two wounded comrades. He set a splendid example of pluck and determination. His work has always been marked by the greatest coolness and bravery.

Jackson was the youngest Australian to win a VC, and he was presented with his medal by the King on 18 November 1916 at Buckingham Palace.

Jackson had been very badly wounded and remained in England until 4 May 1917, when he was invalided home to Australia. He arrived home at Sydney on 5 July on board HMAT *Themistocles*, together with 992 other returning servicemen. On returning to Sydney he was hoisted shoulder high at a reception held at the Anzac Buffet.

Together with Sgt Hugh Camden of the 19th Battalion, who had been awarded the DCM on the same raid as Private Jackson, he returned to Hay for an official reception and welcome from the deputy mayor on 26 July. He later returned to his home at Gunbar, where he was again officially welcomed and was even offered the gift of a farming property as an act of appreciation. However, he did not consider that he could run it properly with the loss of his right arm. He was discharged from the Army on 15 September.

William Jackson (John William Alexander, known as Billy) was born at Gunbar, a settlement of four houses north of Hay, in New South Wales, on 13 September 1897. He was the fourth child and eldest son of John Gale Jackson, a farmer, and Adelaide Ann (née McFarlane). He worked as a farm labourer and enlisted in the Army on 20 February 1915 at Liverpool (Sydney). In May 1915 he sailed with the 17th Battalion (NSW) AIF as a member of B Company, and after a period of training at Heliopolis in Egypt, he was detailed for special duties in Alexandria prior to the landing of the battalion at Gallipoli on 20 August. About six weeks later (suffering from diarrhoea and tooth trouble), he was transferred to hospital and was later transported by hospital ship to Malta, where on 7 January 1916 he was put on board a ship for home, only to suffer from an attack of dysentery and be taken off the ship when it was three days out. By mid-February he was passed fit enough for duty and rejoined his battalion on 8 March before it left for France.

Meanwhile, after leaving the Gallipoli Peninsula in December, his battalion had been operating in the Sinai Desert, where it manned outpost lines. It later embarked for France, arriving in the Armentières sector on 7 April 1916. The battalion was part of the 5th Infantry Brigade of the 2nd Australian Division.

After the war Jackson returned home to Gunbar Station, and later to Merriwa in 1920. He was still connected with farming, selling horses and skins, but it didn't work out, and after six seasons of drought, followed by the Depression, he gave up that line of work in 1927 and took up running the Figtree Hotel at Wollongong, near Sydney, where he remained for eighteen months. He appears to have had considerable difficulties in keeping any job for long after the war: perhaps his serious wounds prevented him from being able to cope properly with work. On 12 January 1932 he married Ivy Alma Morris. The couple were to have one daughter, Dorothea.

Eighteen months after the Second World War broke out Jackson joined up as a corporal/acting sergeant with Eastern Command Provost Company from March 1941 to March 1942. Apparently he requested a discharge from the Army, which was granted, only for him to change his mind and re-apply, until he finally left in 1946. In October of the same year, he was involved in a very serious motor accident south of Sydney involving four vehicles and in which two people lost their lives. He was slightly injured himself, and at the inquiry Jackson, who had been driving a lorry, might possibly have got off lightly because the judge was a former Army colleague.

Jackson left for Melbourne in 1953 and worked as a commissionaire with the Melbourne City Council. His duties involved dealing with enquiries at Melbourne Town Hall. A few months later, on 25 February 1954, he was one of the holders of the VC who were presented to the Queen and Prince Philip at Melbourne Cricket Ground. During the same royal visit he also attended a state banquet and was on parade when the royal couple visited the Anzac Memorial in Hyde Park, Sydney.

Just over two years later, in June 1956, Jackson also attended the centenary celebrations of holders of the VC in London, when he was part of the Australian contingent of thirty-five VCs. Between these two events Jackson and his wife were divorced.

While on the voyage to London he became ill and only managed one of the VC events, the garden party at Marlborough House, after which he was flown home and continued working at Melbourne Town Hall.

William Jackson died of heart disease in Melbourne on 4 August 1959 while in his early sixties, at the Repatriation General Hospital, Heidelberg. He was given a full military funeral before being cremated at Spring Vale Crematorium, Melbourne, where his ashes were placed in the Boronia Gardens and a plaque set up. He is also commemorated at the Australian War Memorial in Canberra and in Albury, New South Wales, where a street is named after him. He is remembered in Hay at the school museum, which has a framed photograph of him and his biography. He is also remembered at his former home town of Merriwa with a memorial bar in the local RSL Club named after him. A highway rest stop is also named after him.

Jackson's medals, which always seem to have been to him a matter of controversy, included the DCM, 1914/15 Star, BWM, VM, 1937 Coronation Medal, 1939/45 WM, 1939/45 Australia Service Medal and 1953 Coronation Medal. The story behind the award of the DCM was that it was awarded to him and then cancelled and replaced by the VC. Owing to a breakdown in communication between Jackson and the War Office in London, the cancellation was never carried out properly. Jackson decided to keep hold of the DCM, although he must have known that he was not entitled to it as the award of the VC upgraded and replaced it. At the present time his VC is not publicly held.

J. HUTCHINSON

Opposite Ficheux, France, 28 June 1916

(David Harvey)

Two VCs had already been won near Blairville in 1916 by members of the 55th Division, and a third was gained close to Blairville Wood, Ficheux, south of Arras, on 28 June, just before the original date for the commencement of the Battle of the Somme. The recipient was Pte James Hutchinson of the 2/5th Lancashire Fusiliers (164th Brigade).

No fewer than six raids were planned to take place in the divisional sector, and the 164th Brigade was allocated two. The objectives were the familiar ones of taking prisoners, bombing enemy dugouts, capturing machine-guns and in these cases investigating the effects that gas had on the enemy.

Hutchinson was a member of one of these raiding parties, which was made up of four officers and between fifty-six and sixty-three other ranks who were instructed to carry out a bombing raid close to the northern part of Blairville Wood. Hutchinson's party, led by Capt L.H. Bloy, had been training for two weeks. Heavy bombardments of the enemy wire had been carried out since the 24th when orders for the operation arrived. Lanes 20 yards wide were cut in the German wire and the enemy billets were also targeted by the artillery.

On the 28th the raiders reached their assembly positions at 5.00 p.m. and remained in dugouts until gas and smoke bombs had been sent across No Man's Land in order to cover their approach. As the wind was not very strong the gas unfortunately hung about between the lines. Twenty minutes later the raiders moved to 'an appropriate spot', and at 5.35 under cover of smoke-bombs began to advance across the 180 yards in quick time, but despite this they suffered considerable casualties. When they came within the range of enemy machine-guns they rushed the last few yards. However, heavy artillery fire and machine-gun and rifle fire failed to deter the raiders, who by then had been split into three groups, and when they managed to reach the wire they found that much of it had already been cut by artillery fire. The enemy retaliated strongly. The enemy machine-gun that was doing the most damage was situated to the left of Ficheux Mill.

Hutchinson's party to the left of the attack was led with great dash by Lt M.H. Young before he fell mortally wounded on shooting a German officer. At this point Private Hutchinson took over as leader of the then small group of nine men. They were then attacked by bombs, and as they failed to get their ladders into the trench, which was 7 feet deep and 8 to 10 feet wide, they jumped down into it. As first bayonet man, Private Hutchinson shot through the head a man who was firing a machine-gun. Next he bayoneted a second and then shot a third and bayoneted two more men when entering a second traverse. In a third traverse he bayoneted or shot three more of the enemy, and in a fourth he ran out of ammunition but somehow managed to subdue the Germans, 'who were too upset to shoot straight'.

Once the objective of reaching behind the enemy lines had been gained Hutchinson undertook an equally hazardous task when he covered the raiders' retreat until the last of them was clear. When it came to his own retirement he first bandaged some of the wounded before escorting them back to their lines. No wounded in his party were left behind, nor were any prisoners captured either. However, Hutchinson did manage to retrieve a German cap, which was described in the 164th Brigade Diary: '. . . This cap was a round grey one having a red band covered with a khaki ribbon. There were two circular badges on the front. . .'. All this time Hutchinson had been exposed to machine-gun and rifle fire at close quarters, and as if he hadn't done enough already he then volunteered to take a message from one end of the battalion lines to the major in the 1/4th Loyal North Lancashires. His own battalion, the 2/5th Lancashire Fusiliers, returned to Bretencourt after two days, returning four days later to front-line trenches in front of Agny.

Maj Gen H.S. Jeudwine of the 55th Division inspected the surviving raiders on 29 June and told Hutchinson 'that he should have something to wear on his breast'.

The official version of his gallantry published in the *London Gazette* of 9 September 1916 was very brief:

James Hutchinson, Private (now Corporal), No. 2579, Lancashire Fusiliers. For most conspicuous bravery. During an attack on the enemy's position this soldier was the leading man, and, entering their trench, shot two sentries and cleared two of the traverses. After our objective had been gained and retirement ordered, Private Hutchinson, on his own initiative, undertook the dangerous task of covering the retirement, as he did this with such gallantry and determination that the wounded were removed to safety. During all this time this gallant soldier was exposed to fierce fire from machine-guns and rifles at close quarters.

Tragically, Frank Hutchinson's brother James took part in the same raid, as a corporal but was one of sixteen casualties. His name is commemorated on the Arras Memorial. Joseph, a third brother, suffered an eye injury during the start of the Somme offensive and he was sent home to a London hospital and lost the sight of his right eye. Three weeks later Hutchinson, like his brother Joseph, also lost the sight of his right eye. In 1917 he won a competition for the disabled.

After receiving his VC from the King at Buckingham Palace on 2 December 1916 Hutchinson returned home to Radcliffe on 9 December to a hero's welcome from a large crowd, accompanied by a brass band, which was followed by a civic reception. He was presented with an illuminated address, together with a gold watch. A short time later he visited his old school.

Owing to the loss of his right eye he did not return to active service, and instead he was promoted to corporal and made company bomb instructor. He was discharged from the Army in 1919 with the rank of lance corporal.

James Hutchinson was born at 18 Bank Top, Radcliffe, Lancashire, on 9 July 1895, fourth and youngest son of Samuel and Ann Hutchinson. He was educated at Radcliffe Parish Church Schools, which included a Sunday school, where he became a teacher and an active member of the Church Lads' Brigade. At some point the Hutchinson family moved to High Bank, Woos Nab, Radcliffe, and regularly attended the parish church at Bury.

Hutchinson was a keen footballer and was employed as a piecer at Mellor's Mill, Warth Fold. He was only five feet four inches tall, and soon after the outbreak of war he enlisted, at the age of nineteen, as a private with the 2/5th Lancashire Fusiliers. He trained in Stockport in Cheshire and left for France on 3 May 1915.

When the war finished Hutchinson continued to live at Bury for a short time before moving to Devon, where he and his wife ran a boarding house in Torquay. At some point he worked as a poultry farmer in Newton Abbot.

In June 1920 he attended the garden party at Buckingham Palace and the House of Lords' dinner in 1929. In 1939 at the age of forty-four he joined up again, and after the war took part in the Victory Parade of June 1946, the VC centenary celebrations of 1956 and other VC/GC functions up to 1968. In 1966 he was one of a small group of VC holders who were invited to France by the Minister of Defence to attend the 50th anniversary of the Battle of the Somme. When interviewed by a *Sunday Times* reporter he said there had been occasions when he had wished he had never gained the supreme award. 'Trying to get back into the building trade after the war, I often lost the chance of a job because it wasn't considered 'good enough' for me.'

When his wife died in 1971 Hutchinson was looked after for nine months by a Mrs Strode, and his final days were spent at Barnshill, Zion Road, Torquay. He was an active member of the British Legion and of the Torquay Social Club. He suffered from chronic bronchitis and died at home on 22 January 1972, and after his funeral was cremated at Torquay Crematorium. The Revd Harold Mason Ainscrow, who had taken part in the raid in which Hutchinson had won his VC in 1916, gave the funeral address. (Ainscow had been taken prisoner and was in captivity for two and a half years.)

Hutchinson's medals are not in the public domain. He is commemorated on the roll of honour at Radcliffe and Bury parish churches. His brother Frank is commemorated on the Lancashire Fusiliers Memorial at Wellington Barracks, Bury.

N.V. CARTER

Boar's Head, Richebourg l'Avoué, France,
30 June 1916

(David Harvey)

The fourth man to win a Victoria Cross towards the end of June 1916, immediately prior to the commencement of the Battle of the Somme on 1 July, was CSM Nelson Carter of the 12th Royal Sussex Regiment (116th Brigade), 39th Division, which was in a sector near Richebourg, north-west of La Bassée.

The 12th Battalion, together with the 13th Battalion, was due to take part in an attack against a pronounced position in the enemy lines called the Boar's Head, north of the Ferme du Bois, close to Richebourg l'Avoué – on the trench maps it had the appearance of a snout. The 13th attacked the enemy position on the right, and its sister battalion, the 12th, attacked on the left, probably with the idea of pinching out a section of the enemy line. A handwritten report in the brigade war diary tells the story of the attack, which turned out to be an utter failure:

The artillery opened at 2.5 a.m. according to programme. At 3.5 a.m. the Infantry Attack commenced. On the right the 13th RSR captured the enemy front line and part of his support line. Information of what was going on after the assault began was very slow in getting back to Brigade HQ. As far as can be ascertained the 13th RSR held on in the enemy line for some time but while there they were very heavily shelled and had to eventually withdraw. On the left the 12th RSR were held up by wire. The two centre companies captured the enemy front line and from reports a few appear to have got as far as his support line. The right company was held up by a ditch. Both battalions lost heavily during the advance to the enemy front line and also between front line and support line from machine-gun fire. The losses of the two battalions are between 200 and 300 each.

12th Battalion lost very heavily in Officers. Officer commanding 13th Battalion on the right of attack reports enemy losses very heavy. Large numbers of dead were seen lying in the trenches and the first troops to enter engaged in hand to hand combat. Enemy losses on left are more difficult to ascertain but were undoubtedly heavy.

A further handwritten account a little later added additional information and stressed once more that the enemy had lost heavily as well and that a large number had been killed by the bayonet as well as by bombs and Lewis gun fire. The reason for the inability to hang on to the captured German positions was due to:

very heavy M.G. fire directed on them as they fought for the front line and support line, and also to the intense artillery fire directed on the enemy's support line during the time they occupied it. The right Battalion was also confused by our smoke which drifted up from the right and made it very dark. The left Battalion encountered cut wire, principally knee-high trip wire which could not be seen in the long grass until getting quite close.

The enemy was undoubtedly well-prepared for the attack. During the night he appears to have brought up fresh troops and had a large number of M.G.s in action.

Although the objective was gained it could not be retained, so the attacking troops had to retreat to their original start line, with casualties of seventeen officers and 350 other ranks for the 12th, and twelve officers and 500 other ranks for the 13th Battalion.

During this attack CSM Nelson Carter, a member of the 4th Coy of the 12th RSR, carried out several acts of extreme bravery and gallantry, and his efforts were later recognised by the award of a posthumous VC. The *London Gazette* of 9 September 1916 published the citation:

For most conspicuous bravery. During an attack he was in command of the fourth wave of the assault. Under intense shell and machine-gun fire he penetrated, with a few men, into the enemy's second line and inflicted heavy casualties with bombs. When forced to retire to the enemy's first line, he captured a machine-gun and shot the gunner with his revolver. Finally, after carrying several wounded men to safety, he was himself mortally wounded, and died in a few minutes. His conduct throughout the day was magnificent.

Four days later the *Eastbourne Gazette* published a letter to Carter's widow from a Capt Harold Robinson of Carter's company:

I take the earliest opportunity of offering you my heartiest congratulations on the great honour that has been bestowed upon your late husband, whose memory I shall always cherish as a good and great soldier. We served together for eighteen months, and for four months preceding his death he was my right-hand man.

. . . On 30 June, he was in command of the last platoon to go over the parapet. When I last saw him he was close to the German frontline, acting as a leader to a small party of four or five men. I was afterwards told that he had entered the German second line and had brought back an enemy machine-gun, having put the gun team out of action. I heard that he shot one of them with his revolver.

I next saw him about a hour later . . . Your husband repeatedly went over the parapet – I saw him going over alone – and carried in our wounded men from 'No Man's Land'. He brought them in on his back, and he could not have done this had he not possessed exceptional physical strength as well as courage.

It was in the going over for the sixth or seventh time that he was shot through the chest. I saw him fall just outside the trench. Somebody told me that he got back just inside our trench, but I do not know for certain.

At F . . ., about a month previously, your husband carried a man about 400 yards across the open under machine-gun fire, and brought him safely into our trench. For this act I recommended him for the Military Cross.

On every occasion – no matter how tight the hole we were in – he was always cheerful and hopeful, and never spared any pains to make the men comfortable and keep them cheery. In fact it would be difficult to imagine a man better qualified to lead his comrades into action under the dangerous conditions . . . .

The site of the Boar's Head is to be found down a track leading off the road between Bethune and Neuve Chapelle quite close to the Indian Memorial. Carter's body was recovered from the lines and taken to the RI Rifles Cemetery three kilometres south-east of Laventie. His grave (VI, C, 17) has the inscription: 'The cherished flowers of France may fall but honour will outlive them all.'

Owing to a muddle in the War Office, Carter's wife Kitty only received official news of his death on 14 December, although she had already been informed that he was missing. However, there could have been little confusion in Kitty's mind about her husband's death as several of his colleagues had informed her in early July.

Probably the very first intimation she had of news of her husband's death was in a letter dated 2 July 1916 from CQMS T.G.D. Grigg of A Coy of the 12th Battalion, in which he stated that her husband was killed in action on the 30th. Another letter dated 2 July came from 2/Lt W.E.C. Spencer, also of A Coy,

R.I. Rifles Churchyard, Laventie
(*Donald C. Jennings*)

expressing the sympathy of the officers.

Kitty received the news of her late husband's posthumous VC in early September, and when interviewed by a reporter from the *Eastbourne Gazette* she told him that her husband had 'loved the Army and his boys – the men in his company – were fond of him. From the officers, too, he received the greatest kindness; and he felt it a great pleasure to serve with Captain Robinson who lives in this neighbourhood.'

Kitty also received expressions of sympathy from a Pte Ellis from C Company of the 12th Battalion and from Maj H. Thrupp. Both writers also congratulated her on her husband's achievements and clearly thought very highly of him as a soldier.

On receiving the official news of Nelson Carter's VC and knowing that his widow was now left with an eight-month-old daughter to bring up, Mrs Rupert Gwynne, wife of the local Eastbourne MP, opened a memorial fund in order to provide assistance for Kitty's and Jessie's expenses. From 12 March 1917 Kitty became eligible for a pension of 17 shillings (85p) from the Army to be paid weekly towards her and her daughter's financial needs.

Nelson's posthumous VC was presented to his widow by the King at Buckingham Palace on 2 May 1917. He had written to her on 26 March 1917 the standard letter of his regret at her loss. On 5 January 1918 she received a further letter from Capt H.C.T. Robinson in which he referred to the committee set up by Mrs Gwynne, which was most anxious that she should not be separated from her daughter or lose her house. Since her husband's death Capt Robinson had acted as a sort of father figure to her and was always prepared to help her in any way. In fact the 12th Royal Sussex was most supportive.

Nelson Carter's name was later commemorated on the war memorial in Hailsham, the regimental memorial in Chichester Cathedral and at the Regimental Museum in Eastbourne where there is a VC display. His deeds were written up in *The Victor* comic on 7 December 1963.

After Jessie's death, her son Geoffrey offered the medals to the Royal Sussex Regimental Museum in Eastbourne and they were unveiled on 28

June 2003. Some of Jessie's ashes were scattered on the grave of her father in Laventie.

Nelson Victor Carter was born in Eastbourne on 9 April 1887 and was one of at least six sons of Richard Carter, an Eastbourne fisherman, and Rhoda Carter from Hailsham, Sussex, where the family had later moved from Eastbourne. Their home address was Harebeating, Batten Road, Hailsham. Nelson was educated in Hailsham and his first job was as a carter with Mr Charles Goldsmith, a local haulage contractor. In 1903 he joined the RFA in Bradford at the age of sixteen, using the name of Nelson Smith, and later attained the rank of bombardier. After three years' service he became ill when in Singapore and was discharged from the Army owing to a haemorrhage of the bladder. He underwent a serious hernia operation in 1906 at the Princess Alice Memorial Hospital, and was then keen to join the police force but was rejected on medical grounds. Instead, he returned to Mr Goldsmith for a time and later got a position at Endcliffe School, followed by a job working at the Burlington Hotel.

At the age of twenty-four Nelson married a former cook, Kathleen (Kitty), née Camfield, at St Mary's Church, Old Town, Eastbourne, on 13 October 1911. The couple were to have one daughter, Jessie Olive, born on 2 January 1916. They lived at 33 Greys Road, Old Town, Eastbourne.

Carter was not only strong, he was also heavily tattooed, a fact that was noted on his attestation papers under the category of 'distinguishing marks'. The range of designs included one of Buffalo Bill, a Japanese lady and the Prince of Wales's feathers. At the outbreak of war in August 1914 he was working as the door attendant at the Old Town Cinema Company in Eastbourne, and promptly re-joined the Army on 5 September. He became a member of the Royal Sussex Regiment, and, possibly owing to his previous service, was immediately made a corporal. He left for training at Cooden in Bexhill and was promoted to sergeant on 29 September 1914 and company sergeant major (2nd Class WO) on 10 November. He was transferred to the 12th Battalion (Lowther's Lambs) the following day and was made a WOII on 28 January 1915 and T/RSM from 20 August to 16 October 1915.

Carter was a fine athlete and a very good boxer, in 1915 winning the regimental championship medal and Silver Cup for the heavyweight championship.

He left for France on 4 March 1916 as a member of A Company of the 12th Royal Sussex Regiment and served for less than three months. Two days before his death on 30 June he wrote home to Kitty for what was to be the last time.

W.B. BUTLER
East of Lempire, France, 6 August 1917

(David Harvey)

The Third Battle of Ypres began in Flanders on 31 July 1917. Elsewhere things were pretty 'quiet on the Western Front', with the day-to-day routine of battalion relief and keeping the enemy in check.

To the south, approximately 10 miles north of St Quentin and west of the Hindenburg Line, the 35th Division was in positions in the Épehy sector. The significance of this area was important to both sides as the enemy wished to keep the Épehy ridge as a sort of outpost to the Hindenburg Line. On the other hand, the British wanted the view of the landscape that dropped down to the St Quentin Canal and then climbed up towards the heavy German defences.

On 1 August 1917 the 17th (S) Battalion (2nd Leeds) West Yorkshires (106 Brigade) relieved the 18th Lancashire Fusiliers (104th Brigade) in positions to the east of Lempire, close to Ronssoy. Brigade HQ was at Ste Emilie and Divisional HQ at Villers Faucon. After being in the line for four days, on 5 August the 17th West Yorkshires were relieved by the 19th Durham Light Infantry, also of the 106th Brigade, and returned to billets at Lempire. The battalion war diary noted that during the day Stokes guns had fired on Falcon Sap, north-east of Little Priel Farm, and that artillery cooperated, firing on enemy trenches at the strongpoints of Bird Cage and Gillemont Farm and an enemy trench mortar was silenced.

Dawn broke on 6 August with a thick mist, which later dispersed to reveal a fine day. The enemy, probably taking advantage of the mist, raided the hilltop Gillemont Farm to the east at around 3.30 a.m., and the West Yorkshires 'stood to' at 4.15 a.m., and later supplied working parties during the day and night. It appeared that the enemy had entered the trenches at Gillemont Farm on all sides in a strength of about 150 men, and as a result the 17th Royal Scots of the 106th Brigade were forced to fall back; but a later counter-attack drove the enemy out of the ground which they had gained.

It was on this day that due to some very quick thinking Pte William Butler of the 17th West Yorkshires, a member of the Stokes mortar battery, probably saved the lives of several of his colleagues. A few weeks later when speaking to the press about 'an accident with a Stokes gun' he said that after it had been firing for forty-eight hours one of the fly-off levers came off 'and started the fuse of a shell in the emplacement'.

> I picked it up and showed it to my mate. 'It's going off', I said. 'I know it is', he replied, and stopped still and never shifted. I hardly knew what I did, but I jumped to the entrance of the emplacement with the shell, which was an eleven-pounder, and there I saw a party of infantry passing.
> I shouted to them to get out of the way, and they did so quickly. Those on the right rushed away, and a man turned about a dozen men back with him. I then threw the shell on to the parados. Not being too far over, it fell back to the bottom of the trench and burst. It damaged the trench, but didn't injure any of the men. . . .

After this incident the 17th West Yorkshires were relieved by the 18th Highland Light Infantry by 10.30 p.m. the following day.

Writing home to his parents in September 1917, Butler said, '. . . I hope the decoration they say I am going to receive comes through before then [mid-October] so that I shall have a bit of something to show for my service. Well, it will only be for what other men have done, or what is being done every week of the year. It will be a surprise to you, I know, but never mind, accidents will happen.' Mrs Butler, his mother, also received a note from the commanding officer of the battalion in which he praised her son's work and deed.

The citation for the VC was published in the *London Gazette* of 17 October 1917:

> William Boynton Butler, No. 17/1280, Private, West Yorkshire Regiment. For most conspicuous bravery when in charge of a Stokes gun in trenches which were being heavily shelled. Suddenly one of the fly-off levers of a Stokes shell came off and fired the shell in the emplacement. Private Butler picked up the shell and jumped to the entrance of the emplacement, which at that moment a party of infantry was passing. He shouted to them to hurry past, as the shell was going off, and, turning round, placed himself between the party of men and the live shell, and so held it till they were out of danger. He then threw the shell on to the parados, and took cover in the bottom of the trench. The shell exploded almost on leaving his hand, greatly damaging the trench. By extreme good luck Private Butler was contused only. Undoubtedly his great presence of mind and disregard of his own life saved the lives of the officer and men in the emplacement and the party which was passing at the time.

The 17th West Yorkshire Battalion left the 35th Division on 16 November for XIX Corps on railway work. On 7 December the battalion was amalgamated with the 15th Battalion. It appears that Butler at some point was wounded and returned to his unit on 18 November 1917.

Butler, the sixth Leeds man to win the VC, was on leave from 2 to 16 December and travelled to his home in Leeds on the 4th, where he found that his parents had already left for London and Buckingham Palace and the investiture which was to take place on the 5th. He was invested by the King, together with Robert Hanna, James Ockenden, Ernest Egerton, Filip Konowal, Michael O'Rourke and Ernest Pitcher. He then returned to Leeds and was met off the train by officials of the Council and was escorted for a brief stop at the Queen's Hotel before going on to the Town Hall, where he was given a civic reception and the Lord Mayor gave an address of welcome on the steps of the building. Another guest was Wilfred Edwards VC. The family were entertained to tea before leaving for St Oswald's School: crowds lined the route and at the school he was presented with a china clock subscribed to by the citizens of Leeds and also a gold medal given by a Mr W. Owen, also of Leeds. A sum of £300 had been subscribed for Pte Butler's benefit, which was invested on his behalf. In the evening he was publicly escorted to his parents' home. Within a few days he was back in France.

Hunslet Cemetery, Leeds (*Donald C. Jennings*)

William Boynton Butler was born in Armley, Leeds, on 20 November 1894. He was one of two sons and three daughters and lived with his parents at 5 Royal Terrace, Royal Road, Hunslet Carr, Leeds. He was educated at St Oswald's School, a National School, which he left in about 1907. He then followed his father into a mining career and worked at Middleton Collieries at No. 2 Middleton Pit.

Butler had 'a quiet and retiring manner'. After about seven years as a miner he managed to enlist in the Army at Leeds on 14 January 1915. He had previously been rejected owing to his short stature, but the formation of a 'Bantam' battalion gave him the opportunity. The 2nd Leeds Battalion

(Leeds Bantams) was raised by the Lord Mayor, and in 1915 the Army took over the running of it, when it became the 17th Battalion West Yorkshire Regiment (The Prince of Wales's Own). Butler was attached to a trench mortar battery and received training at Ilkley. He was based at home until 30 January 1916 and left for France on the 31st and served in the trenches with 106 Stokes mortar battery.

After demobilisation in December 1918 he lived at 314 Belle Isle Road, Leeds, and was employed by the Leeds Corporation gas department (or North East Gas Board), where George Sanders VC also worked.

Butler regularly attended Regimental Association meetings and branch gatherings and was present at the ceremonial opening of the Regimental Headquarters at York by HRH the Princess Royal, as well as the naming of the POWO engine at York Station. He also attended the Buckingham Palace garden party in June 1920 and in 1926 the opening of a memorial hall and unveiling of a memorial tablet to members of the Hunslet Temperance Society. In November 1929 he attended the House of Lords' dinner. In September 1932 he was introduced to Prince George, son of King George, when he was on a visit to Leeds. He was accompanied by two other 'local heroes', Wilfred Edwards and George Sanders. In 1940 Butler became a member of the Home Guard, together with Sanders, and the two men were part of the Gas Board Home Guard. After the war was over he attended the Victory parade of June 1946, followed by the dinner at the Dorchester Hotel and ten years later the centenary celebrations in June 1956. He also attended some later functions of the VC/GC Association.

Butler married Miss Clara Johnson of Lower Grange, Middleton, and the couple had a daughter, Clara, who died in 1964. In his final years Butler was unwell and he died in hospital in Leeds on 25 March 1972.

The former 'Bantam Hero' was given a full military funeral on 29 March, and the bearer party was drawn from senior NCOs and members of the British Legion, together with other organisations that were in attendance. He was buried at Hunslet Cemetery, Leeds, New Section 3 Plot 48. The grave was originally unmarked, but this was rectified after a letter appeared in the *Bulletin* in 1996 and a Mr Alan Coles did some 'digging'. Newton's, a local firm of monumental masons, offered to provide a stone for the grave free of charge, an offer which was accepted. A ceremony was later held at the grave, which was rededicated, and the service was attended by members of the POWO, RBL, and the local MP. A plaque to his memory is outside the City Art Gallery in Leeds.

Apart from the VC, Butler was also awarded the French Croix de Guerre, the BWM, VM, and the 1937 and 1954 Coronation Medals. The medals are held privately.

F. HOBSON, M.J. O'ROURKE, H. BROWN AND O.M. LEARMONTH

Hill 70 near Loos, 15–18 August 1917

During Canadian operations north-west of Lens and the capture of Hill 70 in mid-August 1917 no fewer than six Victoria Crosses were won.

In July Sir Douglas Haig informed General Sir Henry Horne of the First Army that he wanted the coal-mining area of Lens captured. In turn Horne asked the Canadian Corps under Lt Gen Sir A.W. Currie to carry out the task. Currie was unhappy with the objectives given him by First Army, and as Lens was dominated by Hill 70 to the north and from the south-east by Sallaumines Hill he considered that the two heights were tactically more important than Lens itself. To occupy the latter while leaving the high ground in the hands of the enemy was not sensible. Deployment of artillery in the open plain would also be difficult.

At a meeting of corps commanders Currie was able to persuade Gen Horne to allow Hill 70 to become the immediate main objective. He reasoned that Canadian possession of the hill with the resulting observation deep into enemy-held territory would force the Germans to make counter-attacks that could then be effectively dealt with by artillery. An earlier plan to occupy the railway was also altered to one of 'raid and withdraw', and was to be carried out by the 3rd Division.

On 14 August the 1st Corps 'staged demonstration attacks with dummy tanks directly west of Lens'. The treeless Hill 70 was of chalk downland at the end of one of the spurs running north-east from the Artois plateau, which dominated Lens and gave views of the Douai plain beyond. In September 1915 it had been taken by the British, who were unable to hold on to it. The La Bassée–Lens road climbed over its western slopes, short of the bare crest. In the north it fell away towards the Loos valley. The descent was interrupted on the south side by the Cité spur, over which spread four northern suburbs of Lens, which were brick-built company towns of miners' houses. Most of these had been reduced to ruins by shellfire. When fighting among these ruins the enemy were to have the advantage and they also gave a special challenge to the artillery. The final Canadian objective was a series of former enemy trenches that formed an arc around the eastern slope of Hill 70. As far as possible Hill 70 was to be 'a killing by artillery'.

Nine field brigades were to give support to the main assault, four with the 2nd Division on the right and five with the 1st Division on the left. The barrage would be supported in turn by 160 machine-guns. The infantry divisions had two brigades forward from north to south, the 3rd, 2nd, 5th and 4th, giving ten battalions. Their objectives were marked out in three stages and the assault began as dawn was breaking at 4.25 a.m. on 15 August. The engineers began to fire drums of burning oil into Cité Ste Elizabeth and other targets to supplement artillery fire and provide a smoke screen.

It is clear that the enemy were expecting an attack, so that even as troops moved up and into their assembly positions they were met with gas shells. Despite this the speed and strength of the Canadian attack quickly overwhelmed the trench garrisons, and according to the official history, '. . . within twenty minutes the first objective beyond the Lens–La Bassée highway, an average advance of 600 yards, had been reached by the two divisions.' To the right the 4th and 5th Brigades of the 2nd Canadian Division moved through the ruins of the mining villages of Cité St Laurent and Cité St Edouard, and after a pause of half an hour the 4th Brigade followed through the village of Cité Ste Elizabeth and then formed a defensive flank that faced the edge of Lens town. According to the official history it was at this point that Sgt Frederick Hobson of the 20th Battalion won a VC during a strong enemy counter-attack. However, other accounts say that it happened on the 18th, three days later, which is more likely to be the case. The 5th Brigade pushed on further and pressed on through Cité St Emile to the final objective, which was reached soon after 6 a.m. The 1st Canadian Division was equally successful and the 5th and 10th Battalions of the 2nd Canadian Brigade gained the top of Hill 70, and the 16th, 13th and 15th Battalions of the 3rd Canadian Brigade occupied the western side of Bois Hugo and Bois Rase. The Brigade then moved on to its final objective. On the front of the 2nd Canadian Brigade the fresh 7th and 8th Battalions 'reached their intermediate objective along the German Second Position'. Enemy machine-guns in Bois Hugo were quickly dealt with by bombing parties moving round the flanks.

By 6 a.m. the operation had been completed except for a further advance down the eastern slope of Hill 70 by the 2nd Brigade. The necessary pause to allow for the artillery timetable gave the enemy a brief respite, which they made full use of, having 'steadied along the front of Cité St Auguste'. The 7th and 8th Battalions now met intense machine-gun and rifle fire that swept the slope, and the impetus of the Canadian attack was slowed. Casualties mounted as the artillery barrage

Frederick Hobson (*David Harvey*)

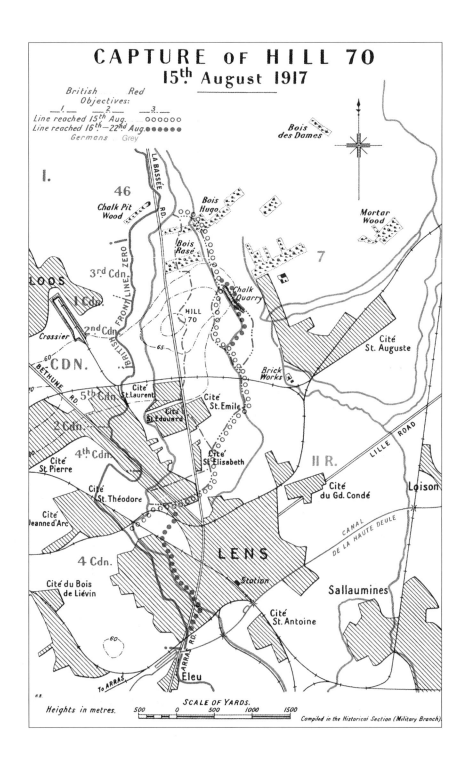

CAPTURE OF HILL 70
15th August 1917

British   Red
Objectives:
___1___ ___2___ ___3___
Line reached 15th Aug. ....oooooo
Line reached 16th–22nd Aug. ●●●●●●
Germans . . Grey

lost its protectiveness. The 7th Battalion left a group of fifty men to hold the northern end of the Chalk Quarry and returned to their previous objective and the 8th Battalion conformed.

On the following day the forward artillery observers were able to look over the Douai plain to the east and to the north-east of Lens. As the ground was being consolidated local enemy counter-attacks were carried out against the 'new front from Bois Hugo, from the wood near the Chalk Quarry, from the Brick Works and from Lens . . .' However, these were broken up by artillery fire, followed by machine-gun and rifle fire. Later in the morning the enemy advanced en masse in extended order on a front behind Cité St Auguste. The Canadians from their positions on the hill witnessed the casualties and disorganisation caused by their artillery barrages.

At 12.45 p.m. further enemy counter-attacks developed against the new Canadian line, and waves of German attackers against the 3rd Canadian Brigade were checked and virtually destroyed by artillery and machine-gun fire. An attack against the 2nd Brigade from the Cité St Auguste also made no headway, but the 7th and 8th Battalions (the two battalions involved) had suffered heavy losses and were exhausted. The order to advance due to take place firstly at 4 p.m. and then postponed to 6 p.m. was therefore cancelled.

Of the sixteen stretcher-bearers with the 7th British Columbia Regiment (2nd Canadian Brigade), 1st Division two were killed and eleven were wounded, most by German snipers. Of the remaining three Pte Michael O'Rourke began his heroic and tireless work in which he was to save the lives of at least forty men over the next three days when, often under very heavy fire, he not only attended to their wounds but also brought them food and water. Several times he was knocked down by shell-bursts and sometimes partially buried. For his work he was later awarded the VC, and the citation below (*London Gazette*, 8 November 1917) gives full details of his heroism. With an Irish brogue he later remarked to the press in later years about his VC: 'Shure I' dint know what it was all about. It was me job, you see, to take out the wounded. There was a lot o' snipin' and machine-gunnin' around but I couldn't do anything else but keep on goin', you know what I mean?'

Michael Jones O'Rourke
(*David Harvey*)

Michael James O'Rourke, No. 428545, 7th Battalion. Canadian Infantry. For most conspicuous bravery and devotion to duty during prolonged operations. For three days and nights Private O'Rourke, who is a stretcher-bearer, worked unceasingly in bringing the wounded into safety, dressing them and getting them food and water. During the whole of this period the area in which he worked was subjected to very severe shelling, and swept by heavy-machine-gun and rifle fire. On several occasions he was knocked down and partially buried by enemy shells. Seeing a comrade who had been blinded stumbling around ahead of our trench, in full view of the enemy, who were sniping him, Private O'Rourke jumped out of his trench and brought the man back, being himself heavily sniped at while doing so. Again he went forward about 50 yards in front of our barrage, under very heavy and accurate fire from enemy machine-guns and snipers and brought in a comrade. On a subsequent occasion, when the line of advanced posts was retired to the line to be consolidated, he went forward under very heavy enemy fire of every description, and brought back a wounded man who had been left behind. He showed throughout an absolute disregard for his own safety, going wherever there were wounded to succour, and his magnificent courage and devotion in continuing his rescue work, in spite of exhaustion and the incessant enemy fire of every description, inspired all ranks and undoubtedly saved many lives.

The capture of the final objective in front of Cité St Auguste was to take place on 17 August at 4 p.m. using two fresh battalions, the 5th and 10th. After an intense bombardment and under a rolling barrage the attack advanced by short rushes down the 400-yard slope. The objective was gained, but not without heavy loss of life as the enemy themselves were in force, massing for a counter-attack. Fierce close fighting took place, especially at the Chalk Quarry, where the Germans left behind a hundred dead, in addition to a hundred wounded and thirty prisoners.

In Norman Trench the 5th Battalion took fifty prisoners and captured eight machine-guns, but by 5.30 p.m. the battalion had run out of ammunition and was forced to fall back. On the right flank the 10th Battalion hung grimly on. Communication between the 10th (Quebec) Battalion HQ and Company HQ had broken down because all wires had been cut. Artillery support was desperately needed. Two runners then attempted to take back messages from the front line: one was killed, but the other, Pte Harry Brown, with his arm shattered, kept on going through an intense barrage until he arrived at the 'close support line', where he looked for an officer at a company HQ in order to deliver his message. All the time an intense enemy barrage was going on. He was so exhausted that he fell down the dugout steps but retained consciousness long enough to hand over his message, saying 'important message' and collapsing. The message received allowed the Canadian artillery to save the situation. Brown died of his wounds a few hours later at a dressing station near Hill 70 and was buried in the same cemetery as Maj Learmonth (see below) in Plot II of Noeux-les-Mines Communal Cemetery, Row J, Grave 29. The battalion war diary mentions Brown in Appendix B: 'This man displayed courage and self-control seldom witnessed. His devotion to duty was of the highest possible degree imaginable, his action undoubtedly saved the loss of the position, at least temporarily and saved many casualties to our troops.'

Brown's citation was published in the *London Gazette* of 17 October 1917:

Harry Brown (*David Harvey*)

Harry Brown, Private, No. 226353, late Canadian Infantry Batt. For most conspicuous bravery, courage and devotion to duty. After the capture of a position, the enemy massed in force and counter-attacked. The situation became very critical, all wires being cut. It was of the utmost importance to get word back to Headquarters. This soldier and one other were given the message with orders to deliver the same at all costs. The other messenger was killed. Private Brown had his arm shattered, but continued on through an intense barrage until he arrived at the close support lines and found an officer. He was so spent that he fell down the dug-out steps, but retained consciousness long enough to hand over his message, saying, 'important message.' He then became unconscious, and died in the dressing station a few hours later. His devotion to duty was of the highest possible degree imaginable, and his successful delivery of the message undoubtedly saved the loss of the position for the time and prevented many casualties.

A series of unsuccessful counter-attacks then took place. With the assistance of artillery and machine-gun fire the line of the quarry was held. However, to the south the 5th Battalion was 'much reduced in strength and short of ammunition, and had to fall back to a shell-hole position about two hundred yards short of the final objective where the 2nd Canadian Division had been established.' During the night the 1st Brigade took over from the 3rd Brigade on the left of the Division and on the following night took over the 2nd Brigade's sector as well.

The minor Canadian actions on the 17th met with 'varying success' and determined German counter-attacks continued. A series of attacks were made against the quarry and many Canadian gunners were put out of action as a result of gas shells. Late on the 17th large numbers of the enemy reached within a hundred yards of the quarry before being stopped by Lewis guns and rifles of the 4th Battalion. German planes were very active and a gas alert was also on. Another attempt was made three hours later, and a third at 4.15 in the morning of the 18th. This third attack coincided with an attack against Chicory Trench on the right flank of the 2nd Division. Only one German company managed to close with the defences of Chicory Trench and was quickly dealt with by an ex-Boer War veteran, Sgt Frederick Hobson of the 20th (1st Central Ontario) Battalion (4th Brigade), who played a major role in repulsing a German attack. His battalion had by now been in the line for three days, with the 18th Battalion to the right and 21st in the centre, and on the first day he, together with members of A Coy, had seen action at Nabob Alley when they bombed along it, pushing back the enemy who were only retreating very slowly, and having captured about 70 yards of trench the Canadians established a post.

On the 18th, however, on seeing an important Lewis gun post wiped out, Hobson rushed forward and dug the gun out, together with a surviving member of the crew, and proceeded to engage the enemy at short range until the gun jammed. Not being a trained Lewis gunner he ordered the wounded survivor of the gun crew to 'remedy the stoppage'. Hobson, now also wounded, rushed forward to attack the enemy with bayonet and clubbed rifle. He was laid low by a rifle shot but by now the Lewis gun was back in action and reinforcements were on their way up. The Lewis gun enfiladed the enemy advance and caused many casualties.

Hobson's VC was published in the *London Gazette* of 17 October 1917:

No. 57113, Frederick Hobson, Sergeant, late 20th Battalion. Canadian Infantry. During a strong enemy counter-attack a Lewis gun in a forward post in a communication trench leading to the enemy lines was buried by a shell, and the crew, with the exception of one man, killed. Sergeant Hobson, though not a gunner, grasped the great importance of the post, rushed from his trench, dug out the gun, and got it into action against the enemy, who were now advancing down the trench and across the open. A jam caused the gun to stop firing. Though wounded he left the gunner to correct the stoppage, rushed forward at the advancing enemy, and with bayonet and clubbed rifle, single-handed held them back until he himself was killed by a rifle shot. By this time however, the Lewis gun was again in action, and, reinforcements shortly afterwards arriving, the enemy was beaten off. The valour and devotion to duty displayed by this non-commissioned officer gave the gunner the time required to again get the gun into action, and saved a most serious situation.

Some fairly lurid accounts survive about Hobson's deed. Here is an example:

When he engaged the enemy in no man's land he bayoneted or club rifled fourteen of them. When men of the company went out after him he was hit by a stick bomb and his middle was torn away . . . the rescuers found the fourteen dead Germans in a semicircle around him.

The 4th Brigade's war diary mentions that the brigade had received a request from the 20th Battalion for a Lewis gun to be sent to it because one had been destroyed in a hostile bombardment. The battalion war diary notes that 'our Lewis Gun posts in Nabob Trench did splendid service until wiped out'. It also states that when a large number of troops came over the fighting 'was of a most desperate nature.'

After Hobson's death the enemy staged another counter-attack, at 5 a.m. on the 18th, to the north of the Chalk Quarry, which mainly affected two companies of the 2nd Battalion (Eastern Ontario Battalion) astride Bois Hugo. Penetrating the more northerly position the German bombers who were using *Flammenwerfer* and bombs were soon driven out. Both company commanders, Maj Spence and Maj O.M. Learmonth, whose company was south of the wood, died of wounds, Maj Learmouth winning the Victoria Cross. Although mortally wounded he stood on the parapet and still directed the defence and hurled grenades at the approaching enemy. He even caught some of the enemy bombs and threw them back at them with good effect. When no longer able to do this he instructed his junior officers in running the battle. The battalion held its ground and further attacks were dealt with by artillery fire, and were relieved by the 3rd Battalion between 10 p.m. and 1.15 a.m.

According to the Skeffingtons' *Thirty Canadian VCs*:

Okill Massey Learmouth
(*David Harvey*)

He saw a number of the Germans, after their advance had been checked within a few yards of our trenches, had found shelter to some extent in a small wood; and to rout them out of the wood a bombing party from No. 3 Company was sent forward. They bombed the Germans out of the wood and down a trench called Horse Alley, driving them into the open, where our snipers and machine-gunners engaged them and cleaned them up. Throughout the whole of the attack Learmonth showed what his Commanding Officer, Major R. Vanderwater, DSO, had named a 'wonderful spirit'. Absolutely fearless, he so conducted himself that he imbued those with whom he came into contact with some of his personality. When the barrage started he was continuously with his men and officers, encouraging them and making sure that no loophole was left through which the enemy could gain a footing. When the attack was launched against the thin Canadian line, Learmonth seemed to be everywhere at once. When the situation was critical, he took his turn at throwing bombs. He was wounded twice, but carried on as if he were perfectly fit and whole. He was wounded a third time, his leg this time being broken, but still he showed the same indomitable spirit. Lying in a trench, he continued to direct his men, encouraging them, cheering them, advising them. At a quarter past six that morning the battalion headquarters received word that Learmonth was badly wounded and was being carried out of the line on a stretcher; but the enemy attack had been repulsed. He had waited till he saw the finish. They brought him down to headquarters, and, lying on a stretcher, he gave valuable information to the officers there before he was taken to hospital. He died shortly afterwards – the man who would not give in.

Learmonth later died of his wounds, and at 11 a.m. on the 22nd the battalion moved from huts at Mazingarbe to Noeux-les-Mines, north-west of Lens, where Learmonth was buried in the Communal Cemetery, II, K, 9, quite near the grave of Pte Harry Brown. According to figures mentioned in the 2nd Canadian Brigade War Diary, O'Rourke's 7th Battalion suffered casualties of thirteen officers and 416 other ranks during the three-day operation, and Brown's 10th Battalion had lost eleven officers and also 416 other ranks. Hobson's 20th Battalion of the 4th Brigade had suffered 182 during operations from 15 to 21 August.

Learmonth's VC citation was published in the *London Gazette* of 8 November 1917:

For most conspicuous bravery and exceptional devotion to duty. During a determined counter-attack on our new positions, this officer, when his company was momentarily surprised, instantly charged and personally disposed of the attackers. Later, he carried on a tremendous fight with the advancing enemy. Although under intense barrage fire and mortally wounded, he stood on the parapet of the trench, bombed the enemy continuously and directed the defence in such a manner as to infuse a spirit of utmost resistance into his men. On several occasions this very brave officer actually caught bombs thrown at him by the enemy and threw them back. When he was unable by reason of his wounds to carry on the fight, he still refused to be carried out of the line, and continued to give instructions and invaluable advice to his junior officers, finally handing over all his duties before he was evacuated from the front line to the hospital where he died.

According to the Provincial Archives in Victoria, Michael James O'Rourke was born in Dublin on 3 March 1874; but in a copy of his attestation papers dated 23 March 1915 he stated that he had been born several years later in Limerick, on 19 March 1878. If the 1874 date is indeed correct O'Rourke was able to maintain the deception until his death, when obituaries gave conflicting dates of birth, making his gravestone incorrect as well. Giving his age as thirty-seven he would have underestimated it by four years. He also stated that he had served in the Royal Munster Fusiliers for seven years. A Roman Catholic and a former miner, O'Rourke applied for enlistment and was passed fit for service abroad at his interview in New Westminster, British Columbia. He gave his next-of-kin as his sister, Mrs K. Mack.

His address in 1915 was at 2564 Broadway, Montreal. He joined the 30th Battalion 1st Reinforcement Draft on 23 March 1915. A few weeks later he was transferred to the 1st Draft of 47th Battalion on 1 May 1915. He travelled to England, transferring to the 30th, and was camped at the Canadian base at Shorncliffe in June. While there he fell foul of the authorities for the first time and had seven days' pay deducted as a result of being drunk and using abusive language. On 28 August O'Rourke left the 30th Battalion for the 7th and arrived in France the following day. He was to spend the whole of his military service as a stretcher-bearer.

O'Rourke was a temperamental Irishman with periods of great gallantry coupled with bouts of drunkenness. In May 1916 he was awarded nine days' leave and at the end of June he was in trouble again, and this time was given fourteen days' field punishment no. 1 for drunkenness. On 6 October he received the MM 'for bravery in the field' from Lt Gen Julian Byng, which was gazetted on 9 December 1916. On 20 November 1916 he was attached to 1st Canadian Division Train until 2 February 1917.

On winning his VC during the fighting for Hill 70 in August 1917, O'Rourke was granted ten days' leave in early October before his VC was gazetted on 8 November 1917 in the *London Gazette*. On 5 December he received his medal from the King at Buckingham Palace during the same investiture as Cadet Hanna, Cpl Konowal, Sgt James Ockenden, PO Ernest Pitcher and Cpl Ernest Egerton were awarded theirs. Soon after he was granted fourteen days' leave, which was extended to a ten-week furlough in Canada between the end of December and the end of March 1918.

From his medical records O'Rourke was clearly no longer fit for foreign service, and in Vancouver, British Columbia, he was discharged from service with the 11th Battalion Canadian Garrison Regiment CEF on 16 July 1918, 'having become medically unfit for further service overseas by reason of disabilities incurred on active service'. His medical records state he was unfit because of 'exposure to cold and wet & strain of service'. He showed: 'fairly marked degree of debility, is nervous and tremulous – somewhat anaemic. The left sciatic is somewhat tender – and there is pain on full extension of leg flexed on abdomen. Can walk 3 or 4 miles at an easy gait; is somewhat dyspnoeac on such exertion as running, climbing hills & c. The sciatica is of slight grade.' He was graded as Class C3 permanent. But despite his bouts of drinking, papers in the file housed in Ottawa described his conduct and character as 'very good'. On release from the Canadian Army on 25 September 1918 he resided for a short time at the Georgian Hotel, 4th Avenue, Seattle.

After the war three of his medals were stolen from his home and he was given assistance by the Prince of Wales in acquiring replacements for them. When working as a stevedore in Vancouver in 1929 he was invited to London for the House of Lords' dinner in November. In the crush he was unable to get near the Prince before the grand dinner, but the Prince did manage to talk to O'Rourke later.

After the Second World War O'Rourke visited London in the summer of 1956 for the VC centenary. He died in the following year at his sister's home, 3410 Point Gray Road, Vancouver, on 6 December. Four days later he was given a full military funeral in Holy Rosary Cathedral. Seven holders of the VC acted as

Forest Lawn Burial Park (*Donald C. Jennings*)

pallbearers, including Robert Hanna and Harcus Strachan. A large congregation of servicemen attended the service and afterwards he was buried at Forest Lawn Burial Park, North Burnaby, British Columbia.

His medals were once in the Officers' Mess of the British Columbian Regiment but are now kept in the Regimental Museum. He is also commemorated by a painting in the Canadian War Museum, Ottawa.

Harry Brown was born to a Roman Catholic family in Ganonoque, Frontenac, Ontario, Canada, on 11 May 1898. He was the son of Mrs Helen McAuliffe, East Emily, RRI, Ontario, and after leaving school became a farmer.

At the age of eighteen Brown enlisted in the Canadian Mounted Rifles in London, Ontario, on 18 August 1916 and was given the regimental number of 226353. As he was about to go overseas he made a will on 10 October 1916 in favour of his mother, and embarked for England on 25 October, arriving there on the 31st. He camped at Shorncliffe and became a member of the 11th Battalion and was briefly transferred to the 4th Canadian Training Brigade.

Brown was briefly in hospital from 23 November to 10 December with tonsillitis. From 5 February 1917 he was shortly with the 11th Battalion, and on 27 May he was transferred to the 10th Battalion and left for France. On 17 August he was admitted to No. 7 CCS dangerously wounded with gunshot wounds and died there after his arm had been amputated.

Noeux-les-Mines Cemetery (*David C. Jennings*)

He was buried at Noeux-les-Mines Communal Cemetery, II, J, 29, in the same cemetery as Okill Learmonth. His medals are kept in the Canadian War Museum, Ottawa.

Frederick Hobson was born in Norwood, South London, on 23 September 1873. He joined the Regular Army and served with the 2nd Wiltshire Regiment from 1897 and took part in the Boer War (1899–1902). He was discharged in the following year with the rank of corporal and shortly afterwards met Louise Moses. In 1904 the couple emigrated to Canada and once there soon married. The couple were to have five children, four sons and one daughter: George (1905), Frederick (1909), Albert (1911), Florence (1913) and John (1915).

Hobson was employed by Dominion Canners, and in 1913 the family were living in Galt at 69 South Street. He then became a storekeeper employed by the City Authorities. Despite being in his early forties and having the responsibility of a pregnant wife, Hobson was determined to return to the Army after the war began, a decision much against his wife's wishes.

Hobson's attestation papers note that he was just short of six feet tall, with blue eyes and a scar on the back of his head. He appears to have joined the Norfolk Rifles at the end of October 1914 and then tried to enlist in Galt several times, without success. But he then decided to try again, this time in Toronto, from his sister Florence's home, who lived at 1381 Lansdowne Avenue. He was successful: on 10 November 1914 he enlisted as a member of the 20th Battalion 1st Central Ontario Regiment, CEF, and was confirmed with the rank of sergeant from New Year's Day 1915. His regimental number was 57113.

On 15 May Hobson sailed for England, arriving on the 24th, and after nearly four months' training he sailed from Folkestone for Boulogne on 14 September. He was to spend two years in France and Flanders. In early February 1916, he was given seven days' leave, and on 16 September was badly wounded by gunshot wounds in his right hip and was admitted to No. 4 Canadian Field Ambulance before being released to his unit. In October he was briefly attached to the 255th Tunnelling Company and in July 1917 was given ten days' leave before returning to the 20th Battalion. He was killed in action while serving in the fighting north-west of Lens on Hill 70 near the La Bassée–Lens Road, where he won the VC on 18 August.

Back in Canada and even while Hobson was still living, Louise seems to have taken up with a widowed neighbour, who was keen to marry her. His name was Thomas George Thorn of Stafford, Ontario, and the couple married on 1 April 1918. He provided for Louise and her five children, but the children, who remembered their father, were forbidden ever to refer to him again. The State provided a pension towards their upkeep.

On 8 May 1918 Hobson's VC was presented to his sister Florence Brown in Toronto by the Governor-General of Canada, the Duke of Devonshire, on the steps of the Legislature. Hobson's name was later commemorated on the panels of the Vimy Memorial on the inside side wall. In 1959 Florence Brown presented her late brother's medals to the Fort Malden National Historic Park, and they

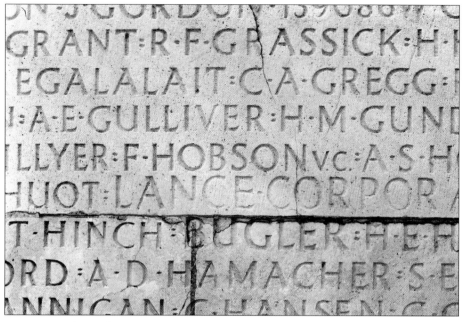

Vimy Memorial (*David C. Jennings*)

were later acquired by the Canadian War Museum in Ottawa. His medals included his Boer War medals, the Queen's South African Medal together with three clasps and the King's South African Medal with two clasps.

In 1995 in Valour Square beside the Armoury in Cambridge (formerly the city of Galt) a Heritage Foundation plaque to Frederick Hobson was unveiled by his grandson Albert Hobson Thorn. Other plaques to VCs in Galt were also unveiled – those to Lt Samuel Lewis Honey and Capt George Fraser Kerr. Another reminder of Frederick Hobson VC was the naming of the Simcoe branch of the Legion after him. His VC is in the collection of the Canadian War Museum.

Okill Massey Learmonth was born in St Louis Road, Quebec, on 22 February 1894 (the 20th according to his attestation papers), the only son of Mr and Mrs William Learmonth. His father was Deputy Lieutenant-Governor of the Province of Quebec and the family was Presbyterian. Learmonth was educated at

Valour Square, Cambridge (*Anon*)

St George's School and Quebec High School. After he graduated he joined the Union Bank of Canada and worked later on Anticosti Island on a private estate. From there he joined the staff of the Provincial Treasurer's Department, part of the Canadian Government Service.

He enlisted in the Canadian Forces on 29 September 1914 and his Regimental number was 22893. He was mobilised for service with the 84th Regiment Royal Rifles and left Canada for England on 3 October as a member of the 12th Battalion. After his arrival in England in mid-October he was transferred to the 2nd Battalion, with whom he was to serve with great distinction. He left for France on 6 February. Two weeks later he made a will in favour of his mother. In mid-June he was made a lance corporal. In the last few weeks of the year he was being treated for gonnorrhoea, and returned to his unit on Christmas Day after several weeks' treatment. Learmonth was awarded eight days' leave between 10 and 18 April and in May was promoted to corporal. He was commissioned as 2/Lt on 18 June 1916. While serving in the Ypres Salient he was wounded by gunshot to his hand and right leg. After a day in 7 Stationary Hospital he was invalided to England, where he became a patient in the Royal Free Hospital, London. On the 30th he went before the medical board, although his wounds were not yet healed. The form notes that Learmonth 'is suffering from the strain of constant duty and this board recommend that he be permitted to spend his leave in Canada'. He was therefore granted leave to Canada until 14 September, and after a two-week extension was awarded another medical board on 28 September at 86 the Strand. After his right index finger had healed he was found to be fit for service. At the time he was attached to the 12th Reserve Battalion at Shorncliffe.

On 17 October 1916 he was taken on the strength of the 2nd Battalion once again and joined them in the field on the 20th. On 10 December he went on a Lewis gun course, returning a week later.

On 15 April 1917 he was promoted to acting major while in command of a company. In the following month he was allowed to go on leave to Paris for ten days from 25 May. He was promoted to lieutenant and was awarded the MC, which was published in the *London Gazette* in mid-August 1917.

Noeux-les-Mines Communal Cemetery (*Donald C. Jennings*)

> Finding himself the senior officer of his battalion present after reaching the final objective of an attack, he showed great skill in handling the situation, directing the consolidation and making daring personal reconnaissances under heavy fire. His resource and coolness were responsible for repulsing a strong counter-attack, and he set a splendid example throughout.

On 21 March 1917 Learmonth made another will to replace the one made in favour of his mother earlier in the war. This time it was in favour of a nursing sister whom he might well have met during some of the spells he had spent in hospital. Her name was Irene Winifred Lamarche, and at one point she may have served in the Canadian Nursing Service at No. 8 Canadian General Hospital.

The couple probably planned to marry in Paris but never did so as Learmonth visited the Consulate-General and postponed the ceremony. In his will he also set aside £10 to be awarded to his batman Pte E.A. Insley. During 1917 Nursing Sister Lamarche was released on medical grounds and returned to North Bay.

On 25 July 1917 Learmonth was granted four days' leave. He was promoted to captain and acting major and won his posthumous VC at Hill 70 near Lens on 18 August 1917, dying of his wounds the following day at 7 CCS. He was buried four miles south-east of Bethune at Noeux-les-Mines Communal Cemetery, II, K, 9. Harry Brown VC is buried close by.

In *The Victoria Cross 1856–1920* by Creagh and Humphris, an entry on Learmonth quotes a misleading newspaper account from 9 November 1917:

> There is a poignant romance connected with the late Capt. Learmonth, of the Canadian Forces, who came from Quebec, and whose award of the Victoria Cross was in the Gazette published yesterday. Capt. Learmonth went to France as a ranker with the Canadians, and was promoted a non-com. On the field. He received his commission just over twelve months ago, and about the same time married Miss S. W. Tamarche [*sic*], who belonged to his province, and was attached to the Canadian Nursing Service. Mrs. Learmonth was invalided back to Canada some time back, and her gallant husband died of wounds three months ago.

Learmonth's next-of-kin was his mother Martha Learmonth. She was sent her son's medals, plaque and scroll in 1921/2 at her home address at 65 Murray Avenue, Quebec City.

Okill Learmonth is commemorated in Quebec City by Learmonth Avenue, with a painting by James Quinn at the Canadian War Museum and at the Okill Learmonth Chapter of the Imperial Order of the Daughters of the Empire. His VC is with the Governor-General's Foot Guards.

R.H. HANNA AND F. KONOWAL

Lens, France, 21–23 August 1917

The first three days of the Canadian operations against Hill 70 and Lens yielded no fewer than four winners of the Victoria Cross, and before the operations were completed six days later there were to be two more, won by CSM Robert Hanna on the 21st and Acting/Cpl Filip Konowal between the 22nd and 23rd.

Lt Gen Currie, in charge of the Canadian operations at Hill 70 and Lens, was keen to clear up the situation in front of the town on the lower half of the southern slope of the hill. The plan was now to close in from the north and west by occupying the enemy front line on a 3,000-yard frontage from Eleu (on the Arras–Lens road) to the east of Cité St Emile. The attack was scheduled to begin at 4.35 a.m. on the 21st and would be carried out by the 10th and 6th Brigades of the 4th and 2nd Divisions respectively.

However, the enemy was very active from 4 a.m. and dropped shells all along the front line and assembly area, causing casualties. The shelling then increased and the left flank of the 29th Battalion (6th Brigade) suffered particularly badly. In addition, the Canadian artillery was dropping short close to the junction of Commotion and Carfax Trenches. At 4.30 the enemy opened up a heavy bombardment with 'fishtails' and trench mortars on the left flank of the 29th Battalion The enemy also used what was described as 'a square box bomb which on bursting emitted large flame and dense smoke'.

It was still dark when the Canadian attack began; and it happened to coincide with a German counter-attack. The 2nd Division found the enemy either advancing or about to advance. After fierce hand-to-hand fighting in the western environs of Lens the 10th Brigade retained most of its objectives. However, north of the Lens–Bethune road the 27th (Winnipeg) and 29th (Vancouver) Battalions of the 6th Brigade had been caught by enemy artillery and became involved in difficult fighting in a triangle between the Lens–Bethune and Lens–La Bassée roads. The 29th Battalion, south of Cité St Emilie, met a strong force of enemy infantry who were without rifles but were loaded with bombs, and were about to attack. In fifteen minutes, using their bayonets in the dim light and ground mist, the 29th forced back members of the 1st Foot Guard Regiment beyond the trench that was the battalion objective. The left company of the 29th Battalion, when held up, requested artillery support. Fighting for possession of Cinnabar Trench continued for the rest of the morning and it was during this fighting that 75631 CSM Robert Hanna of B Coy won his VC.

Robert Hanna (*David Harvey*)

When all the officers had been either killed or wounded, quoting Nicholson's book on the history of the Canadian Expeditionary Force 1914–1918, he 'assumed command and led a party against a German strongpoint that three assaults had failed to capture. He personally killed four of the defenders, seizing the position and silencing its machine-gun. He then made good a portion of Cinnabar Trench and held it against repeated counter-attacks.' The 2nd Division's war diary notes that Cinnabar Trench was continuously fought for and that Hanna's B Coy held part of it with a block and ninety men, together with some members of A Coy as well. The enemy had been pushed back to the section of Cinnabar Trench, which was close to a water tower, and later they captured the right flank of the trench. Casualties were very heavy.

It appears from the 6th Canadian Brigade's war diary that 'The enemy reinforced his line and continuously from C.T.s and houses from CITÉ DU GRAND CONDÉ and houses along AUGUSTE CITÉ ROAD, men appeared to pour in from every direction.' 'Enemy snipers from positions in this area caused heavy casualties as well and the houses along the AUGUSTE CITÉ ROAD were full of machine-guns.'

Part of the account in the Skeffingtons' *Thirty Canadian VCs* notes that after Hanna had assumed command he saw:

> . . . that the crux of the position was a German post protected by a heavy wire and armed with a machine-gun. He collected a party of his men and led them against the post amid a hail of rifle and machine-gun fire. Rushing through the wire he bayoneted three of the Germans, brained a fourth, and overthrew the machine-gun. The redoubt was captured. The Germans arrived in force, and counter-attacked. Hanna, who was now short of bombs, built a block. Again and again the enemy tried to rush his position; but he and his handful of men held it until they were relieved later that day . . .

Despite Hanna's heroism the enemy still held nearly 500 yards of Cinnabar Trench and several other smaller trenches, which made the Canadian position in this sector precarious, and so the 27th and 29th later withdrew to their original line. The two battalions were relieved in the line on the night of 22/23 August by the 52nd Canadian Battalion, and then proceeded to Fosse 10.

Hanna's citation was published in the *London Gazette* of 8 November 1917:

Robert Hanna, Company Sergeant-Major, No. 75361, 29th Battalion. Canadian Infantry. For most conspicuous bravery in attack, when his company met with most severe enemy resistance and all the company officers became casualties. A strong point, heavily protected by wire and held by a machine-gun, had beaten off three assaults of the company with heavy casualties. This Warrant Officer, under heavy machine-gun and rifle fire, coolly collected a party of men, and leading them against this strong point, rushed through the wire and personally bayoneted three of the enemy and brained the fourth, capturing the position and silencing the machine-gun. This most courageous action displaying courage and personal bravery of the highest order at this most critical moment of the attack, was responsible for the capture of a most important tactical point, and but for his daring action and determined handling of a desperate situation, the attack would not have succeeded. Company Sergeant-Major Hanna's outstanding gallantry, personal courage and determined leading of his company is deserving of the highest possible award.

The sixth member of the Canadian Forces to win the VC in the Hill 70/Lens operations in August 1917 was Acting/Cpl Filip Konowal, a Ukrainian in the Canadian Army. He was a member of the 47th Battalion (10th Brigade), 4th Division, and he gained his medal over 22/23 August. Some accounts say 22–24 August, but he was being treated for his wounds on the 23rd at a CCS.

On 21 August three battalions of the Canadian 10th Brigade were also as deeply involved in the fighting as the 6th Brigade, and the brigade orders were to capture Green Crassier, a large heap of mine refuse between the railway station and the Lens Canal 350 yards beyond the 10th Brigade's right. The brigade gained and held on to all its objectives in the western environs of Lens after bitter hand-to-hand fighting in the ruined houses. One section on the left had not been captured by the 50th Battalion to the south of the Lens–Bethune road, where they had been caught in a barrage thirty minutes before zero hour at 4.35 a.m. and suffered a hundred casualties. It therefore became necessary to alter the movements of the assaulting companies. A feint attack halfway to the objective at Aloof Trench had put the enemy on the alert. Only small groups of men managed to reach the objective, which was the junction of the La Bassée–Bethune road. After retiring, most of these men did not reach their own lines.

The 46th Battalion in the centre had suffered heavily from German shelling the previous night, and their forward company officers became casualties and had to be replaced. In spite of this and the failure of the 50th Battalion, the 46th

Filip Konowal (*David Harvey*)

managed to reach its objective. They were now in Aconite Trench and positions in a row of houses to its east. The 47th to their right had escaped the shelling but carried out bitter fighting all day through the Cité du Moulin towards the Lens–Arras road and Alpaca Trench, from which the enemy machine-gunners took a heavy toll. By evening one company had reached the Arras road and by 10 p.m. all the battalion objectives had been gained. Advance posts were set up a little way out in front. It was during the extremely fierce fighting that Cpl Konowal of the 47th Battalion was heavily involved in the mopping-up of cellars, craters and machine-guns, gaining the Victoria Cross for two specific deeds in the period 22/23 August.

The battalion war diary notes:

. . . Later, during the day, we assisted the 44th Battalion on their attack on the GREEN CRASSIER by raiding a Machine Gun nest in a tunnel in the vicinity of Fosse 4. The party under leadership of Captain D.B. Wedon destroyed part of the tunnel with two ammonal charges, and Corporal Konowal single-handed killed the entire Machine Gun crew and captured one gun, establishing a post in the tunnel, but was forced to withdraw late under heavy enemy counter-attack, the enemy counter-attacked our positions on the Lens–Arras Road no less than six times during the day . . .

Single-handed Konowal took on two further attacks in which he killed several Germans, and on the following day, when involved in a minor operation, he destroyed another machine-gun. All told he killed sixteen men. The battalion war diary noted in chilling fashion, 'The situation made it unwise to take many prisoners.'

Cpl Konowal's deeds were written up in Skeffingtons' *Thirty Canadian VCs*, in which a colourful account is painted:

. . . The buildings about the Lens–Arras road proved difficult enough to clear. The main body of our troops had passed through and continued to the objectives beyond, but a couple of buildings still held Germans and German machine-guns, and there was heavy fighting upon the rear of our advancing men. Entering one of these houses Konowal searched for the Germans, and finding no living traces of their occupation, dropped daringly into the cellar.

Three men fired at him as he landed, but this he escaped unharmed. Then ensued a sanguinary battle in the dark, a mêlée of rifle fire and bayonet, with the odds three to one. Finally the scuffling ceased and Konowal emerged into the daylight – he had bayoneted the whole crew of the gun! But this is all taken for granted in the business of mopping-up, and the corporal and his section continued their way along the road, every sense alert to locate the close rifle-crack that might betray the wily sniper. There was a large crater to the east of the road, and from the bodies of our good men before the edge it seemed obvious that a German machine-gun had been in position there. Halting his men Konowal advanced alone. Upon reaching the lip of the crater he saw seven Germans endeavouring to move the ubiquitous machine-gun into a dugout. He opened fire at once, killing three, and then, charging down upon them, accounted for the rest with the bayonet. These drastic methods rapidly concluded the clearing of their section of the line, and the corporal and his men moved on up to our new front, where the enemy was delivering heavy and incessant counter-attacks. Heavy fighting continued throughout the night, and in the morning troops of the 44th Battalion, who were making an attack upon the Green Crassier, requested the aid of a party of the 47th in a raid upon a machine-gun emplacement in a tunnel about Fosse 4. Corpl. Konowal was an expert in this subterranean fighting, and his party succeeded in entering the tunnel. Two charges of ammonal, successfully exploded, somewhat demoralized the German garrison and then Konowal, dashing forward in the darkness with utter disregard of his own safety he had displayed all through the fighting, engaged the machine-gun crew with the bayonet, overcoming and killing them all. Altogether this good fighting man killed sixteen men in the two days of the actual battle, and continued his splendid work until he was severely wounded.

The 10th Brigade war diary notes than on the 23rd the 47th repelled several bombing attacks on their right flank and inflicted heavy losses on the enemy. On the 24th the battalion 'consolidated on the right flank'. On the 26th the 47th Battalion returned to Niagara Camp, Château de la Haie, for a 'hot breakfast'. Their casualties during August totalled 242 and those of the 10th Brigade were 1,081, although many of these were for the slightly wounded. The battalion had captured fifty-three Germans, including twelve wounded, as well as three machine-guns and the destruction of two more.

The following extract also comes from *Thirty Canadian VCs*:

The fighting about Lens in Aug 1917 called for more individual dash and initiative on the part of the troops engaged than had been required before. The house-to-house fighting, the repeatedly isolated and difficult positions, the many knotty problems which required instant solution – all these combined to make leadership, whether of a section or a battalion, more arduous and responsible . . .

Konowal's citation was published in the *London Gazette* of 26 November 1917:

Filip Konowal, Acting Corpl., 47th Infantry Battalion. Canadian Expeditionary Force. For most conspicuous bravery and leadership when in charge of a section in attack. His section had the difficult task of mopping up cellars, craters and machine-gun emplacements. Under his able direction all resistance was overcome successfully, and heavy casualties were inflicted on the enemy. In one cellar he himself bayoneted three enemy and attacked single-handed seven others in a crater, killing them all. On reaching the objective, a machine-gun was holding up the right flank, causing many casualties. Corpl. Konowal rushed forward and entered the emplacement, killed the crew, and brought the gun back to our lines. The next day he again attacked single-handed another machine-gun emplacement, killed three of the crew, and destroyed the gun and emplacement with explosives. This non-commissioned officer alone killed at least 16 of the enemy, and during the two days' actual fighting carried on continuously until severely wounded.

Robert Hill Hanna was a son of Robert Hanna, farmer, and was born in Kilkeel, County Down, Ireland, on 6 August 1886. He was brought up as a Presbyterian and educated at Balliran's School. He emigrated to Canada in the early years of the new century and settled in British Columbia to work in the forests as a lumberman.

At the age of twenty-eight, on 1 November 1914 Hanna decided to enlist in the Canadian Infantry, in Vancouver. He was posted as a private to the 29th (Vancouver) Battalion British Columbia Regiment, CEF, with a regimental number of 75361. His mother, whose address was Aughnahoory, Kilkeel, Co. Down, was his next-of-kin.

On completing his training Hanna left for England at the end of August 1915, and from there embarked for France on 17 September, arriving in Boulogne the following day. After six months' active service he caught German measles and was admitted to Number 7 General Hospital at St Omer on 1 April 1916. He was discharged on the 13th. On 24 June, he was slightly wounded on the cheek by shrapnel, which was quickly removed.

Masonic Cemetery, Burnaby Plot (*David C. Jennings*)

Judging from his promotions in rank Hanna was a good soldier. On 20 August he was appointed lance corporal and made up to sergeant in the field on 9 October. Shortly afterwards he was granted a week's leave of absence. On 21 August 1917, the day he won the Victoria Cross, he was appointed acting CSM, and six days later he was promoted in the field.

Hanna's winning of the VC led to his being considered good enough to be considered for a commission, and he returned to England for officer training on 20 September. Although he would of course not have known it at the time, he was never to return to active service in France.

Following the announcement of his VC in November he attended an investiture at Buckingham Palace on 5 December. Other men who had also won the VC were present, including William Butler, Ernest Egerton, Filip Konowal, James Ockenden, Michael O'Rourke and Ernest Pitcher. Hanna then returned to Northern Ireland for a brief visit to his family home at Kilkeel and was given a hero's welcome. Returning to England for officer training, he was commissioned on 26 January 1918 and appointed a temporary lieutenant on 12 February 1918, serving with the 1st Canadian Reserve Battalion.

THIS BENCH IS DEDICATED TO THE GLORY OF GOD
AND TO THE MEMORY OF OUR ORANGE BRETHREN
WHO FOR THEIR VALOUR WERE AWARDED THE VICTORIA CROSS
BRO GEORGE RICHARDSON V.C.   BRO ABRAHAM ACTON V.C.
BRO ROBERT QUIGG V.C.   BRO ROBERT H HANNA V.C.
BRO REV JOHN WEIR FOOTE V.C.

Ulster Tower, Thiepval (*Author's Collection*)

When the war was over he returned to Canada, sailing on 10 May 1919, and was demobilised in Ottawa on the 24th. Once home he returned to the lumber industry and managed a logging camp. In the 1930s he got married and had at least one son, and at the end of the decade he decided to give up managing a logging camp and return to farming. In June 1956 he attended the VC centenary celebrations in London, and according to one witness was seen to be 'a great big, fine chap, always smiling'. The following year he was one of seven VC pallbearers at the funeral of, and attended the requiem Mass for, the late Michael O'Rourke on 10 December. Harcus Strachan was another of the VC pallbearers.

Hanna died in his eightieth year on 15 June 1967 at Mount Lehman, British Columbia, and was buried in the Masonic Cemetery, Burnaby Plot 49, Section C, Grave 2. The inscription on his gravestone is 'Life's work well done'. The grave gives his date of birth as 1887.

Hanna was a Mason and a member of the Orange Order, and is commemorated by a wooden bench at Helen's Tower, Thiepval, on the Somme, together with four other VC winners, members of the Orange Order.

There are many variant spellings of the place in the Ukraine where Filip Konowal was born, but in his service records it is noted as Kutcowce, Podolskoy. Many accounts say that he was born on 15 September 1888, but on his attestation papers he wrote down the date of 25 March 1887.

Konowal was the son of a Russian farmer, Miron, and his wife Eudkice, and grew up as a Greek Catholic. On 25 July 1909, when he was twenty-two, he married Anna Stanka, of Russian parentage, and the couple had one daughter, Maria, born in 1909. Also in 1909 he was conscripted into the Imperial Russian Army and became an expert in close-quarter combat. He remained with the Army for four years before emigrating to Canada, arriving in Vancouver in April 1913. He left his wife and daughter behind while he sought to make his fortune.

Notre Dame Cemetery (*David C. Jennings*)

Seeking employment Konowal became a lumberjack in Western Canada before moving, after a few months, to Eastern Ontario, where he worked in the Ottawa Valley. On 12 July 1915 he enlisted in Ottawa, giving up his job as a labourer to join the Canadian Expeditionery Force as a member of the 77th Battalion. His regimental number was 144039. Also on his attestation papers Konowal spelt his christian name as Filip and for the rest of his life was sometimes known as Philip and at other times Filip. At five feet six inches he was on the small side, with brown eyes and brown hair. He trained in Canada until leaving Halifax for Liverpool on 19 June 1916. At Bramshott Camp he was transferred to the 47th British Columbia Battalion on 6 July and made a lance corporal sixteen days later. On the same day he made his will in favour of his wife, although he had first written down his mother's name before changing his mind.

Konowal left for France on 10 August 1916, arriving there the following day. He took part in the Battle of the Somme and in mid-September became a casualty when a tendon in his right hand was severed. He spent a brief period in hospital, and when released on the 18th was attached to No. 4 Canadian

Sanitary Section for five weeks. In February 1917 he was in hospital again, this time with diarrhoea and dysentery. On 6 April he was promoted to acting corporal, and took part in Vimy Ridge fighting. Later in the summer he went further north to the Loos area, where he was to win a VC on 22/23 August. In carrying out his VC actions he was seriously wounded by gunshot wounds to his face and neck and was admitted to 6th CCS on the 23rd and invalided back to England on the 27th. Once in England he was taken to Beaufort Hospital, Bristol, before being transferred to a convalescent hospital in Wokingham, where he was a patient for ten days, being discharged on 22 September.

On 1 November he was taken on the strength of the 16th Reserve Battalion and on 6 December he proceeded on command for duty with the Military Attaché in the Russian Embassy, London. On the 30th he was appointed to acting sergeant. A few days later he was decorated with his VC at Buckingham Palace on 5 December 1917 in the same investiture as six other holders of the VC – William Butler, Ernest Egerton, Robert Hanna, James Ockenden, Michael O'Rourke and Ernest Pitcher.

On 19 January Konowal was granted permission to wear a Russian medal, the Cross of St George, 4th Class. On 15 February he was transferred to the 1st Canadian Reserve Battalion. He returned from working at the Russian Embassy on 8 July 1918 and his rank reverted to corporal. For a short period from 1 August he served with the Canadian Forestry Corps. A few weeks later he left for Canada and was taken on the strength of the Canadian Siberian Expeditionary Force on 18 September. He was appointed acting sergeant on 1 October 1918.

Leaving Vancouver on 11 October, he disembarked at Vladivostok. In rank he reverted to corporal on 16 December 1918 after he had been absent without leave for less than 24 hours, and his pay was docked for a day. He served on command to Omsk from 28 March to 1 June 1919. He embarked for return to Canada on 5 June 1919, arriving on 20 June.

When the Russian campaign was over he was demobilised (4 July 1919) with the rank of corporal, but before he left the Army he was medically examined and was clearly still affected by his wounds, both mental and physical. He suffered from partial paralysis of a facial muscle on the left side as a result of bullet wounds at Lens and his left hand was partly crippled as a result of wounds received at Ypres. He also suffered from fluttering of the heart and periodic pains on exertion.

He clearly had a 'short fuse', for in Hull, Quebec, in the same month that he left the Army, he killed a man, an Austrian called William Artich, who either insulted Canada or its national flag. Using his war wounds as an excuse Konowal pleaded insanity. Two years later he was brought before the Court of the King's Bench, Crown Side, District of Hull, and on 20 April the jury returned a verdict of 'Not Guilty', accepting the plea of insanity as a result of war wounds. Nevertheless, the court ordered that he should be kept strictly in custody until the 'pleasure of the Lieutenant-Governor was known'. There was no other indictment against him.

Altogether Konowal spent nine years in various hospitals, including St Jean de Dieu Hospital in Quebec, and from around 1927 he was confined in the Hospital for the Criminally Insane in Bordeaux, Quebec. On release he found it very difficult to get employment, but he was able to enlist as one of the Governor-General's Foot Guards in Ottawa in 1928. He was well enough to travel to London in 1929 for the House of Lords' dinner in November. He was unemployed in the early 1930s but in 1936 he did manage to get a job in the Canadian House of Commons as a junior caretaker, probably owing to the assistance of Milton Gregg VC, who was Sergeant-at-Arms from 1934 to 1944. One of his duties was to keep the floor of the Hall of Fame clean, and at this time he was spotted by the Prime Minister, William Mackenzie King. He was then promoted and allowed to take charge of Room 16, the Prime Minister's Office.

Konowal's first wife died of starvation in the Ukraine and his daughter disappeared in Russia, probably dying in a Soviet work camp, and he later married a widow, Juliette Leduc-Auger, in 1934. In 1939 he was invited to attend a garden party for King George VI and Queen Elizabeth, when the royal couple were visiting Canada. The party took place at the Rideau Hall in Ottawa, and the King shook hands with Konowal during the Dedication of the National War Memorial.

After the end of the Second World War, when he was too old to serve, Konowal became a member of the Quebec branch of the Canadian Legion of the British Empire Service in December 1945. In 1953 the Toronto branch of the Royal Canadian Legion number 360 invited him to be their patron. This honour was confirmed during a Remembrance Day Dinner held on 7 November in Toronto.

When the VC centenary celebrations to take place in London were being planned, Konowal knew that he would be unable to raise the amount of money needed for the trip. In order to assist with his expenses he asked the Ukrainian branches to contribute, despite the Ottawa War Museum saying that they would help with his transport costs. He duly attended the VC centenary celebrations, which included a tea party at Westminster Hall on 25 June hosted by the Prime Minister, Sir Anthony Eden, the Hyde Park review on the 26th and the subsequent garden party at Marlborough House.

Back once more in Canada, Konowal continued his cleaning job at the House of Commons and his income was also helped by a small disability allowance. When asked by a reporter of the *Ottawa Citizen* dated 16 June about his job as a janitor he replied, 'I mopped overseas with a rifle, and here I must mop up with a mop.' Of his VC he remarked, 'I was so fed up standing in the trench with water to my waist that I said the hell with it and started after the German army. My captain tried to shoot me because he figured I was deserting.'

Konowal, who in his later years must have been 'a bit of a character', died in Ottawa on 3 June 1959 in the Veterans Pavilion, Civic Hospital, Ottawa. He was given a funeral with full military honours, which took place at St John the Baptist Ukrainian Catholic Church. He was buried in Lot 502, Section A, at Notre Dame Cemetery in Ottawa. His widow died in 1987 and is buried beside him. Initially his grave was marked with a small tablet, and thirty-six years later it was replaced by a standard Commonwealth War Graves stone at a wreath-laying ceremony on 6 December 1995.

On Konowal's death his medals were entrusted to a Ukrainian Canadian Veteran, Mr G.R. Bohdan Panchuk, who served with the RCAF in the Second World War and became a leading light in the Ukrainian Canadian Veterans' Association. It appeared that the medals were later acquired by the Canadian War Museum in Ottawa. Since his death at least five historical plaques have been set up in the Ukrainian's memory during the last fifteen years, mostly in the mid-nineties: one in Ottawa at Cartier Square, a second at the Drill Hall of the Governor-General's Foot Guards (15 July 1996), a third at the Royal Canadian Legion Branch 360 in Toronto on Queen Street West (21 August 1996) (the branch also sponsored a small booklet on Konowal's life, in three languages) and a fourth in the armoury of the Royal Westminster Regiment, New Westminster, British Columbia (1997). The regiment emerged from the 47th Battalion. The plaques are written in English, French and Ukrainian. A further tribute to his memory was the issue of a new 46-cent postage stamp featuring his portrait, issued in July 2000.

These memorials were not confined to Canada, as on 21 August 2000 a plaque and statue of Konowal (prepared by Petro Kulyk) was unveiled in his home village of Kutkiw in the Ukraine. In addition a 9 ft high bust, as well as a trilingual plaque commemorating his bravery, was unveiled. A dual ceremony took place in Ottawa, where he was posthumously awarded the National Council of Veteran Associations Order of Merit, which was presented to Claudette Wright, his granddaughter. The Canadian War Museum in Ottawa has a painting of Konowal and might well still have his medals, which appear to have been mislaid. The story is that they bought them from a dealer in 1969 and displayed them until 1972, and between 1972 and 1974 they went missing.

The Ukrainian community contributed a great number of men to the Canadian Expeditionary Force in the First World War and probably feel that this fact has been insufficiently acknowledged. In this context Filip Konowal VC has become a great hero to the community.

H.F. PARSONS

Near Épehy, France, 20/21 August 1917

(*David Harvey*)

Although in August 1917 the Épehy sector to the north-west of St Quentin was considered relatively quiet, it was still very important to both sides as it stood on the crest of a ridge. To the enemy it could be used as an outpost position to the Hindenburg Line, which was to the east of it. To the Allies, however, it was a position which if held provided an excellent place of observation over ground that fell away in a series of valleys dropping down to the St Quentin Canal. Part of the Hindenburg front line indeed crossed the canal to the south of Vendhuile. Observation was the prize, and one of the major enemy strongpoints was a position known as the Knoll, a sort of hump in the ground to the south-west of Vendhuile. The site looks very innocent today, just part of a rather ordinary field of wheat or sugar beet, but it was a very different story in August 1917, and again in September 1918, when the ground was bitterly fought for.

On 18 August two companies of the 15th Sherwood Foresters and 15th Cheshires (105th Brigade), 35th Division were involved in a desperate struggle to capture and hold onto the Knoll position. Following a barrage the assaulting companies captured the position within fifteen minutes, and if more troops had been available then the German trench which ran down to the Vendhuile –Lempire road might have been taken as well. The resulting casualties came to over 150 and two communication trenches were established that ran back to Battalion HQ. Not giving in, the enemy made several counter-attacks over the next two days, and as a consequence fierce fighting continued.

During the night of the 20th the four companies were relieved by the 14th (S) Gloucester Battalion, and they returned to their billets at St Emilie. The Gloster Battalion, originally a Bantam battalion, was in the 105th Brigade of the 35th Division and had first landed in France in January 1916.

According to the battalion's war diary, 'the relief was carried out without incident. . . . At 4 a.m. the enemy attempted to recapture the Knoll. The attack was made in three salient points, assisted on the right by *Flammenwerfer*.' The diary noted that there were about twenty casualties, including one officer killed. The diary does not mention T/2/Lt H.F. Parsons as being the dead officer. However, the 105th Brigade War Diary is much more informative and noted:

> the enemy made a determined attack on the Knoll at four [*sic*] different points simultaneously; the left and right Bombing Posts and the Left and Right forward Companies being attacked by parties each about 40 strong. The attack on the Right Bombing Post was led by *Flammenwerfer* which forced the garrison to fall back down the trenches a short distance. Lieutenant Parsons, 14th Gloster Regiment, however remained at the Post and although scorched by the *Flammenwerfer* checked the enemy for a long enough period for a counter-attack to be organised. This gallant officer was burnt to death but undoubtedly prevented the enemy from penetrating further into our position and was afterwards recommended for the V.C. for his action.

Holding the position for even the short time that they did allowed detailed observation of a section of the Hindenburg line, which could be added to information already gathered.

A telegram to Parsons' father, the Revd J. Parsons, dated 25 August 1917, from the WO informed him that his son had died four days before. A further cable informed him that his son had been buried north-east of Péronne at Villers Faucon Communal Cemetery Extension (German). The subsequent grave reference in the Communal Cemetery was A 16 and the inscription is 'TO LIVE WAS CHRIST TO DIE AGAIN'. The grave of another holder of the VC, 2/Lt John Dunville VC (The Royal Dragoons), who died of wounds in Épehy a few weeks before Parsons, on 26 June, is in the same cemetery in row A 21.

Villers-Faucon was captured by the 5th Cavalry Division in March 1917 and lost in the German Offensive a year later, then retaken in early September 1918. The cemetery has 317 graves, including 90 German.

On 8 November 1917 King George V held an investiture on Durdham Down, Bristol, which 126 'heroes' attended and where the Revd J. Parsons was presented with his son's posthumous VC. Later those who had taken part in the investiture on the Downs were given tea and entertainment at the Museum Art Gallery. Parsons' effects, a wrist ID, two watches and strap were returned to his father in early 1918 by registered post. The recommendation of a VC for Parsons was approved and the citation appeared in the *London Gazette* of 17 October 1917:

> Temporary Second Lieutenant Hardy Falconer Parsons, late Gloucester Regiment. For most conspicuous bravery during a night attack by a strong party of the enemy on a bombing post held by his command. The bombers holding the block were forced back, but Second Lieutenant Parsons remained at his post,

and single-handed, and although severely scorched and burnt by liquid fire, he continued to hold up the enemy with bombs until severely wounded. This very gallant act of self-sacrifice and devotion to duty undoubtedly delayed the enemy long enough to allow of the organization of a bombing party, which succeeded in driving back the enemy before they could enter any portion of the trenches. This gallant officer succumbed to his wounds.

Hardy Falconer Parsons was born in Rushton, Blackburn, Lancashire, on 30 [*sic*] June 1897, the son of the Revd J.A. Ash Parsons, a Wesleyan minister, and his wife Henrietta. He was the eldest of three brothers and attended King Edward VII School, Lytham, and Kingswood, Bath. He then became a first-year medical student at Bristol University and was preparing to become a medical missionary. He was also a member of the OTC. His family moved fairly regularly, and there are addresses at Arnside, Westmorland, where the Revd Parsons worked at the Leysian Mission in City Road, and in Bristol, where he worked at a Wesleyan Chapel in Old King Street and resided at 54 Sawbury Road, Redland.

Villers-Faucon Communal Cemetery
(*Peter Batchelor*)

Hardy Parsons joined the 6th Officer Cadet Battalion at Balliol College, Oxford, on 5 October 1916 and was appointed as temporary lieutenant with the Gloucestershire Regiment (LG 15 February 1917). He was then attached to the 14th (S) Battalion. His medical records state that prior to the war he had suffered from pneumonia on two occasions and had a spinal curvature. Of his two brothers, one served in the RFC, and a third, who was born in 1902, was born too late to take part in the war.

After the war Hardy Parsons was commemorated at King Edward VII School, Lytham, and at Kingswood School, Bath, and his medals are with the Gloucestershire Regiment. His deeds were featured in an issue of *The Victor*, dated 11 July 1970.

S.J. DAY

East of Hargicourt, Parvillers, France, 26 August 1917

(David Harvey)

On 24 August 1917, after the 11th Suffolks had been transferred to III Corps from the XVIIth, they moved into positions to the east of the Hindenburg Line near the village of Hargicourt and occupied part of the front and 'Brown Line', leaving two companies in Priel Wood.

The 11th Suffolks were one of six battalions belonging to the 34th Division who had been given the task of clearing the enemy from a position known as Cologne Farm Ridge, which concealed a commanding view of a section of the Hindenburg Line east of Hargicourt. The land they were to advance across was an open and rolling countryside with slag heaps, with the enemy occupying trenches on the western side of the loftiest ridge. A prominent feature in the objectives would be a position known as Malakhoff Farm.

On the 26th the Suffolks formed up in what in places was a sunken road between the ruins of a farm known as Unnamed Farm and a position called Huzzar Post. At this point the opposing lines were comparatively close together with the enemy front line including Cologne Farm. To the north and south the area of No Man's Land was much wider, which made patrols much easier.

The following account of the action draws heavily on the battalion war diary of the 11th Suffolks who were on the left of the line. To their right were the 15th and 16th Royal Scots and the 10th Lincolns. Prior to the attack a covering party initially went out for a distance of about 120 yards. Then at 2.30 a.m. on what was a very cold night, D, B and A Companies went forward, leaving most of C Coy in reserve. The covering party quickly 'mopped up' the first obstacle, Rifle Pit Trench, which was found to be empty. Malakhoff Trench and Sugar Trench were then occupied and there was fierce hand-to-hand fighting and bombing at the junction of Malakhoff Trench and Sugar Trench. A machine-gun caused several casualties but its crew were quickly dealt with.

Malakhoff Farm (*Peter Batchelor*)

Members of D Coy noticed that Triangle Trench was strongly occupied, and Capt Wright, the company commander, decided to take it, and in so doing captured thirty prisoners. A trench was then quickly begun to connect it with Malakhoff Support. B Coy lost ground passing through Malakhoff Farm owing to the bad going, but as planned, troops on either side of the farm quickly bombed down Malakhoff Support and a block was established close to the junction of Malakhoff Trench and Malakhoff Support. Between 3 and 9 p.m. the Suffolks consolidated Malakhoff Support Trench and had by now gained observation down the valley. The road that ran south-west of the farm was an objective. The rest of the divisional attack against Cologne Ridge was successful except that the right flank of the 15th Royal Scots to the right of the line was briefly held up by a counter-attack.

A copy of a report on the role of the 34th Division makes the following comments on progress of the positions captured by the Suffolks:

Malakhoff Support Trench has been dug down 6 feet and firestepped. There is a good field of fire down the valley in the direction of Quennemont Farm. Sugar Trench is 6 feet deep, firestepped, and has a field of fire of about 150 yards. The South end of Triangle Trench is held up for 100 yards. From the North point held at Triangle Trench a trench has been dug to Malakhoff Support Trench. This will be completed tonight and gives a good field of fire down the valley . . . . The left of Malakhoff Support Trench was overlooked from Quennemont Farm.

Two days later machine-guns in Triangle Trench were still giving trouble, and a sniper from the Suffolks managed to put one of them out of action. 15092 Cpl Sidney Day was a member of D Coy, and during the attack against the enemy strongpoint of Malakhoff Farm the attackers, who were moving through smoke and fire, began to falter owing mainly to an enemy machine-gun, which was causing them heavy casualties. In the words of his VC citation, published in the *London Gazette* of 17 October:

> Corpl. Day was in command of a bombing section detailed to clear a maze of trenches still held by he enemy; this he did, killing two machine-gunners and taking four prisoners. On reaching a point where the trench had been levelled, he went alone and bombed his way through to the left, in order to gain touch with the neighbouring troops. Immediately on return to his section a stick bomb fell into a trench occupied by two officers (one badly wounded) and three other ranks. Corpl. Day seized the bomb and threw it over the trench, where it immediately exploded. This prompt action undoubtedly saved the lives of those in the trench. He afterwards completed the clearing of the trench, and establishing himself in an advanced position, remained for 66 hours at his post, which came under intense hostile shell and rifle-grenade fire. Throughout the whole operations his conduct was an inspiration to all.

On carrying out his heroic work at Malakhoff Farm on 26 August 1917, Cpl Day was recommended for the VC by Lt Col G.L.J. Tuck, when he was a major, having in April taken over command of the battalion from Lt Col E.H. Kendrick, commanding officer of the 11th Battalion, when the latter was sick.

In a letter home dated 4 September to his parents, Day told them the story of how the VC came about:

> . . . In about six weeks' time you will, I hope, be informed of great news, which will make you the proudest parents in Norwich. I am recommended for the coveted honour, the V.C., the first one in the battalion up to the present. Now I know you want to hear all about it, and what I did to get it. Shall be able to tell you more about it when I come home. Am sure it cannot be a greater surprise to you that it has been to me. You cannot imagine how honoured I feel to break the news to you all. Last Sunday week, August 26th, we went over to the attack. Everything went off successful, and, thanks to God's mercy and care, I came through untouched. When we got back to our billets my platoon officer, who is a perfect gentleman, broke the news to me.

He called me aside, and told me that he was very pleased with what I had done in the attack, and was recommending me for a reward. At first, he said I was in for a M.M., but the captain and himself decided on a D.C.M., but initially the colonel and captain thought me worthy of the Victoria Cross, as he told me personally I thoroughly deserved it, and he hoped I would get it. Well, when my officer told me that, you might have knocked me down with a feather, for little did I dream that I should ever be the one to gain that much coveted honour . . . The colonel congratulated me personally. He came to my billet, and said, 'Corporal, I have come to congratulate you on the splendid work you did last Sunday. I am very pleased with and proud of you. Up to the present everything has gone off well, and I hope you will get what you thoroughly deserve' . . . When it comes in orders I am to be made sergeant, and then I shall come to dear old Blighty to receive my medal . . . There are to be several decorations given in the battalion; anyhow, the recommendations have gone through, and I hope they will be granted . . . Above all, I have my officer to thank for what he has done for me. I shall never be able to repay him. Anyhow, he seems to think that I am worthy of what I am to get and says I have earned it.

On 25 September the 11th Suffolks moved from the neighbourhood of Vandencourt Chateau to Péronne by road and rail to Bienvillers-au-Bois. Day was initially granted leave from 14 to 29 December, during which time he was given a hero's welcome in Norwich and given a civic reception at the Guild Hall, where he was presented with an 'Illuminated Address'. On 19 December he was the guest of St Mark's School, accompanied by his sister, and was presented with a 'handsome clock'. He also attended a Church Lads' Brigade Social at the St Mark's Mission Hall in Trafalgar Street, probably on the 20th, and on the following Sunday, the 23rd, as a former sergeant in the CLB he attended a service at St Helen's before marching with them to the Market Place.

Day's leave was later extended by the War Office, and he was invested with his VC by the King at Buckingham Palace on 9 January 1918, in the same investiture as when the Australian L/Cpl Walter Peeler received his. It appears that soon after the visit to London Day fell ill, which led to his being detained at Shoreham and spending nine weeks at Bury St Edmunds before returning to France on 21 March at the time of the German March offensive.

On 9 or 10 April 1918 he was taken prisoner, and his 'Burnt File' states that he was injured by a bullet in his right thumb, although it seems that his wounds were far more serious. For a couple of months Day was thought to be missing as there was no word from him. However, according to a brief report in the *Eastern Daily Press* of 8 June, Day was no longer thought to be missing but was imprisoned in Langensalza, a German prisoner-of-war camp, having been in

Church Lads' Group, Norwich 1917 (*Anon*)

hospital after being captured. The news came from a colleague who wrote to Day's family on his friend's behalf, possibly because Day's injuries made writing impossible. The communication was dated 1 May. The last sighting of Day on the field of battle was noted by an officer in his battalion who saw him 'in a wounded condition'.

At the war's end Day was repatriated to Hull on 23 December 1918 and demobilised on 18 March 1919.

Sidney James Day was born at 4 St Ann Lane, King Street, in the Conesford District of Norwich on 3 July 1891, youngest of nine boys and one girl: the family lived at 119 Ber Street. His father had been head cellarman at Morgan's King Street Brewery, which was only yards from St Ann Lane. He was later the landlord of the Jolly Butchers public house and lodging house at 125 Ber Street. The inn was possibly owned by Morgan's Brewery and was noted for its 'fine ales'.

Sidney was educated at St Mark's School, Hall Road, Lakenham, less than a mile from his home, and worshipped at the nearby church, attending Sunday School and joining the Church Lads' Brigade. According to an article in the *Eastern Daily Press* of 18 October 1917 Day was '. . . always regarded as a smart, robust lad, but modest withal, and gained the esteem of the vicar, his teachers, and all with whom he came into contact'.

After leaving school Day entered the butchery trade as a trainee, and firstly worked at Miller's in nearby St Catherine's Plain. Prior to the war he moved to Suffolk and worked as a butcher in Saxmundham. It was from there that he enlisted in the 9th Sussex Regiment on 14 September 1914 at the age of twenty-three. His attestation papers described him as being fractionally over five feet seven inches tall, with brown hair and blue eyes. He trained at Shoreham and Aldershot and left for France on 31 August 1915 in time to serve in the Battle of Loos, where on 26 September he saved the life of the badly wounded Lt T.T. Stevens of the 9th Suffolks and 'took him in his arms and was proceeding to carry him to a place of safety, when a bullet from a sniper's rifle rendered further effort in that direction useless. The lieutenant was dead.' Later Stevens's family presented Day with a silver cigarette case, which carried an inscription of the event. Day was promoted to lance corporal in December 1915 and went to Belgium and took part in the fighting during the winter months in the Ypres Salient. He was promoted to corporal on 17 August 1917.

During the Battle of the Somme Day was seriously wounded by gunshot wounds in four parts of his body, including one just above his heart. His life was possibly saved through the presence of two or three pocket books and a packet of postcards and field service cards in his breast pocket. The bullet passed through them all 'but was deflected and, entering his side, came out at his back. Another bullet struck him near the groin, but became embedded in the leather case of a range finder and inflicted nothing worse than a bruise. A third passed through his thigh and came out of his groin; and a fourth went through his left side and came out of his back. Thus wounded and exhausted he lay in a shell-hole from seven o'clock in the morning till it became dark, when he crept three miles to a dressing station.'

Day was fortunate to have escaped death, and was sent home to Norwich and spent the next two months in the Norwich War Hospital at Thorpe, only a couple of miles from the family home in Norwich. He next travelled to Wymondham, on the west side of Norwich, for a period of convalescence. On his discharge he returned to his unit and later left for France and joined the 11th Suffolks of the 34th Division.

After he was repatriated to England, Day appears to have found adjustment to peacetime life very difficult. Possibly he expected to find 'a land fit for heroes' instead of one where soldiers were no longer wanted and jobs were hard to come by. In May 1919 he was given a warm welcome home by the Loyal Amicable Lodge of Oddfellows at a meeting held at the Cricketer's Arms, a public house in Orford Place, which was probably later destroyed by enemy action in 1942.

However, in May 1919, when still not wishing to claim unemployment benefit, he had two interviews with Sir G.M. Chamberlin, the owner of a local drapery store and warehouse and current Lord Mayor of Norwich. What Day said at these interviews has not been recorded, but Chamberlin was unable to offer the VC hero a job, as 'I found his ideas as to the nature of the work he could take up, and the salary, or wages, he should receive, made it impossible for me to offer him employment.' However, the Lord Mayor did agree to make an initial donation of £10 to a fund for the local hero. The fund was called the 'Corporal Day, V.C.' Subscription Fund and was to help Day to start up a business of his own. When asked about his response to the appeal Day said, 'I consider it excellent. I don't think employers in general have had that consideration for ex-servicemen that they ought. They have shown too great a tendency to take for granted all that these men went through in the war. They don't seem to realise what the men really endured.'

Meanwhile, Day had placed his name on the list of applicants for the government training scheme for ex-servicemen, presumably having given up the idea of returning to the butchering trade, and was employed by the Norwich Electricity Department at its Duke Street Works, 'changing plugs and things'.

In June 1920 he attended the VC garden party in the grounds of Buckingham Palace and on Armistice Day in the same year the service for the Unknown Warrior at the Cenotaph and subsequent burial at Westminster Abbey. In November 1929 he was one of the guests of the Prince of Wales at a dinner given at the House of Lords and on the next day attended a special performance of R.C. Sherriff's *Journey's End* at the Prince of Wales Theatre, and a special service at the Cenotaph the following day. He had been given free travel for his trip to London by United Automobile Services.

In the early 1930s Day moved to Portsmouth, probably as he had friends there, and took out a lease on the property called the Arcade Restaurant off Queens Street in Landport, Portsmouth city centre. He renamed it the 'Sidney Day VC tearoom'. It is not known when he met Doris Ena, but the couple married on 21 June 1939 and lived above the café until they were bombed out on 10 January 1941. Day then took a job as a messenger for the Admiralty in HM Dockyard on 6 February. It is possible that the couple then lived with a sister of Mrs Day for a short time before taking up rented accommodation at 192 Kirby Road, North End, where their son Michael was born in 1943. After the war they moved to a prefab at 37 Penhale Road, Fratton.

Suffering from tuberculosis, Day retired from work at the Dockyard on 9 March 1956, in the same year as the family moved to 18 Fraser Road in a large council estate in Bedhampton, Havant, outside Portsmouth.

Day was clearly very proud of winning the VC and never lost an opportunity of mentioning it in correspondence, signing his name Sidney Day VC. After the

Milton Cemetery (*Donald C. Jennings*)

Second World War ended he attended the Victory Parade in June 1946 and the dinner at the Dorchester Hotel. Ten years later he also attended the 1956 VC centenary celebrations in London.

Three years after giving up work at the age of 68, Sidney Day died in Queen Alexandra's Hospital, Cosham, Hampshire, on 17 July 1959. He was given a full military funeral when he was buried at Milton Cemetery two days later. A former Drum Major of the 1st Suffolks sounded the Last Post and Reveille. Day's widow Doris died on 18 June 1982 aged seventy-six and was buried next to her husband.

According to a note made by Canon Lummis in his VC files, a few days after Day's death Col Tuck told Lummis, 'Corporal Day did not subsequently prove a very satisfactory NCO and was sent home', a view that Lummis had often heard Tuck express previously. These comments were not made in any way to denigrate Day's heroism on 26 August 1917 when he won his VC, but were more to do with his rank and perhaps leadership qualities.

As for commemoration, at some point a memorial tablet was erected in St Mark's, Day's former school, which subsequently disappeared, probably when the building ceased to be used as a school. In the early 1970s former boys at the school later arranged for a replacement to be placed this time in the memorial chapel at St Mark's Church in October 1971, together with a copy of Day's citation and his portrait. However, this too went missing and was later found in the church vestry. The couple's son, Michael, who served as a WO in the RAF survives, and his father's VC is not publicly held.

At the time of writing there are active plans afoot by a group of dedicated volunteers to erect a more lasting memorial to commemorate Day's life close to where he was born in Norwich. In addition, a new memorial is also (at the time of writing) being planned for St Mark's, Lakenham. There are no buildings left belonging to Malakhoff Farm, but the outline of what was a rectangular-shaped complex is clearly visible in the ground during autumn and spring. Formerly part of the Hindenburg defence system, the land on which the farm once stood has been ploughed many times, yet there are many signs of former buildings in the soil – brick and tiles and other building materials. The replacement buildings of Gillemont Farm, now protected by a screen of conifers, can be seen on higher ground to the north-east.

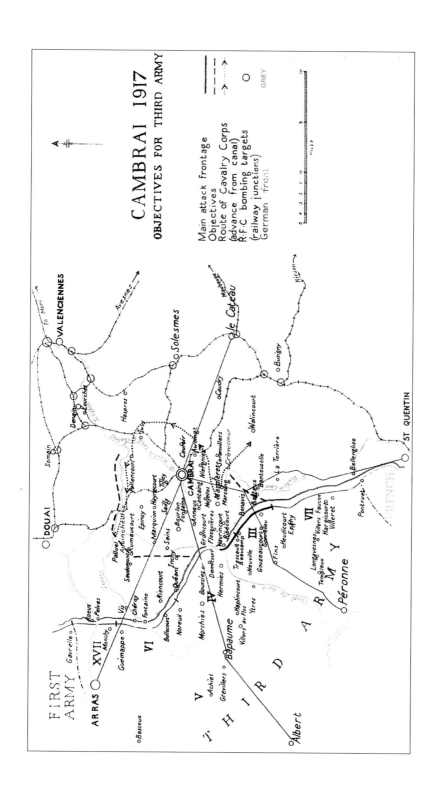

CAMBRAI 1917
OBJECTIVES FOR THIRD ARMY

Main attack frontage
Objectives
Route of Cavalry Corps
(advance from canal)
R.F.C bombing targets
(railway junctions)
German front

A.E. SHEPHERD

Villers-Plouich, France, 20 November 1916

(*David Harvey*)

On 20 November 1917, the first day of the Battle of Cambrai, the 20th Division was in the British front-line positions at Villers-Plouich and to the west of the German-held village of La Vacquerie. The 12th Division was to its right and the 6th Division to the left.

At Villers-Plouich at 6.10 a.m. precisely the leading eighteen tanks in sections of three began to move forward towards the German-held Hindenburg Line. Following the long line of tanks in the mist of the early dawn, the infantry with fixed bayonets moved forward in silence ten minutes later, the enemy seemingly unaware of their presence. However, when the British support lines were reached by the tanks the enemy suddenly 'woke up' and quickly responded with machine-gun and trench-mortar fire. Simultaneously the British barrage came crashing down on the Hindenburg Line. Field-guns and heavy howitzers had been recently brought up to Villers-Plouich and set up within 1,000 yards of the enemy front line. A smoke barrage beyond the enemy line was also put down. The German artillery reply was 'very ineffectual'.

Men from the 12th (S) King's Royal Rifle Corps (60th Brigade) formed up in the Station Quarry, Villers–Plouich (which can still be traced and has given way to housing and a sports field) and at 6.10 a.m. attacked Farm Trench which they captured without much resistance after the tanks had smashed down the thick wire in front of it. Here D Coy remained as the rest of the battalion moved on towards Welsh Ridge and the village of Marcoing. Reaching Good Old Man Farm, C Coy on the right was held up by heavy machine-gun fire. However, despite the loss of two officers, the company following the tanks managed to reach its next objective. It then captured four machine-guns. A Coy also carried its objective, though with greater casualties, and seized six machine-guns.

B Coy under Captain Hoare, which had not been in action up to that point, moved forward in a northerly direction with the support of a Stokes mortar that had been attached to the battalion. It crossed the first enemy trench, but then in

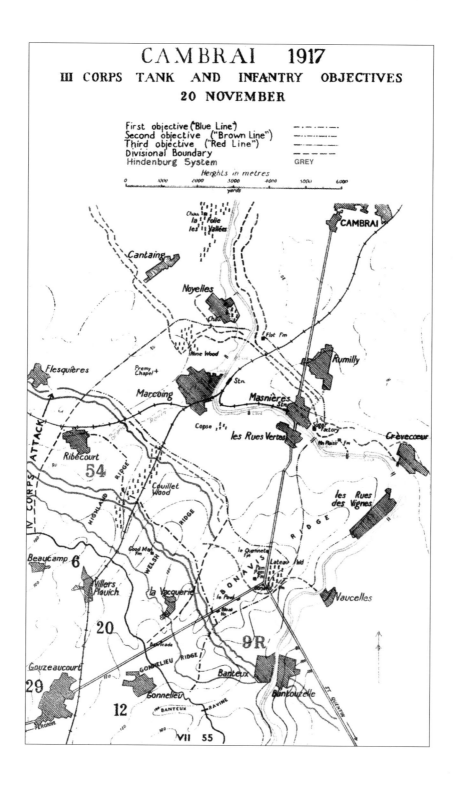

an enemy support trench came under enemy fire and fierce hand-to-hand fighting ensued. A mound in the enemy third line concealed a dugout holding snipers and machine-guns, and the riflemen began to suffer from severe fire. The mound was probably about 350 yards north-east of the track intersection that led to Good Old Man Farm. The 6th Ox & Bucks, also in the same brigade, were to their right and had not pushed far enough forward at this point, and as a result the attackers of the KRRC took the full brunt. The innocent-looking mound resulted in the deaths of fifteen men and the wounding of many other riflemen. The most serious event was the mortal wounding of Capt Hoare, after which the last remaining NCO became a casualty. This left Captain Hoare's orderly and company runner Rifleman Shepherd to take charge.

Planning to capture the mound and ordering the remaining men to keep up a steady fire, Shepherd managed to walk back over 70 yards of open ground under heavy fire in order to hail a tank that he saw approaching. After he had attracted the attention of the tank crew and given instructions, the tank moved forward to deal with the enemy position while Shepherd returned to his company, once more under heavy fire. With the members of the 6th Ox & Bucks, the remaining riflemen managed to capture the mound with no further losses.

While this was happening to B Coy, D Company was moving forward on the left down the Couillet Valley, reaching its objectives by 2 p.m. In mid-evening orders from Brigade HQ instructed the battalion to reach out to its right as far as the crossroads in La Vacquerie Valley. All battalion objectives had now been met, but not without a day of very heavy casualties.

After a wet night, which made the trenches muddy, the battalion received orders from brigade in the late afternoon to move up to former enemy positions 1,000 yards to the north-west of La Vacquerie, south-south-east of Marcoing.

Capt Archibald Hoare was taken to a CCS, where he died a week later, possibly at Tincourt, as he was buried at Tincourt New British Cemetery to the east of Péronne.

Rifleman Shepherd was recommended for a VC, which was published in the *London Gazette* of 13 February 1918:

No. R.15089, Albert Edward Shepherd, Private, King's Royal Rifle Corps. For most conspicuous bravery as a company runner. When his company was held up by a machine-gun at point-blank range, he volunteered to rush the gun, and although ordered not to, rushed forward and threw a Mills bomb, killing two gunners and capturing the gun. The company, on continuing its advance, came under heavy enfilade machine-gun fire. When the last officer and the last non-commissioned officer had become casualties, he took command of the company, ordered the men to lie down, and himself went back seventy yards under severe fire to obtain the help of a tank. He then returned to his

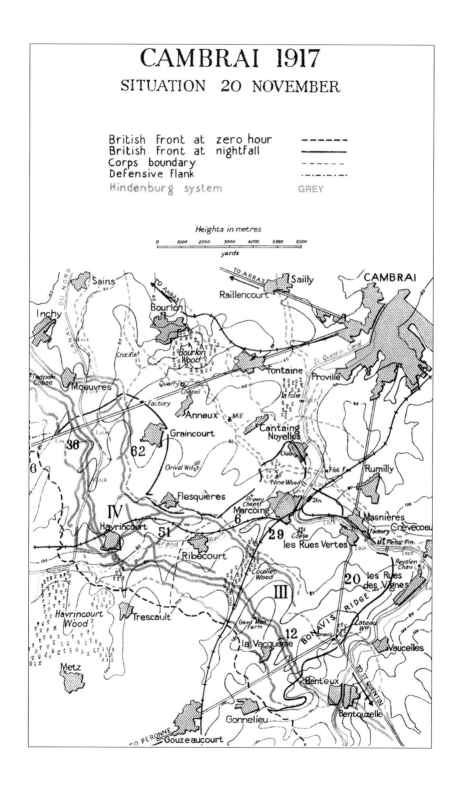

company, and finally led them to their last objective. He showed throughout conspicuous determination and resource.

After these deeds Shepherd let his family know that he might be awarded a medal 'for something he had done out yonder'. He returned home to Royston a few days after his award was published in the *London Gazette*. Perhaps not wanting a fuss, he had asked his father to keep quiet about the time of his intended arrival at Royston station, but, nevertheless, the news of his return must have got out as there was a large crowd of people waiting for him there. The local newspaper described them as 'enthusiastic inhabitants, who turned out in their hundreds and cheered the gallant young fellow to the echo'. In addition to this warm welcome, the village of Royston was bedecked with flags and bunting. The reception party was headed by the Royston Subscription Band and the crowd that followed it escorted Shepherd to the Palace Picture House, where he was welcomed by the chairman of Royston District Council, the vicar and other local dignitaries. Several speeches of congratulation were made, to which Shepherd replied in brief. The Patriotic Fund gave him a gold watch and chain and the scholars of the Primitive Methodist Chapel presented him with a Bible.

On the following day, and seemingly not to be outdone, the neighbouring and much larger town of Barnsley also prepared to provide the ex-mineworker with an official welcome. The distance between his home and Barnsley was four miles, and a large crowd formed a procession, once more headed by a local band, to make the journey. En route the local hero was acclaimed and carried shoulder-high by a relay of admirers. Once at the town the procession was met by another large group representing the town. The procession was destined for Peel Square, where Shepherd was greeted by the Deputy Mayor at the *Chronicle* building, which was bedecked with patriotic flags, and the speeches were made at one of the open windows. This time not only the local council but Shepherd's Colliery employers and also the Army all took part with their speeches of congratulations. In reply Shepherd told the enthusiastic crowd, '. . . I consider I was one of the lucky ones. I am glad, of course, and I am glad to be a native of Barnsley and district.'

Shepherd was then taken to an upper floor of the building, and when he made his appearance at another window 'he was received with wild enthusiasm'. Later he was again paraded shoulder-high through the crowded streets and received 'with the greatest cordiality'.

The hero was presented with his VC by the King at Buckingham Palace on 9 March. He was promoted to lance-corporal on 28 August 1918 and to full corporal a month later. On 2 January 1919 he was discharged from the Army.

Albert Edward Shepherd was born in Royston, Barnsley, in South Yorkshire on 11 January 1897, the son of Noah Shepherd, a miner, and his wife Laura (née Darwin). His mother died on 7 November 1911. Albert was educated at Royston West Riding School and probably left school when he was fourteen or fifteen years old, when he became a pony driver at New Monckton Colliery in 1911. His chief recreations were boxing and running. When he was still only seventeen years old he enlisted (on the first day of the war) and was drafted to one of Lord Kitchener's service battalions, the 12th (S) Battalion King's Royal Rifle Corps. In 1916 he took part in the Battle of the Somme and fought in the Battle of Passchendaele in the autumn of 1917.

Royston Cemetery (*Donald C. Jennings*)

During his war service he was seriously wounded in the arm and twice gassed and later qualified for an Army pension. After he left the Army Shepherd returned to the colliery and was employed as a caretaker. Later he joined the Corps of Commissionaires.

As late as 17 March 1920 he heard that he had been awarded the French Médaille Militaire, but eight months later on 21 January 1921 this award was cancelled and replaced by a Croix de Guerre. In between these two dates he attended the Buckingham Palace garden party on 26 June 1920 and nine years later the House of Lords' dinner on 9 November 1929.

Shepherd retired from work in 1945, and in the following year attended the Victory parade on 8 June, followed by the VC dinner at the Dorchester Hotel. In fact he attended most of the VC/GC functions, including the Hyde Park Review on 26 June 1956 and a review of the Corps of Commissionaires on 13 May 1959.

Shepherd survived until his seventieth year, dying on 23 October 1966 at his home at Oakwood Crescent, Royston. At his death he left a widow, two sons and a daughter. He was given a full military funeral at John the Baptist Parish Church, Melbourn Street, and as the cortège moved into the church it was given a guard of honour provided by the Army and members of the local British Legion. The Union-Flag-draped coffin also had his VC and Croix de Guerre on it. The 'Last Post' and 'Reveille' were played at the graveside by a corporal. Later

Shepherd's name was insribed on a wooden archway to the churchyard paid for by public subscription. In 1968 Mrs G.M. Shepherd, Albert's widow, presented her late husband's VC and other medals to the Royal Greenjackets at Winchester on 1 April; they included the 1915 Star, BWM, VM and Coronation Medals of 1937 and 1953.

In August 1983 the then Royston vicar, the Revd John Hudson, made himself very unpopular when he used part of the archway to the War Memorial, which is a memorial to Shepherd, as a clothes post for his washing line. He was taken to task by the local British Legion, whose spokesman said, 'I was absolutely disgusted . . .'.

The village of Villers-Plouich has associations with another holder of the VC, namely Cpl Edward Foster of the 13th East Surreys, who won his medal during fighting in the village on 24 April 1917 in the Battle of Arras. Foster came from Wandsworth, and in 1920 the Wandsworth Borough Council made the decision to adopt the devastated village under the scheme arranged by the British League of Help. Links made with the village eighty-three years ago survive, and the author saw a wreath at the local war memorial from Wandsworth only a short while ago during a visit.

R.W.L. WAIN

Marcoing, France, 20 November 1917

(*David Harvey*)

Unlike many of the tanks being concealed in various woods, including Havrincourt and Dessart, the tanks from A, C, F and I Battalions had no wood to shelter in and instead were concealed in brick-coloured camouflaged netting in and about the villages of Villers Guislain and Gouzeaucourt.

At dawn on 20 November 1917 when the tanks moved forward to their assembly positions, they used low gears in order to reduce throttle noise, and on the previous day the ground had been reconnoitred and tapes laid down. The eve of the 20th was very cold, and an order was given that to defeat any frost hazard tank engines should be started up and run for a quarter of an hour every two hours and the vehicle moved slightly in order to avoid its tracks from freezing. Each tank was to carry a fascine, which would allow it to move more easily through the Hindenburg Line, including the wide trenches and gaps.

No fewer than 378 tanks took part in the first day of the Battle of Cambrai on 20 November 1917, in a line which was 13,000 yards long between Trescault, in front of Havrincourt Wood, and Gonnelieu, to the south of La Vacquerie. However, by the end of the day and in spite of the element of surprise, close to half the tanks had either broken down, failed to make progress or were destroyed by the enemy.

Eight divisions took part in the initial assault and the 3rd Tank Brigade had four tank battalions working with the 12th, 20th and 29th Divisions. Their objectives were the village of La Vacquerie, the Brown and Blue Lines beyond and the canal crossings from Masnières to Marcoing. Crèvecoeur was their most easterly objective. The assault of the 60th Brigade (20th Division) was to be led by tanks of A and I Battalions. The other tanks of the 3rd Tank Brigade were C and F Battalions. Although in the misty November morning many of the enemy were terrified by the new war machine, there were pockets of resistance – in particular at Flesquières, where enemy artillery were picking off Allied tanks at point-blank range as they reached the summit of the ridge, and also at Grand

121

Ravine between Havrincourt and Ribecourt, where sixteen tanks were also knocked out.

Capt Richard Wain was in command of a section in No. 1 Company of the 1st Tank Battalion, and at first light was travelling in the leading tank, No. 2399 Abou Ben Adam II, of the three-tank section under the command of Lt C.W. Duncan MC. Their 'orders were to proceed in the direction of Good Man Farm [*sic*] towards Marcoing and assist Infantry in advance'. Prior to the explosive start of the British artillery barrage, and using their fascines to drop into the trenches of the Hindenburg Line, the tanks of 1st Tank Battalion made good progress and reached 'Good Man Farm' where there was no infantry hold-up. One of the tanks in the section, A 3 A-Merry-Can, crossed the Hindenburg front line by using the fascine dropped by Abou Ben Adam II. They moved on, clearing the way of enemy defenders as they went, until they were held up by a strongpoint in the Hindenburg support line. At this point, one by one, Wain's tank section was knocked out by fire from an enemy trench mortar battery, and Duncan's tank was hit five times before it was stopped. Duncan was killed, as were other members of his crew, including the first driver, Pte J.A. Browning, and others were wounded. The actual position was about 1,300 yards north-north-east of Good Old Man Farm.

Wain, though also badly wounded, jumped out of the tank accompanied by another member of the crew, seized a Lewis gun, and although only 50 yards from the enemy position and 200 yards in front of the infantry, advanced towards the strongpoint, firing as he went, managed to capture the enemy position, together with several prisoners, and put four trench mortars and two machine-guns out of action. Though he was bleeding profusely from his first wound he refused the attentions of stretcher-bearers in order continue his task of clearing the enemy out of the strongpoint. Picking up a rifle he continued to fire at the retreating enemy until he was mortally wounded in the head by a sniper. He had undoubtedly saved the lives of many of the accompanying infantry, who were now able to advance towards Marcoing, which was captured later in the day.

Many men would have witnessed Capt Wain's gallant deeds, and the war diary of the 12th Rifle Brigade (60th Brigade), 20th Division reported the events in the following way after one of its companies had been held up within 200 yards of the Hindenburg support line by a nest of five machine-guns and a trench mortar:

> . . . At this stage Captain Fraser commanding A Coy managed to get hold of a stray tank which at once advanced on the next . . . The tank got within 50 yards of the nest when it received a direct hit from the T.M. which killed 5 of its crew and severely wounded the officer and remaining men. The officer, however got out of the tank and rushed at the Germans with a Lewis Gun . . . The officer was killed in the melée, but the party of Germans who survived

Good Old Man Farm (*Peter Batchelor*)

immediately surrendered. Only 1 of the 5 MG was fit for use and it was
immediately turned on parties of the Germans who were running away . . .

The bodies of Capt Wain and other tank crew members were later buried about
200 yards south-east of their tank beside the Villers-Plouich–Marcoing road, or
325 yards east of Couillet Wood. Orchard Road was the name of the position on
the trench maps of the period, and today the site is close to a bridge under which
the A 26 Autoroute passes. Wain's name is commemorated on Panel 13 of the
Louverval Memorial.

In recent years the accounts of Wain's deed in several books have stated that
he gained his VC at Good Old Man Farm, and it is difficult to pin down just
where this error first occurred. Certainly it is made in volume one of Liddell
Hart's *The Tanks*, published in 1959, but it might have occurred earlier
elsewhere and then for ever repeated as fact. The other problem is that Good
Old Man Farm is sometimes named in war diaries or on maps by another name,
such as Goodman Farm or Good Man Farm. As we have seen, the evidence
points to Wain winning his VC about 1,300 yards away to the north-east of the

Welch Ridge (*Peter Batchelor*)

derelict farm building, which in 1917 and 1918 was sometimes used as a Battalion HQ. The farm is now known as Ferme du Bois Veillard, on a slope overlooking Villers-Plouich, and certainly was the last-named location close to where Wain's action took place.

Wain's posthumous VC was the second to be won by a man serving with the Tanks Corps, the first having been won at Zonnebeke, Belgium, nearly seven weeks earlier. The citation was published in the *London Gazette* of 13 February 1918, and his parents were presented with the medal at an investiture at Buckingham Palace on 20 April; it remains in private hands. The VC citation was as follows:

Richard William Leslie Wain, Temporary Lieutenant (Acting Capt.), late Tank Corps. For most conspicuous bravery in command of a section of Tanks. During an attack the Tank in which he was, was disabled by a direct hit near an enemy strong point which was holding up the attack. Capt. Wain and one man, both seriously wounded, were the only survivors. Though bleeding profusely from his wounds, he refused the attention of stretcher-bearers, rushed from behind the Tank with a Lewis gun, and captured the strong point, taking about half the garrison prisoners. Although his wounds were very serious, he picked up a rifle and continued to fire at the retiring enemy until he received a fatal wound in the head. It was due to the valour displayed by Capt. Wain that the infantry were able to advance.

Wain was a member of the 25th Manchester Regiment attached to A Battalion Tank Corps.

One of Wain's senior officers wrote to his parents:

. . . Your son has been in my company since last Christmas [1916] and saw the whole of this year's [1917] fighting with it. He had already distinguished himself on several occasions, and always showed the very greatest gallantry. On November 20, after passing the Hindenburg Line, the Tank in which he was, attacked a trench mortar battery and three machine-guns. It received five hits from T.M. shells. The fifth shell stopped it and killed everyone except your son, who leapt from the car with a Lewis gun and engaged the three machine-guns and T.M.s in the open. He succeeded in putting them all out of action, but was afterwards killed by a sniper. He is buried on the Hindenburg line by his Tank, with a Lieutenant, whose commander he was, and the crew . . . . in conclusion I will only say that you have the heartfelt sympathy of every officer and man in the company, for the loss of so gallant a man. He was extremely popular with everyone in the battalion, and his loss is keenly felt both at work and play.

In the same account an unnamed Cardiff gunner in the Tank Corps who knew Capt Wain well stated that 'he was the bravest of the brave' and before he too was wounded on the 30th, 'he heard it whispered that Capt. Wain had been recommended for a high distinction. . . He certainly deserved it, because all the men who were around him that day came back from the fight speaking in glowing terms of his gallantry.'

After his son's death, according to papers which remain in his file in the National Archives, Wain's father seemed anxious to obtain suitable compensation from the War Office to cover the loss of some articles of clothing formerly used by his son. He considered that £6 was a suitable sum to cover the loss of a fur-lined trench coat, Sam Browne and revolver. An eyewitness confirmed that everything left in the tank was destroyed. Cold night though the 20th had been, it is very unlikely that Wain was actually wearing his coat in the tank or even found time to put it on when he left the vehicle in such a hurry. Wain's other effects were returned to his father via Cox & Co.

On 5 December 1964 Wain's gallant action was written up in *The Victor* in comic form. Good Old Man Farm was rebuilt after the war but is now derelict once more.

Cambrai Memorial (*Donald C. Jennings*)

Richard William Leslie Wain was a son of Harris Wain, a Cardiff solicitor, and his wife Florence, and was born in 4 Victoria Square, Penarth, Glamorgan, South Wales, on 5 December 1896. The family home was later Woodside, 4 The Avenue, Llandaff, Cardiff. He was educated at Llandaff Cathedral School and St Bees School in Cumberland (1911–14), where there is a plaque with his name inscribed, together with two other VCs, John Fox-Russell and William Leefe Robinson. Wain is also commemorated at Llandaff Cathedral.

In 1912 Wain joined St Bees' OTC and was in camp when war broke out two years later. He was the holder of a house scholarship and had gained the Higher Certificate for Oxford and Cambridge and planned to go to Oxford University. Instead, when still only seventeen years old, he joined a 7th (Cyclist Battalion) TF of the Welsh Regiment in September 1914. On 30 December he enlisted in Woldingham with the 16th (S) Battalion of the Middlesex Regiment (the public schools' battalion), from which he was gazetted to a commission on 16 July 1915 as a second lieutenant in the Manchester Regiment. He served in France and was wounded on the first day of the Battle of the Somme. He was promoted to lieutenant on 12 July 1916 and acting captain on 12 November. He became a member of the 25th Manchesters, and was deeply interested in mechanics and engineering and qualified himself for work with the tanks. He was attached to A Battalion of the Tank Corps on 2 January 1917.

R. McBeath

Ribecourt, west of Cambrai, France,
20 November 1917

(*David Harvey*)

On 19 November 1917 the 51st (Highland) Division occupied the British front line to the north-east of Havrincourt Wood, close to the village of Trescault. To its right was the 6th Division and to its left the 62nd Division. In preparation for a tank-led advance to take place early on the following morning, six platoons drawn from the 1/5th (The Sutherland & Caithness Highland Territorials) Seaforth Highlanders (Ross-shire Buffs, The Duke of Albany's) (152nd Brigade) spent time between 11 a.m. and midnight preparing the ground and cutting the wire, thus creating gaps in the British wire to facilitate the smooth passage of tanks. The objective was to cross the Hindenburg Line and reach as far as the railway line on the western side of the village of Ribecourt prior to moving up the rising ground northwards towards the village of Flesquières. The 6th Division was to capture the village itself. At midnight the battalion – less the above platoons – moved into assembly positions via Winchester Valley and Shaftesbury Avenue. The battalion war diary stated that there were no casualties during the assembly.

At 6.20 a.m. the guns of the artillery began to open out and two sections of the Seaforths began to advance behind a tank which was about 100 yards in advance of their section of the British front line. By 8.55 a.m. two companies had made rapid progress and captured part of the German front line, Triangle Support and Mole Trench. Four machine-guns, 208 men and 12 officers were soon captured. Contact was maintained with the 1st Leicesters (71st Brigade) 6th Division to the right and the 8th Argyll and Sutherland Highlanders (152nd Brigade) 51st Division to the left, and as soon as the tanks had crossed German trenches they were quickly filled in and wire cut in order to facilitate the passage for all arms. One company was delayed for a short period at Grand Ravine, west of the village of Ribecourt, when pausing in order to allow a tank to get ahead.

Although the Seaforths made a rapid advance towards their objective, they came up against a system of enemy dugouts with a machine-gun post to the west of the village. These strongly held positions in Station Road had been set up to guard the railway, and the enemy machine-gunners were taking toll not only of the Seaforths but the 1st Leicestershires to the left and the 9th Norfolks (71st Brigade) 6th Division, who were advancing on the right. In the prose of the Seaforths' war diary: '. . . the situation in the village of Ribecourt was not entirely cleared up and a patrol under Lance/Corporal R. McBeath which was sent out to reconnoitre captured 5 M/Gs, killing 3 and capturing 30 of the enemy including 2 officers. . . .' The 1st Leicestershires were in contact at Ribecourt Station and the 8th Argyll and Sutherland Highlanders to the left. Already thirty tanks had managed to cross the railway. If one visits Ribecourt today it is possible to pinpoint where McBeath won his VC, to the south-west of the village where the houses end. The local church nearby, which has been rebuilt, replaces an earlier one, which was used as a German hospital during the war.

In Appendix F in the 152nd Brigade war diary, dated 1 December 1917 and signed by Brig Gen H.P. Burn, the brigade commander, the story of McBeath's role is told in much greater detail:

Lance/Corporal McBeath advanced with his company towards the RIBECOURT-HAVRINCOURT Railway, which formed the final objective of his battalion. On reaching the railway a nest of German M/Gs on the western outskirts of RIBECOURT opened fire both on ourselves and on the 9 /Norfolk Regiment who were advancing on our right and held up the advance causing casualties in both battalions. Captain Mackenzie commanding Lance/Corporal McBeath's Coy called for a Lewis gun to deal with the m/gs. Lance/Corporal McBeath volunteered for the duty, and alone immediately moved off with the Lewis gun with 2 magazines and his revolver. Near the western houses of RIBECOURT he encountered one of the m/gs in action. He worked his way towards it and shot the gunner with his revolver at 20 yards range. He was already a distance of 150 yards from his Coy There were several other hostile m/gs in action, but, with the assistance of a tank, he likewise attacked them and drove the gunners to ground in a deep dugout. McBeath rushed in after them, and when he was down four steps one of the Germans turned and fired at him, the bullets grazing his hand. McBeath bounded down the steps after him and shot him and then drove the remainder of the garrison of the dugout, in all 3 officers and 39 men (it was a Battalion HQ) out by another exit into the trench above. These prisoners were directed towards the rear, and McBeath once again entered the dugout, placing a sentry at the entrance. He thoroughly searched it single handed and shot the only 2 men he could find.

There were in all 5 m/gs mounted round the dugout. By putting them out of action McBeath cleared the way, not only for our advance but for the 9/Norfolks in the Brigade on our right as well.

The conduct of Lance/Corporal McBeath not only in the action above described, but throughout the fighting from 20th–23rd was beyond praise.

Lance/Corporal McBeath has already lost 3 brothers in the war and he is absolutely regardless of his own safety so long as he can kill Germans.

The Seaforths had captured four lines of trenches and reached their objectives in under three hours, and apart from the dugouts so admirably dealt with by McBeath were hardly given any trouble by the enemy and were able to eject them from the houses and streets in the village.

Nearly eight weeks later, in a special order given by the battalion commander, Maj A.C. MacIntyre MC, dated 14 January 1918, the announcement of McBeath's award of the VC was announced. The VC citation was published in the *London Gazette* of 11 January 1918:

Robert McBeath, No. 240171, L.-Corpl., 1/5th Battalion. Seaforth Highlanders. For most conspicuous bravery on 20 Nov. 1917, when with his company in and approaching final objective, a nest of enemy machine-guns in the western outskirts of a village (Ribecourt) opened fire both on his own unit and on the unit to the right. The advances were checked and heavy casualties resulted. When a Lewis gun was called for to deal with these machine-guns, L-Corpl McBeath volunteered for the duty, and immediately moved off alone with a Lewis gun and his revolver. He located one of the machine-guns in action, and worked his way towards it, shooting the gunner with his revolver. Finding several of the hostile machine-guns in action, he, with the assistance of a tank, attacked them and drove the gunners to ground in a deep dugout. L.-Corpl. McBeath, regardless of all danger, rushed in after them, shot an enemy who opposed him on the steps, and drove the remainder of the garrison out of the dug-out, capturing three officers and 30 men. There were in all five machine-guns mounted round the dug-out, and by putting them out of action he cleared the way for the advance of both units. The conduct of Lance-Corpl. McBeath throughout three days of severe fighting was beyond praise.

After the fall of Ribecourt the village of Flesquières, 1,000 yards to the north-east, proved a much harder objective to capture. It was on high ground and protected on its west side by part of the Hindenburg support line. Haig's despatch dated 20 February 1918 noted that heavy fighting took place and mentioned an obstacle on the top of the ridge where:

The stout brick wall skirting the Chateau grounds posed a formidable obstacle to our advance, while German machine-guns swept the approaches. A number of tanks were knocked out by direct hits from German field batteries in position beyond the crest of the hill . . . . Many of the hits upon our tanks at Flesquières were obtained by a German artillery officer, who remaining alone at his battery, served a field gun single-handed until killed at his gun. The great bravery of this officer aroused the admiration of all ranks.

On 21 November the Seaforths formed up on the railway at 6.10 a.m. and moved up the slope to Flesquières, only to find it abandoned, so they moved on a further 1½ miles to the village of Cantaing. Soon it was possible to look down on the German-held town of Cambrai. The much vaunted Hindenburg Line had been broken.

Robert McBeath was born in Kinlochbervie, Lairg, Sutherlandshire, Scotland, on 22 December 1897, and lived with his adoptive parents, Robert Mackenzie and his sister Barbara McBeath. He was educated at Inshegan School, Kinlochbervie.

On 12 August 1914, when he was still only sixteen, he enlisted in the Army as a private in the 1/5th Seaforth Highlanders. He was made a lance-corporal on 24 July 1917. He was discharged from the Army in 1919.

Mountain View Crematorium, Vancouver (*Donald C. Jennings*)

When he returned home after the announcement of his VC McBeath was given a hero's welcome and was presented with a silver tea service. He was presented with his VC by the King at Buckingham Palace on 16 February 1918. He renewed his friendship with Barbara McKay, daughter of John McKay, and the couple married on 19 February in Edinburgh. McBeath had also been presented with a farm as an award for winning the VC as a result of a scheme organised by the Duke of Sutherland.

In June 1920 he attended the Garden Party at Buckingham Palace for holders of the VC and shortly after he emigrated to British Columbia with his wife. Once in Canada he joined the British Columbia Provincial Police, and a few months later the Vancouver City Police, which he joined on 12 August 1921. On 9 October 1922, when patrolling the Granville Street beat with a Detective Quirk, a colleague, the two men tried to stop the driver of a car that was being driven erratically. Fred Deal, the negro driver, was determined not to be apprehended and struggled with McBeath while his colleague interviewed Marjorie Earl, the female passenger left in the car. Deal then shot both officers and Quirk gave chase, but was hardly in a fit state to catch the criminal and returned to his dying colleague. Both men were taken to St Paul's Hospital, and McBeath died soon after arriving.

Deal was arrested by another constable after he had cast away the murder weapon, which was quickly retrieved. Three days later McBeath was given the 'largest official funeral in Vancouver's history'. His body was later cremated and his ashes were interred in the Masonic Section 193, Lot 6, Mountain View Crematorium, Vancouver. McBeath was commemorated in Jasper National Park, Alberta, where one of the peaks is named after him, as was a police launch, *R.C. McBeath VC*, which was used as a patrol boat for policing the waters off Vancouver. Later a mural was produced which features the former policeman.

After her husband's death Barbara McBeath not surprisingly felt homesick and decided to return to Scotland, where she later married Alex MacDonald. She died in her mid-forties and was buried at Scourie, Sutherlandshire.

As for Deal, he was committed for trial and was convicted of McBeath's murder and the attempted murder of Quirk. He was sentenced to hang in January 1923, but the conviction was overturned and at the retrial he was sentenced to life imprisonment. He served sixteen years in Canada before completing his sentence in a prison nearer his home in Florida.

McBeath's VC is kept at the Highlanders Museum, Fort George, Invernessshire, and in more recent times a housing development in Kinlochbervie, McBeath Court, has been named after the local hero.

C.E. SPACKMAN

Marcoing, France, 20 November 1917

(David Harvey)

The 1st Border Regiment of the 87th Brigade (29th Division) arrived at the village of Fins on 18 November and moved north-eastwards into tents in Dessart Wood, arriving at about 1 a.m. The battalion war diary noted that 'everyone very tired'. The next day was a day of rest and preparation for the battle that was to begin on the following day.

At 1 a.m. on the 20th the battalion moved up to its concentration area, arriving about two hours later. The men then bivouacked and lay down to wait for dawn and zero hour. It was bitterly cold. The battalion was one of four belonging to 87th Brigade, which formed the centre of the planned 29th Divisional advance from the Gouzeaucourt sector towards the village of Marcoing and Masnières via Couillet Wood Valley, with four tanks from A Battalion leading the way. The 86th Brigade was on the left and the 88th on the right. In addition twenty tanks were to act independently of the brigade in the capture of Marcoing.

After the British barrage began at 6.20 a.m., the Borders moved forward behind the 1st King's Own Scottish Borderers, keeping on the west side of the Gouzeaucourt–Marcoing railway to the 'jumping-off' place, which was in a sunken road to the north of Villers-Plouich, where they arrived at about 8 a.m. They were able to advance along the Couillet Wood Valley at 10.05, having heard that the Hindenburg support line had fallen. During the time in the sunken road they suffered several casualties in its southern portion.

After passing silent enemy gun positions and their first two objectives, they reached the outskirts of Marcoing and halted while the 1st KOSB approached the village. They met opposition from snipers and machine-guns firing from the houses until, with the assistance of tanks and by working round the flanks of the houses, the enemy were forced to retire across the canal. One company of the 1st KOSB battalion crossed the canal by the main railway bridge and another crossed via a lock bridge to the left that led to the railway station. A bridgehead was then formed. The two other companies continued to deal with any remaining

Railway at Marcoing (*Peter Batchelor*)

opposition in the village, where two tanks had been held up by mechanical problems. Other tanks belonging to B Battalion remained in the village.

Quickly following the KOSB, two companies of the Borders crossed the canal by the railway bridge and a third by the lock bridge that led to the station. It was at this point that an enemy machine-gun began to threaten the advance. With a very clear field of fire, the enemy gun was operating in the open from a position on the station platform. However, with the minimum of fuss this threat was soon dealt with by Sgt Charles Spackman, who, attacking the gun single-handed, managed to kill the gunner with his first shot from a distance of 200 yards. He then dealt with the replacement gunner and lastly bayoneted the third member and captured the team, thus allowing the advance to continue.

The flanking battalion, the 1st Royal Inniskilling Fusiliers, had not yet arrived at the ammunition pits that were one of their objectives, as there had been difficulties in crossing the canal lock about 1,000 yards to the east, and the Borders' advance was therefore checked on a defensive line facing west. An urgent message was sent to Sherwood-Kelly, commanding officer of the 1st RIF, to ask him 'to push on with all possible speed'. Soon after 1.30 p.m., A Coy, assisting the RIF, did succeed in clearing the ammunition pits, and a line of 500 yards was established north-east of the railway station.

The Borders' HQ was established at the railway station when Kelly arrived there and informed them that his right was now being held up by enemy machine-guns firing from positions to the north of Masnières. Four tanks were called for in order to silence these guns, but Kelly later considered that their arrival, at about 4 p.m., was too late in the day, and the attack was called off. Although the Borders had also received orders to attack, in the changed circumstances it was considered best not to, but unfortunately C Coy was unaware of the change of plan, and although it successfully attacked the enemy line to the south of Flot Farm and captured nineteen prisoners and two machine-guns, it had then to fall back as its right flank was in danger from an enemy machine-gun.

During the night the battalion line was consolidated and three companies held positions to the north-east of the Sunken Road. By the following day the enemy were found to have been strongly reinforced, and two other battalions from the 87th Brigade began an advance from the station, only to be heavily fired on from Flot Farm and the north of Masnières as soon as they showed themselves.

Pte Spackman's VC was announced in the *London Gazette* on 11 January 1918 as follows:

C.E. Spackman, No. 9522, Sergeant, 1st Battalion. Border Regiment. For most conspicuous bravery when, in action, the leading company was checked by the heavy fire of a machine-gun mounted in a position which covered the approaches. The ground was absolutely devoid of cover of any description. Sergeant Spackman, realizing the position, and seeing that it would be impossible for troops to advance, went through the fire to attack the gun. Working forward gradually, he succeeded in killing all but one of the gun crew. He then rushed the gun and captured it single-handed, thereby enabling the company to advance. The behaviour of this non-commissioned officer was gallant in the extreme, and he set a fine example of courage and devotion to his men.

The war diary of the 29th Division notes on 12 January 1918 that three members of the division had been awarded the VC for their gallantry during the Battle of Cambrai on 20–30 November 1917: Capt Gee of the 86th Brigade, Col Sherwood-Kelly and Sgt Spackman. Ceremonial parades for the 86th and 88th Brigades were held to mark the event on 12 January at Wizernes.

Spackman was presented with his VC at Buckingham Palace on 23 February 1918 during the same investiture as Lt Col Arthur Borton and Capt Robert Gee. Spackman was demobilised at the end of the war and joined the Territorial Force.

Charles Edward Spackman was born in Fulham, London, on 11 January 1891. He enlisted in the Army in 1908/09 and during March 1915 embarked for

Gallipoli with the 1st Border Regiment. He served as a private in no. 3 platoon of A Company. When he left the Army he married (in December 1919) a girl who used to live next door to him in Fulham. Her name was Miss E.A. Copeland, and the couple were to have four sons. In June 1920 Spackman attended the June 1920 Garden Party at Buckingham Palace and in November the House of Lords' dinner. After the Second World War he attended the Victory Parade in June 1946, the 1956 VC centenary in Hyde Park, and later, other VC/GC functions.

Still a member of the Territorials as a sergeant in the Queen Victoria Rifles, Spackman volunteered on the outbreak of the Second World War and served as a sergeant-major in the KRRC based at Swindon in Wiltshire. He moved to Southampton in 1958 and was seeking employment as he and his wife were unable to live just on their old-age pensions. Of the £10 allowance for being a holder of a Victoria Cross, Spackman said that it didn't keep him in cigarettes.

Gardens of Remembrance, Swaythling Crematorium (*Donald C. Jennings*)

His home was at 32 Priory Road, Netley Abbey, and his wife predeceased him, dying on 14 January 1969. Spackman died sixteen weeks later on 6 May in Southampton General Hospital. He was given a full military funeral at South Stoneham Church on the 9th, and his body was later cremated at the nearby Swaythling Crematorium and his ashes scattered in the Gardens of Remembrance. The Border Regiment, KRRC, British Legion, and National Provincial Bank were among those who sent wreaths to the funeral service, at which all of Spackman's four sons were present.

On his death, and in addition to his VC, Spackman left the French Médaille Militaire, 1914–15 Star, BWM, VM, Defence Medal 1939–45 and the 1953 Coronation Medal. They were offered for sale by Glendinings on 17 December 1969, who described the £1,200 bid by the coin dealers Baldwin & Sons as 'quite good'. The VC is not publicly held.

J. SHERWOOD-KELLY

Marcoing, France, 20 November 1917

(David Harvey)

The 29th Division was to take part in the Cambrai operations on 20 November 1917 with the initial objectives of capturing the canal crossing the villages of Marcoing and Masnières. The division would not take part in the first day of the battle until the Brown or Second Line had been taken by tanks. Of three infantry brigades due to take part, the 88th was to the right, the 86th to the left and the brigade which we are concerned with here, the 87th, was in the centre. This brigade was not only to have the assistance of four tanks but a further force of twenty additional tanks, which, although independent, were also to assist in the capture of Marcoing.

The 87th Brigade consisted of the 2nd South Wales Borderers, the 1st Royal Inniskilling Fusiliers, 1st King's Own Scottish Borderers and the 1st Borders. Battalion orders given at 10.30 a.m. to the 1st Royal Inniskilling Fusiliers instructed them to advance behind the 2nd South Wales Borderers. The objective was Marcoing copse on the south-east corner of Marcoing, together with the nearby canal crossings. Once the canal was crossed, the RIF, together with the assistance of tanks, were to capture their allotted portion of the Red Line and consolidate. This sector was beyond the village of Masnières, to the east of the Cambrai Road, and was part of the Hindenburg Line trenches.

The RIF, who had been kept in the dark about the forthcoming battle, had arrived at Basseux on 17 November and on the night of the 19th were stopping at Fins to the south-west of Havrincourt. Moving through Gouzeaucourt in the early morning of the 20th, they observed that the deserted houses were in fact sheltering tanks. At 5 a.m. they arrived at their appointed assembly positions and rested on the damp grass until 6.45 a.m., when they moved off towards Villers-Plouich. Passing through an enemy barrage they suffered several casualties. In mid-morning, when it was still misty, the division moved forward and the 87th Brigade in the centre moved northwards towards Marcoing. On reaching Marcoing copse the 2nd SWB had the task of clearing several snipers. The Escaut River was then crossed by a light railway bridge, but when they reached the canal and lock (Ecluse de Bracheux) they came under heavy machine-gun fire from the eastern edge of Masnières. This fire was also holding up the Newfoundland Regiment, which was also attempting to cross the canal, but a tank arrived on the eastern side of the copse and successfully engaged the offending machine-guns, which then allowed three companies to cross the canal by a light bridge at a point about 400 yards to the west of the lock. The RIF soon arrived at the canal crossings, and although the lock bridge crossing had been captured by the SWB, who had then formed up on the opposite side, the enemy now had a machine-gun post set up in a building on the opposite side of the canal, with a clear view of the bridge, and this prevented them from making the crossing.

Undeterred, Lt Col J. Sherwood-Kelly, in command of the 1st RIF, ran under fire to a tank, which he ordered to fire against the enemy-held building. He then stormed across the lock bridge and captured the enemy position. It was now 2.30 p.m. and the battalion proceeded to form up on the enemy side of the canal. They were on 'dead ground' adjacent to the canal. From the top of the bank the ground sloped gently upwards for a distance of about 2,000 yards. This slope had been used as an ammunition dump by the enemy and was full of gunpits, which had been used for storage. A force of motor machine-guns from Cambrai garrisoned the pits. Kelly came forward to see the situation for himself, and immediately gave orders to his four companies, two in the front line and two in the second. The RIF, no longer protected by the canal bank, moved forward up the slope only to be met with heavy rifle and machine-gun fire. The battalion paused and then advanced in platoon rushes for a distance of about 500 yards, when Kelly returned to lead his men forward against the nearest gunpits. However, they were then faced with the problem of how to get through thirty yards of barbed wire.

Under covering fire the RIF, assisted by a company of the 1st Borders on its flank, quickly set about cutting through this obstacle and with a rush carried the first line. The battalion war diary tells of one officer 'who placed a Lewis gun on the shoulder of a man and used it that way'. All the companies were involved in the fighting and two of them worked their way round the enemy flanks. Most of the enemy had retired to the rear, and after another rush the pits were taken and the defenders retreated to the Marcoing–Rumilly road. Those Germans who remained were either killed or captured. Two other strongpoints were also captured after the enemy held on stubbornly, one with two machine-guns and the other with three. Three dead German officers were later found.

No time was lost after the pits were captured, and the RIF then moved quickly up to the enemy wire of the Masnières–Beaurevoir Line, which the tanks were meant to have dealt with but hadn't. They then came under heavy fire from German positions in houses on the Masnières–Cambrai Road, and as they could not get through the wire Kelly decided to move back 100 yards and consolidate.

They had possibly advanced too far as no troops could be seen on their right flank. They remained in this position at nightfall. During the day fifty-four Germans were taken prisoner, including five officers, together with five machine-guns. Battalion casualties included six officers and 141 other ranks. Later it was learnt that the 88th Brigade to the right had taken most of Masnières and was in position across the canal, and to the left 86th Brigade had taken its objectives and was in front of the canal.

The RIF remained in their positions, from where they could see the towers of Cambrai, for five days awaiting further orders. Later they moved back to Marcoing for two days and were then involved in the great German counter-attack, which began on the 29th. At first the main German thrust was to the right and south of the 29th Division positions, and they only had to repel a few minor attacks. However, their turn came on the following day and over the next few days the division, together with the flanking 20th Division, was gradually pushed back towards its original start line.

After the end of the Battle of Cambrai in early December, it was felt that the 29th Division's 87th Brigade had achieved a great success by seizing the canal crossings at Marcoing on 20 November, and in particular the attack reflected great credit on Kelly's organising ability and his 'hands-on' military leadership. It was probably the high-point of not only his military career but also his whole life. The citation for his VC, published in the *London Gazette* of 11 January 1918, gives an unusually detailed account of what he achieved at Marcoing on the opening day of the Cambrai battle:

John Sherwood-Kelly, C.M.G., D.S.O., Major (Acting Lieutenant Colonel), Norfolk Regiment, Commanding a Battalion, Royal Inniskilling Fusiliers. For most conspicuous bravery and fearless leading when a party of men from another unit detailed to cover the passage of the canal by his battalion were held up on the near side of the canal by heavy fire directed from the bridge. Lieutenant-Colonel Sherwood-Kelly at once ordered covering fire, personally led the leading company of his battalion across the canal, and, after crossing, reconnoitred under heavy rifle and machine-gun fire the high ground held by the enemy. The left flank of his battalion advancing to the assault of this objective was held up by a thick belt of wire, whereupon he crossed to that flank, and with a Lewis gun team forced his way under heavy fire through obstacles, got the gun into position on the far side, and covered the advance of his battalion through the wire, thereby enabling them to capture the position. Later he personally led a charge against some pits, from which a heavy fire was being directed on his men, captured the pits, together with five machine-guns and 46 prisoners, and killed a large number of the enemy. The great gallantry displayed by this officer throughout the day inspired the greatest

Marcoing (*Peter Batchelor*)

confidence in his men, and it was mainly due to his example and devotion to duty that his battalion was enabled to capture and hold their objective.

On 12 January 1918, a ceremonial parade was held to mark the awards of the VC to Col Sherwood-Kelly, Capt Gee and Sgt Spackman at Wizernes. Kelly was presented with his VC by the King at Buckingham Palace on 23 January 1918.

John Sherwood-Kelly, later known as Jack, was the eldest son of Capt J.S. Kelly of Lady Frere, and was born on 13 January 1880 in Queenstown, Cape Province, South Africa. He was a twin of Hurbert Henry, who died as the result of an accident in July 1893. He was educated at Queenstown Grammar School and Dale College, seemingly not taking kindly to school discipline, as he was expelled. When he was sixteen, in 1896, he enlisted as a trooper in the Cape Mounted Police and served in the British South African Police (Rhodesian) during the Matabele rebellion. He then returned to school, this time at St Andrew's, Grahamstown, and was later expelled again.

Kelly was in Rhodesia when the Second South African War broke out in 1899, and during that war he served with the Imperial Light Horse and Kitchener's Fighting Scouts. Together with another VC holder, William Bloomfield, he was part of the Mounted Bodyguard for Sir Alfred Milner, High Commissioner to South Africa when he visited Transkeill in 1899. He took part in the Relief of Mafeking, when a member of Col Plumer's force in operations in Rhodesia, the Orange Free State and the Transvaal. He had been commissioned in the field on 8 January 1901 when serving with the Imperial Light Horse, but resigned it on 5 June 1901 and became a private, as he was keen to take part in the Somaliland campaign, which he did, serving in the Burger Contingent in the third expedition against the 'Mad Mullah' between November 1902 and July 1903. He was also in business in the period 1902–4. Kelly was Mentioned in Despatches and was awarded four clasps to his Queen's Medal and two to his King's Medal.

Ten years later, when he was thirty-four years old, he left South Africa for England, where he enlisted in the Sherwood Foresters, hoping to serve against the Irish insurgents. At some point he added a hyphen to his name, becoming Sherwood-Kelly. A short time later, when war broke out, Kelly left the Foresters, and as he wished to reach the front in the shortest possible time he joined the 2nd King Edward's Horse as a private on 31 August 1914, having had a medical four days earlier. On his papers he gave his occupation as Civil Servant.

After about seven weeks serving with the King Edward's Horse he was offered a temporary commission as a lieutenant in the Norfolk Regiment on 4 November. With his pre-war experience it was not surprising that he received rapid promotion and was gazetted temporary major on 10 November. During 1915 Kelly was a member of the 29th Division and served in Gallipoli from 23 July 1915 with the 1st King's Own Scottish Borderers, to which he had been attached.

He had developed into a very imposing figure, just over six feet in height, broad shouldered and weighing thirteen stone. His first appearance in the battalion was noted in a diary note attributed to Capt Shaw, which was later published in *The KOSB in the Great War*:

A new major has joined us. The new major was a Herculean giant of Irish-South African origin, with quite a remarkable disregard for danger and a gift for bombing, as for all branches of hand-to-hand combat. But more than that, his interest in ballistics extended to catapults, to obtain greater range. Such things would have been out of date on the Western Front, but on the Peninsula the catapult came into its own . . . . The range of this ingenious but only fairly reliable weapon rarely exceeded 120 yards. The bold major won the soubriquet of 'Bomb' Kelly, and excelled in 'stunts', on occasions alarming his own side . . . . It may be added that he was what is called in Scotland a 'character', and possesses a strikingly if not specially wealthy vocabulary . . . .

Kelly was severely wounded by gunshot wounds in the right leg while at Suvla Bay on 21 August but was back on duty on 15 September. He remained on the Peninsula for ten months, having taken over command in mid-October when the CO, T/Lt Col G.B. Stoney DSO, was killed by a shell. Kelly, now acting lieutenant-colonel, used very different methods from his predecessor, and while on the Peninsula won a DSO (*London Gazette*, 2 February 1916) 'for his fine leadership and remarkable gallantry displayed during an attack on a Turkish trench, when despite being wounded twice, he led his men to capture an enemy position; only six men returned from the action.'

Kelly was briefly in Egypt when recuperating, and left the Dardanelles in early 1916. Arriving in France in May, he was given another command within the 29th Division, when he was attached to the 1st Royal Inniskilling Fusiliers. In April 1916 he married, in London, Nellie Green, daughter of the Hon. G.H. Green from New South Wales, Australia. Two months later, on 4 June, he was severely wounded in France with gunshot wounds to his chest and right shoulder when taking part in a raid with 88th Brigade. When bleeding profusely his life was saved by a stretcher-bearer named Johnson, whom Kelly was to track down seven years later to thank him. At the time he was temporarily in command of the 1st Essex, who were not taking part in the raid. The 29th Division History has this to say about him:

> . . . Nevertheless, there he was, out in No Man's Land, assisting the raiding party back to their trenches. It was then that he was struck by a shrapnel bullet which pierced his shoulder and penetrated the lung, breaking some ribs en route. It was a terrible wound, and little hope was held out for his recovery. However, he made a miraculous recovery and missing the 1st July, was able to participate in the campaigns in Artois and Flanders, and to render services to the division at the Battle of Cambrai . . . .

In June Kelly's wife left for Rouen and accompanied him home to a London hospital, where he 'made a wonderful recovery'. In July the couple left for South Africa, where the marriage began to show signs of breaking down, possibly because Kelly took up with various ladies, some of whom he had known before the war. Later the couple returned to England.

On 29 March 1917 Kelly, still with the 29th Division, replaced Maj Richard Willis VC, commander of the 1st Royal Inniskilling Fusiliers, who had left the Battalion as temporary lieutenant-colonel. In April he was based near Monchy-Le-Preux and on one occasion, on the 15th, was gassed when in the act of descending the steps of 87th Brigade HQ, the site being possibly at Airy Corner. He was back from hospital a few days later on the 18th, the day that the village of Wancourt fell. Wounded a fourth time on 18 July 1917, he returned to duty soon afterwards.

On 4 December the RIF moved back to Sorel and then Beaufort and Kelly left its command after being gassed on the 5th and was sent to Treport Hospital before being returned home to hospital. His place was taken by Major Dent. He was given a medical board on 27 February 1918, and when a resident at the Hotel Rubens, Buckingham Palace Road, London SW, wrote on 4 March for permission to spend some time in South Africa once more. He was given permission to travel but he was not accompanied by his wife. Kelly blotted his copybook in June when travelling on board the *City of Karachi*, and his behaviour was reported on by a Lt Baxter in a letter dated 21 June 1918. Apparently Kelly was 'alleged to have made references to the South Africans as 'damned South Africans' whose discipline was 'bad' and he described the DCO's staff as 'undisciplined rabble'.' Later, apologies for Kelly's behaviour were made to the High Commissioner for South Africa. However, that was not all, and when taking part in a recruitment meeting he made an injudicious speech. This time the report was made by a Mr B.B. Cubitt, who stated that Kelly got into bad favour with the English section of the meeting, and Kelly's leave was probably curtailed as a consequence. Brig Gen Martyn gave the opinion that in future that Kelly should not be allowed to make speeches.

On 23 September 1918 Kelly took over as acting lieutenant-colonel when commanding the 12th (S) Battalion The Norfolk Regiment, which was in the Ploegsteert region, from Maj M. E. Barclay. On 6 October he left in order to command a brigade. After the Armistice in November 1918 Kelly was appointed to command the regular battalion of the 2nd Hampshires (30 April to 17 August 1919) as part of an Allied Force to Russia at Archangel. They were to relieve troops already there. The expedition was the brainchild of Winston Churchill, Secretary of State for War in Lloyd George's government. Churchill detested Lenin and the Bolsheviks, who had brought down the Tsar in 1917, and wished to use Allied soldiers to assist the troops of the disorganised White Russian armies who were involved in a civil war with the Bolsheviks. Churchill's stance was not popular at home, as many thought it a continuance of the war. Lloyd George, though also not in favour of the intervention, was too busy at the Paris Peace Conference to keep his War Minister on a tighter rein.

Eventually 30,000 Allied troops were on Russian soil and about half of them were under General Ironside in the Arctic ports of Archangel and Murmansk. Thousands more troops were to the south under the White Russian General Denikin with their headquarters at Omsk. On 20 June, during a two-pronged attack on Troitsa, Kelly decided to withdraw his battalion without firing a single shot, as he considered it was vulnerable and likely to be cut off. He had no desire to risk the lives of his men. This decision not to commit his troops in itself was perhaps forgivable, but his next step was a grave mistake, considering that he was a serving officer in the British Army. He wrote a letter home to a friend in which he roundly condemned the whole North Russian escapade, together with its leaders.

We may have a clue as to the state of Kelly's mind during his time in North Russia from the privately published memoir of Charles Hudson VC. In this account Hudson (who was later sacked from the Army himself) does not actually name Kelly, but it could only be him. He describes the 'newly arrived colonel' as boisterous and overbearing in manner but good company. But it was not until Hudson accompanied him on a tour of the blockhouses one day that he realised that Kelly's nerve had completely gone, since even a light shell some distance away caused him to shake with fear and turn white.

The second-in-command of the 2nd Hampshires reported to Hudson that Kelly had stated in the mess that before the Hampshires embarked he had been assured that his troops would not be used for offensive action. 'He proposed therefore to refuse to carry out any offensive action . . . .' By this time the letter that Kelly had written to a friend in England (a Mr Charles Martin, who ran the Rubens Hotel in London, where Kelly often stayed when on leave) was published in an English newspaper. When questioned, Kelly originally denied writing it, but later broke down and admitted that he was indeed responsible. He was subsequently relieved of his command on 18 August by General Rawlinson. According to notes in his file in the National Archives the letter gave away military information. Kelly had also insulted Ironside by saying that he was 'a much overrated man and in my opinion has made a hash of things'. For his part Ironside described Kelly as 'a very hot-headed and quarrelsome man'. Churchill said of Kelly, 'he is not normal, and suffers from an uncontrollable temper'. He was sent back to England 'for serious offences under the Army Act' and informed that he had committed an offence that warranted a court-martial, but he was let off with a warning because of his excellent war record.

Having made two mistakes in North Russia and got off lightly, he then compounded his misdemeanours once he was back in England. Using the *Daily Express* as a platform for his views, in September/October 1919 he published three letters which were critical of the handling of the North Russia Expedition under General Ironside. This time he was not to escape from being court-martialled for contravening King's Regulations. In the articles he especially chastised Winston Churchill. Concerning the military policy of the British government in North Russia, Kelly '. . . accused them of engaging our troops irregularly in a civil war, and of gross mismanagement'. He considered that the Allied relieving force was required solely for rescuing their comrades of the original army of occupation, but instead they were kept on for offensive operations after the relief had been achieved. As a postscript troops were about to be withdrawn soon anyway.

Kelly's indiscretion led to a court-martial, which took place on 28 October 1919 at the Middlesex Guildhall. Pleading 'Guilty', Kelly was convicted, the sentence of the court being that he should be 'severely reprimanded'. During the proceedings he was described as 'a tall stoutly built man' and wore three rows of medal ribbons, together with five wound stripes. He had suffered constantly 'from the effects of a wound in the lung which he received during the early part of the war'. After the court-martial Kelly relinquished his commission on completion of service. A few weeks later in November he and his wife were divorced.

Kelly left the Army with the rank of lieutenant-colonel. After the war he was short of work and money and was desperate to try to get back into the army, where he had only been a temporary officer in the first place. However, despite badgering the War Office and even Winston Churchill, the then surfeit of officers (together, one feels, with his reputation for blunt speaking) prevented him from getting his wish. In addition he tried, without success, to reopen his court-martial proceedings. He attended the Buckingham Palace Garden Party in June 1920. However, within two years he fell on hard times and was admitted to hospital for an operation. With only his Army pension to live on and with his wounds preventing him from being fully fit, he was unable even to afford to pay his gas bill. In 1922 he decided to stand for Parliament, and stood unsuccessfully as a Conservative candidate for the Clay Cross division of Derbyshire. He came third in the voting. In November he was admitted to hospital. In December the following year he stood again and this time was second. In October 1924 he tried a third time but lost again. During one of the campaigns at a 'public meeting one of an organised gang of hecklers called him a liar and declined to withdraw. Sherwood-Kelly thereupon left the platform and gave the man a thrashing amid the applause of the audience.' Not succeeding in entering Parliament, he was always keen to return to the Army, but was rejected; at one point he even applied to join the French Foreign Legion.

In October 1926, together with Sgt Oliver Brooks VC, he laid a wreath at the Cenotaph on the occasion of the Memorial Service held on the Horse Guards' Parade under the auspices of the Ypres League. In November 1929 Kelly attended the VC Dinner at the House of Lords.

He must have recovered from his war wounds to a certain extent, as in 1927 he went out to Bolivia to open up the country with a view to the settlement of British colonists. Roads and railways were built and for the first time direct communication with Buenos Aires was established up the great Paraguay River, and a new port was made 6,000 miles inland. Later, however, the colonisation scheme was abandoned.

After the King left Bognor Regis, where he had been convalescing in the late 1920s, Kelly became an agent for the owner of Craigwell House, Bognor Regis, Sir Arthur De Cros, where the King had recuperated. Within a short time 13,000 visitors had visited the rooms formerly occupied by Their Majesties. In 1930 Kelly contracted malaria while he was in Tanganyika, and on his return to

England died, at the age of fifty-one, on 18 August 1931, in a Kensington nursing home where he had been for two or three weeks. His file includes a reference to an enquiry from a Mr Ernest Short of Kensington Court, London, asking the War Office if Kelly was going to be given the customary honour of a military funeral. The Army agreed to provide such a funeral if the expenses were covered. The funeral took place on the 21st and the coffin arrived at Brookwood Station at 12.30 and was met by a gun carriage provided by Aldershot Command, who also provided a Union Jack. London District provided a bearer party, together with two buglers. There was, however, no band. The 18-lb gun carriage was manned by men from the RFA, and the Grenadier Guards provided the guard of honour and firing party. The banners of the branch of the local British Legion were carried in the cortège on its way to Brookwood Cemetery. The two buglers sounded the Last Post at the graveside. No relatives were able to attend the service as most of them lived in South Africa. The inscription on his gravestone is 'One who never turned his back but marches breast forward'.

Whatever way history passes judgement on Jack Sherwood-Kelly, there can be simply no question about his soldierly qualities, his courage and leadership. However, he was clearly 'burnt out' by his experiences in the First World War, and found it impossible to settle down in a peacetime world. As for his character, he was clearly 'larger than life' and very much a man who did not take kindly to orders that he did not agree with. One of his obituaries, published in *The African World* of 22 August 1931, stated that ''Bomb' Kelly won the VC not once, but half a dozen times. He was brimful of bravery and initiative. . . .' Apart from being an extremely gallant soldier, Kelly was 'a great sportsman' and 'an intrepid hunter of game'. He was also a keen horseman and good at tennis, cricket, rugby and golf.

After his death his medals were acquired by the National Museum of Military History, Johannesburg, South Africa, and their miniatures remain in family hands. He is commemorated at St Anne's Cathedral, Belfast, and at Delville Wood, France. He is also remembered at the Royal Norfolk

Brookwood Cemetery (*Donald C. Jennings*)

Regimental Museum in Norwich, and the National Portrait Gallery has a portrait of him.

Apart from his being Mentioned in Despatches during the First World War on 2 February 1916, 13 July 1916 and 4 January 1917, the complete list of his decorations and medals is as follows:

DSO 2 February 1916
CMG 1 January 1917
VC 11 January 1918
Queen's SA Medal with Clasps
Queen's Relief of Mafeking
Queen's Rhodesia
Queen's Orange Free State and Transvaal
King's SA Medal with Clasps
King's SA 1901 & 1902
African General Service Medal with Clasps 1902–20
African Somaliland 1902–4
Allied Victory Medals 1914–20

H. STRACHAN

Masnières, France, 20 November 1917

(*IWM*)

On 20 November Maj-Gen J.E.B. Seely, in command of the Canadian Brigade (5th Cavalry Division), was waiting for a chance to follow in the wake of the day's successful tank sorties, which stretched across a 4-mile front. The brigade had started out at Gouzeaucourt and before 2 p.m. had arrived at Les Rues Vertes, close to the canal crossing at Masnières. After conferring with Brig Gen H. Nelson (88th Brigade), who informed him that he thought the tanks had already crossed the canal, Seely, whose squadrons were halted south of Les Rues Vertes, decided to send his leading regiment, the Fort Garry Horse, to continue the advance across the canal. He then went forward with his brigade major, Geoffrey Brooke, and his aide-de-camp, Prince Antoine d'Orleans, together with six orderlies. The group was close behind a tank that was making for the canal bridge. In his memoir *Adventure* Seely wrote his version of events:

My instructions were, as soon as the tank had crossed the bridge, to take my Brigade over and gallop towards and beyond Cambrai. As the event proved, had the bridge remained intact, this we could easily have done. With the thousands of horsemen and machine-guns supporting us, the results might well have spelt a disaster of the first magnitude to the German Army. The tank rumbled along the street leading straight to the bridge, I, on my faithful Warrior, cantering along behind it. It got on to the middle of the bridge, but then there was a loud bang and crash, and down went the tank and bridge together into the canal. At the same moment there was a burst of rifle fire from the opposite side of the canal, and one or two of my orderlies were hit. I sent back a message at once reporting this disaster, saying that I would endeavour to bridge the canal elsewhere. At the same time I sent for my Brigade to come to the outskirts of Masnières. One squadron was sent to try to find a means of bridging the canal further to the south. That redoubtable soldier, Tiny Walker, my machine-gun officer . . . took on the job. He managed

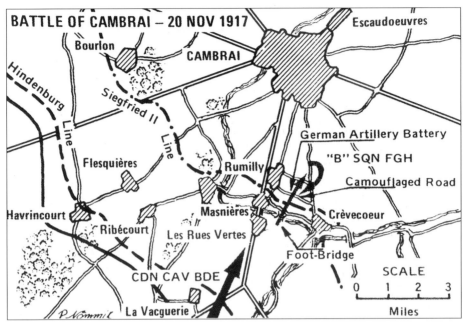

Battle of Cambrai, 20 November 1917 (*Anon*)

to find two baulks of timber near a demolished lock, and, under cover of continuous rifle fire directed on every nook and cranny in the buildings opposite, got this narrow structure into position. The squadron, commanded by Strachan [*sic*, Captain Duncan Campbell], of Fort Garry Horse, led their horses across and galloped into the open country, with the intention of silencing a German battery that was firing at us at about eight hundred yards' range.

Following an infantry advance into Masnières, there were still a number of the enemy holding out in the northern part of the village. Just beyond the village and still on the main Cambrai road stood the village of Rumilly and part of the Beaurevoir-Masnières line to the south of it. Having already travelled 10½ miles, the advance guard of the Fort Garry Horse had entered Masnières with the intention of moving forward to Rumilly and attacking the enemy lines, including a battery that was being a nuisance, as well as hoping to capture the German Corps Command Post at Escaudoeuvres. The Canadians crossed the river bridge before reaching the canal bridge and found the latter had already been damaged by German demolition, although it could be used by infantry, until it collapsed owing the weight of the Tank Flying Fox II of F Battalion, when the bridge was

De-Saint-Quentin Ecluse de Masnières Lock (*Peter Batchelor*)

no longer possible for it to be used by cavalry. Under heavy fire an alternative bridge was found to the south-east at the De-Saint-Quentin Ecluse de Masnières Lock, a few hundred yards from the main bridge, and the cavalry began to cross a 20-inch bridge under heavy fire at about 3.45 p.m. Two companies of the Hampshire Regiment had already used it, and with the help of machine-gun detachments and French civilians the bridge was made suitable for the passage of horses. It seems that those on the spot were unaware of the existence of a second and much more suitable bridge close to Mon Plaisir Farm, which was 1,600 yards south-east of the main bridge and hidden from fire, although its map reference was clearly marked on the divisional operation order, which clearly did not reach Cavalry Corps HQ.

Capt Duncan Campbell was in command of B Squadron, and moved off towards the Rumilly-Niergries ridge and attacked the enemy lines. They came under heavy machine-gun fire and 'were hard put to it on the marshy ground about the canal'. A gap had been previously cut in the enemy wire and they charged through this from the swampy ground near the canal. It was at this point that Campbell was mortally wounded and Lt Harcus Strachan took his place. In an interview fifty years later Strachan stated:

As I rode up Dunc was coming riding slowly back crouched in the front arch of his saddle and I thought he was wounded, but I just shouted 'Okay' and galloped up to the head of the squadron. And the time I saw him was early the next morning when the small party was returning over the narrow bridge and we came on Dunc's body. Right at the bridge where we had crossed. I buried him there.

South-east of Rumilly the Fort Garrys came across a mile-long camouflaged road that was used as a German supply route. In an interview with the author John Gardam, published in *Seventy Years After 1914–1984*, Strachan said:

We got up to this narrow road along the crest and found the Germans had been using it for their supply route and they had it camouflaged, shutting it off from the side of our people. Well, you know it's awkward, we had to dismount there and cut our way through it and open it up and make arrangements for the rest of the Regiment to come through. The order was that when we got through the hedge we were able to dribble through, we would form in line of troop columns, no squadron front, not to present a good target. Then I told each troop commander, 'Let your troops straggle. I don't care if they don't look well, let them straggle. Don't give the enemy machine-guns a good target.' I also said, 'Now every troop commander has full authority to proceed in any way he likes suitable to the opposition and the ground, but he must not get out of touch with the squadron. . . . We then thought, 'well, we're over the worst of it' and lo and behold we saw a cavalry man's dream of heaven, an unprotected battery of guns. So we got up over the hill and lo there was our dream, four 77 mm guns. They are lined roughly with gun teams all behind and the crews congratulating each other about the fine shooting they were doing. Boy, they did not know what was going to happen! Well, we didn't need an order. We just were riding with swords drawn that way and we went in with swords. The Germans made a grave mistake, I think. I don't know how they were trained in foot fighting, but they all left their guns. For me, I would have crept under a gun and sat down and hid. They all straggled away and were sitting ducks. There was no opposition from them whatsoever, and it was all over in a moment.

Strachan then gathered together his remaining men and continued his move towards Rumilly. They came under fire from blockhouses on the outskirts of Masnières and then halted in a sunken road half a mile to the east of the town. Realising that they were now alone, with no other cavalry, let alone infantry troops, in sight, and in failing light, Strachan had to decide what action to take. The slight pause allowed the enemy to recoup, and soon the remaining cavalrymen became almost surrounded. By now the squadron was down to fewer than fifty men, and two troopers were sent back to HQ in Masnières with messages. Simultaneously, in order to cause greater confusion, Strachan set his men to cut three main telephone cables that ran along the edge of the sunken road. The light was still just strong enough for Rumilly church tower to be seen, and Strachan took a compass bearing and made the decision to gather up the remaining horses and deliberately try to cause them to stampede and thereby cause confusion in the enemy's mind as they fired at the riderless horses, although in reality, far from stampeding, the horses simply wandered off into the darkness. He then decided to lead his men back to Masnières on foot by using the straightest possible route in the growing darkness. At least four groups of Germans were encountered during the return journey to brigade, but each time the dismounted cavalrymen routed their foe and also collected a few prisoners while doing it. The remaining members of the squadron, now in two groups, reached the makeshift bridge of wooden beams carried up on tanks where their adventure had all started, in the early hours of the night. However, Strachan's troubles were not yet over, for when making his way across one of the two tanks which supported the wooden structure he fell off it into ten feet of canal water. Presumably still damp, he then reported to Col Patterson, who promptly burst into tears as he had assumed the worst and that the whole of B squadron had been 'scuppered'. When it had been decided earlier in the afternoon to call off the cavalry action, Patterson had in fact crossed the canal and ridden for half a mile in a vain search for B Squadron in order to recall them, but had failed to find them.

Capt Campbell's body was later recovered from the lock and reburied at Flesquières Hill British Cemetery.

Strachan was awarded a VC for his gallantry and leadership, which was published in the *London Gazette* of 18 December 1917:

Harcus Strachan, M.C., Fort Garry Horse, Canadian Cavalry. For most conspicuous bravery and leadership during operations. He took command of the squadron of his regiment when the squadron leader, approaching the enemy front line at a gallop, was killed. Lieutenant Strachan led the squadron through the enemy line of machine-gun posts, and then, with the surviving men, led the charge on the enemy battery, killing seven gunners with his sword. All the gunners having been killed and the battery silenced, he rallied his men and fought his way back at night through the enemy's line, bringing all unwounded men safely in, together with fifteen prisoners. The operation – which resulted in the silencing of an enemy battery, the killing of the whole battery personnel and many infantry, and the cutting of three main lines of telephone communications two miles in rear of the

Fort Garry Horse. B Squadron, Fort Garry Horse, led by Lieutenant Harcus Strachan, passing through Épehy, 30 November, 1917 (*IWM*)

enemy's front line – was only rendered possible by the outstanding gallantry of this officer.

A second announcement was made in the *London Gazette* of 23 March 1918, when his Christian name was altered. Strachan was presented with his VC by the King at Buckingham Palace on 16 January in the same investiture as that of Frederick Booth, William Hewitt and Arthur Hutt. While in London he gave several sittings for 'a portrait in oils' commissioned by the Canadian Government, which now hangs in the Canadian Parliament House in Ottawa.

A few days after his investiture he returned to his birthplace and was given a public reception by the Bo'ness Town Council at the Town Hall. After sitting through a long speech given by the Provost, Strachan was presented with a sword of honour on behalf of the Burgh. After the presentation 'a distinguished baritone' gave a rendering of 'Scots Wha Hae'. Strachan then gave a brief response and was followed by a speech from Lord Rosebery and others.

On 17 January 1918 Strachan was given a month's leave and was later allowed compassionate leave to Canada for two months between 23 February and 24 April, which was later extended to 23 May. He left France for England on

18 April 1919. At one point when he had been visiting his home town he had been invited to join the Freemasons, into which he was initiated. The ceremony was completed over a year later when he was once more visiting his home town in May. He kept in touch with the Lodge in the ensuing years, and a portrait of him hangs in a room of the Douglas Lodge.

At the end of the war Strachan held the rank of temporary major, serving with the 19th Dragoons, dated 1 August 1918, being demobilised on 30 April 1919. He returned to Canada with 2,000 other soldiers in May 1919.

Harcus Strachan (pronounced Strawn) was born in Hollywood, a large house in Dean Road, Borrowstounnes (Bo'ness), West Lothian, Scotland, on 7 November 1887 (as he noted on his attestation papers, not 1884). He was the third son of William Strachan, a solicitor and sheriff-clerk of the County of Linlithgowshire. He was educated at Bo'ness Academy and at Royal High School, Edinburgh, and then Edinburgh University in 1903, where he studied medicine. He 'was considered a good all round sport', especially in rugby and cricket. He left his home in Scotland for Canada at some time between 1905 and 1908, accompanied by his brother Alexander. Together they had decided to emigrate and take up as homesteaders, so they purchased a ranch in Chauvin, Alberta. Strachan later left the farm in the hands of his brother, mother and two sisters.

When he was twenty-seven Strachan enlisted in the Canadian Army, leaving for England on 9 June 1915, as a private with the 7th Canadian Mounted Rifles: his number was 15585. (His service records confuse as they state that he enlisted in Canterbury, Kent, on 15 July 1915.) He was transferred to the Fort Garry Horse as a trooper on 22 January 1916 and became a lance-corporal in February, when he left for France, arriving there on the 25th. He was promoted in the field to corporal on 16 April, made a lance-sergeant in the field in mid-June and sergeant on 23 June. As a trooper he soon made his mark and was commissioned as a lieutenant in the field on 1 September 1916. At the end of January/early February he had ten days' leave, and a month later was able to spend a further few days in Paris. In May of the same year he won an MC, which was published in the *London Gazette* of 16 August 1917:

> For conspicuous gallantry and devotion to duty. In command of a party which attacked the enemy's outposts (south of St Quentin). He handled his men with great ability and dash, capturing eight prisoners and killing many more. The operation was carried out without a single casualty to the party.

On 8 July Strachan took part in a raid in which he was wounded by gunshot wounds to his right arm and thigh and also gassed. He was admitted to 55 CCS and then the 34th. He was later transferred to No. 12 Stationary Hospital at Etaples and on to No. 8 General Hospital in Rouen, followed by a period of convalescence in Dieppe, until he was discharged on the 22nd. He rejoined his unit in the field on 30 August. He was able to return to Canada in September for ten days' leave and convalesce at the family home. In September 1917 he returned to France and took part in the Battle of Cambrai in November.

After the war, when he returned to Canada, Strachan changed careers, joining the Canadian Bank of Commerce to become a bank manager. He was also an officer in the militia with the 19th Alberta Dragoons, and by April 1922 was a major, second-in-command. The year before he attempted to enter Federal politics on behalf of the Liberal Party for the Wainwright constituency, but was defeated by 'the tide that swept the United Farmers of Alberta to power'. He later said in an interview, 'Not a damn soul voted for me.'

In 1926 he transferred from the Dragoons to the 15th Canadian Light Horse, and a year later went on reserve. In November 1929, together with two VCs from Edmonton's 49th Battalion, John Kerr and Cecil Kinross, he attended the VC dinner at the House of Lords hosted by the Prince of Wales.

Moving to Calgary in the late twenties, he married a Calgary lady, Betsy Stirling, who worked in the bank in Chauvin. The couple were to have one daughter, Jean. Strachan, together with six other VC holders from Alberta, was presented to the King and Queen during ceremonies in the Alberta Legislature during the Royal couple's visit to the province in 1939. Strachan was by now ADC to the Governor-General. After the Second World War broke out he returned to active service, becoming Lieutenant-Colonel of the 15th Alberta Light Horse. In early 1940 he accepted an appointment as major in the South Alberta Regiment, and in July he became Lieutenant-Colonel Commanding of the former Edmonton Fusiliers and served in Europe for a time. Towards the end of 1944, when he had turned sixty, he returned to reserve status in Canada, and in July 1946 went on the retired list. He had rejoined the bank in 1945, and retired to Vancouver with his wife Bess in 1950.

He was invited to London as part of the Canadian contingent for the VC centenary celebrations in June 1956, and on 10 December 1957 was one of seven VC pallbearers at Michael O'Rourke's funeral at Mount Lehman, British Columbia. On 19 November 1959 he attended a dinner in Toronto at the Royal Canadian Military Institute.

Strachan's wife predeceased him, and he was proud of being able to cope by himself without 'being a nuisance to anybody'. His main hobbies were golf and the study of military subjects. He survived to an advanced age, dying in his ninety-fifth year at the University of British Columbia Hospital, Vancouver, on 1

May 1982 after a long illness. He requested that he should be given no funeral service, and was cremated at North Vancouver Crematorium.

Strachan was a strong character and an excellent leader of men. A friend whose father served with him during the Second World War described him as 'a real fine person around here'. He could also bristle if someone dared to address him as 'Strachan', as opposed to 'Strawn'. According to an article in *The Canadian Star Weekly* of 3 September 1966, he had a new enemy to upset him, the 'permissive welfare society'. 'I live out here in this paradise on earth, Vancouver, and I spend a lot of my time chewing tobacco, spitting on the lawn and disagreeing with a great deal of what I hear.'

His VC is not publicly held.

J. MCAULAY

Fontaine-Notre-Dame, France, 27 November 1917

(*David Harvey*)

Despite the British successes of 20 November, on the 27th the city of Cambrai was still in German hands. The Third Army was well aware that until Bourlon Wood and village were totally in its control the city could not possibly be captured. The wood on high ground to the west was in effect the door to Cambrai. However, equally important was the high ground to the immediate south-east of the city, which gave the German artillery an excellent view of the Bourlon Ridge, as well as the countryside as far west as the village of Flesquières. No serious progress could be made without these positions being taken first.

However, the Third Army decided on another attempt to capture Bourlon Village and Fontaine-Notre-Dame, the latter being the last western village before Cambrai. Maj Gen G.P.T. Feilding of the Guards Division had serious doubts about the merits of the plan, and requested a meeting with Gen Woollcombe, who was later joined by Gen Byng of the Third Army, as well as Haig himself. Despite his objections, Feilding was overruled. This important meeting on the 26th took place in a wooden shed in the grounds of Havrincourt château, where the 62nd Division used to have its HQ until it was blown up.

The situation on the 27th was that the 62nd Division held much of Bourlon Wood and the enemy the northern portion, as well as Bourlon village. More importantly, the enemy had a series of entrenched positions close to the railway that ran on the eastern side of the wood. In addition, intelligence reports indicated that the enemy was bringing up more guns to the north of the wood, which would allow them to fire on any forces attacking the ridge from the front and the rear, as well as the flank. Facing Fontaine-Notre-Dame and the north-west of Bourlon Wood, the 2nd Guards Brigade attacked with the 3rd Battalion Grenadier Guards to the right, the 1st Battalion Coldstream Guards in the centre and the 2nd Battalion Irish Guards to the left.

The Grenadiers moved forward on both sides of the Bapaume–Cambrai road towards the village, and the Coldstreams attacked towards the section of railway

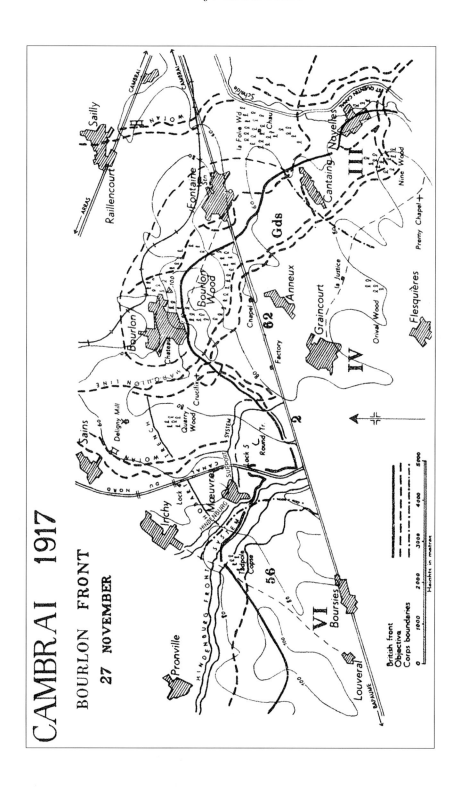

CAMBRAI 1917

BOURLON FRONT
27 NOVEMBER

line to the north of the village. The remaining battalion of the 2nd Guards Brigade, the 1st Battalion Scots Guards, was made responsible for the right flank of the attack and occupied a trench line about 1,000 yards to the south of the village. C Coy had arrived in the line at 5 p.m. the previous day and had spent the night in cold and damp trenches. As soon as the Guards had made progress to their first objective, a company of the Scots Guards was to move up the sunken road to the village, taking a machine-gun with them.

La Folie Wood to the south-east of Fontaine was known to contain several strong enemy machine-gun positions that had a clear view towards the advance of the Grenadiers and parts of the sunken road. The barrage began at 6.20 a.m. The overnight snow showers had turned to rain and the Guards decided not to wait for the tanks, which were slightly late in forming up. Machine-gun fire from La Folie Wood immediately caused havoc in the ranks of the Grenadier Guards, and only one NCO, a sergeant, was able to reach as far as the village church. Once there he joined two other companies of the battalion, which had suffered badly despite being assisted by several tanks. Many of the houses and cellars in the village remained in German hands and the enemy were firing from trenches south of the road and from two disused tanks. In addition a machine-gun was operating in order to cover the sunken road from Cantaing to the south. This road was being held by the 1st Scots Guards holding up the right of the divisional front.

When it appeared that the first objective had been reached, C Company of the Scots Guards was sent forward at about 7 a.m. to assist the Grenadiers. They moved along the partially sunken Fontaine–Cantaing road, taking advantage of its banked sides. However, the cover only lasted for about fifty yards before the road became the same level as the surrounding fields. The Scots Guards were then exposed to very destructive enemy fire, in particular from La Folie Wood, and officers and men fell quickly. Enemy machine-gun fire came from Fontaine as well. Many of the Guardsmen crawled forward on their stomachs in order not to be seen. One of the officer casualties was the company commander, Lieutenant the Hon. Arthur Kinnaird MC, who was hit in his leg and back. Seeing what was happening, Sgt John McAulay was determined to try and save his commander and to bring him back 400 yards to the safety of a dugout on his back. In carrying out this brave act he was knocked down by bursting enemy shells, and in vain, as Kinnaird succumbed to his wounds. Owing to the casualties, command soon devolved upon McAulay, and he managed to beat off several counter-attacks and hold on to the position until ordered to hand over to the South Staffordshires. However, the Scots Guards failed to get any closer to the village than 150 yards and were unaware at the time that the enemy were planning to carry out a strong counter-attack on the same day as the Guards' attack. Forming a defensive flank, McAulay took up a machine-gun to a position from which he could best repel further German attacks. Unfortunately the gun failed to work and he returned for a Lewis gun, which accounted for fifty of the enemy. Despite the heroism of the Guards, the day had been a failure, and neither Bourlon Wood nor the village of Fontaine-Notre-Dame had been completely captured, and as a result the Battle of Cambrai had virtually ended.

McAulay deservedly gained the VC, which was published in the *London Gazette* of 11 January 1918:

John McAulay, Sergeant, D.C.M., Scots Guards. For most conspicuous bravery and initiative in attack. When all his officers had become casualties, Sergeant McAulay assumed command of the company, and under shell and machine-gun fire successfully held and consolidated the objectives gained. He reorganized the company, cheered on and encouraged his men, and under heavy fire at close quarters, showed disregard of danger. Noticing a counter-attack developing in his exposed left flank, he successfully repulsed it by the skilful and bold use of machine-gun, aided by his men only, causing heavy enemy casualties. Sergeant McAulay also carried his Company Commander who was mortally wounded, a long distance to a place of safety under very heavy fire. Twice he was knocked down by the concussion of a bursting shell, but, nothing daunting, he continued on his way until his objective was achieved, killing two of the enemy who endeavoured to intercept him. Throughout the day this very gallant non-commissioned officer displayed the highest courage, tactical skill and coolness under exceptionally trying circumstances.

A comrade writing of McAulay's soldierly ability said:

. . . Jack McAulay doesn't need me to sing his praises; in fact, like the rest of us in the Scots Guards, we are not keen on spreading about what we consider as our duty. But I am simply echoing Major Sir Victor Mackenzie's words about him when I say Sergeant McAulay is an ideal soldier. Both of us hail from the same town, we have both been miners, and we are both in the Scots Guards. I saw the great deed he did, and know what the regiment thinks of it. But it is only one of the many great deeds my comrades have done. He has won the V.C. not once, but several times.

McAulay was presented with his VC ribbon on 13 January 1918 by his Division Commander, Lt Col Sir Victor Mackenzie, and two months later on 16 March he was presented with the actual medal by the King at Buckingham Palace while home on leave in April, when he married Catherine Thomson in

Glasgow New Eastern Cemetery
(*Donald C. Jennings*)

Glasgow on the 23rd. He was also presented with a silver cigarette case by Maj the Earl of Stair on behalf of the sergeants' mess of the Scots Guards at Wellington barracks.

John McAulay, a son of John and Isabella McAulay, was born in Kinghorn, Fife, Scotland, on 27 December 1888. He was educated at Plean, Stirlingshire. He was employed as a miner until, on 27 February 1911, he joined the Northern Police Force in Glasgow as a constable. Three years later he decided to enlist in the Army, joining the Scots Guards on 4 September 1914. He was made a lance-corporal in 1914 and full corporal the following year. In 1916 he was promoted to lance-sergeant and sergeant. On the first day of the Battle of Passchendaele he won a DCM, which was published in the *London Gazette* of 17 September. The citation ran: '. . . For clearing pill-boxes at Ypres on 31 July, 1917, accounting for several snipers single-handed, and taking charge of his platoon after his officer was killed . . . .' This citation was followed by a Mention in Despatches on 13 November 1916.

After demobilisation McAulay rejoined the Glasgow police service on 13 January 1919, and in June 1920 was promoted to sergeant. In the same month he attended the VC Garden Party at Buckingham Palace. On 27 September 1922 he was promoted to Inspector and moved to the Central Division. In November 1929 he was one of the guests at the House of Lords' dinner given by the Prince of Wales. At the time of the King's Silver Jubilee in 1935 McAulay was awarded a medal that commemorated the event on 8 May. Two years later, on 19 May 1937, he was awarded a Coronation Medal.

McAulay was one of the four VC holders to attend the funeral at Riddrie Cemetery of Lt Henry May VC, who died in Glasgow on 26 July 1941. On 31 January 1946 McAulay retired from the police with a pension. On 8 June he attended the Victory parade and the VC dinner at the Dorchester Hotel the same evening. At the end of the month the King and Queen visited Scotland and attended a 25th anniversary parade for members of the British Legion. John McAulay was one of the people presented to the Royal couple.

McAulay died at the age of sixty-seven at 915 Aikenhead Road, Burnside, Glasgow, on 14 January 1956 and was buried at Glasgow New Eastern Cemetery, Section L-VII or Vll. He had been a keen follower of athletics and 'a wrestler of considerable repute'. His wife Catherine died in 1963 and in 1964 his sister Isabella presented her late brother's VC to the Scots Guards.

G.W.B. CLARE

Bourlon Wood, France, 28/29 November 1917

(David Harvey)

By 27 November the Third Army in the Cambrai sector was beginning to run short of fresh troops, and it was decided to make more use of cavalry, whose role in the battle so far had been only in a dismounted capacity.

The 2nd Guards Brigade attacked the village of Fontaine-Notre-Dame on 27 November but, partly owing to a lack of men, it failed to hold on to it. On the left the 62nd Division occupied much of Bourlon Wood and was ordered to capture the northern part and to move forward to the eastern end of the village of Bourlon itself. With the assistance of tanks it made some progress, reaching as far as the village street, but was then unable to make further progress as the enemy were entrenched next to the railway line, a position which ran down the eastern side of the wood. The heavy British bombardment of the previous day had not included Bourlon village, and therefore the attacking forces were faced with a system of very strong defences and were forced to withdraw after two hours.

During the evening the dismounted 5th Lancers moved up towards Bourlon Wood and established their HQ at a château. Having passed through a heavy barrage, they set about relieving a company of the 2/7th West Yorkshire Regiment of the 62nd Division They were about 150 yards from the north of the wood in a support line. On the following day large numbers of enemy aircraft flew overhead at very low altitude. At 4 p.m. the Lancers were ordered up to the front line to relieve the Oxfordshire Yeomanry. On the 29th the front line was heavily bombed and a heavy barrage of gas shells was put up on the southern edge of the wood. At about 5 p.m. the Lancers were relieved by the 17th London Regiment of the 47th Infantry Division.

The 47th Division had taken over the Bourlon sector at 10 a.m. on the 29th, and the three dismounted regiments of cavalry remained with them for twenty-four hours. During the relief the enemy poured high explosives and gas shells into the wood and as a consequence casualties were very high.

Pte George Clare, acting as a stretcher-bearer with the 5th Lancers, won a posthumous VC during this period when serving in the wood: his action was announced in the *London Gazette* on 11 January 1918. Clare began his heroic deed on the 28th, when working with units operating in shell holes in the trenches and shell holes in and around Bourlon Wood. All approaches to the wood, as well as the British sector of the wood, were frequently bombarded.

No. 6657 George William Clare, Private, 5th Lancers. For most conspicuous bravery and devotion to duty when, acting as a stretcher bearer during most intense and continuous enemy bombing. Private Clare dressed and conducted wounded to the dressing station about 500 yards away. At one period, when all the garrison of a detached post, which was lying out in the open about 150 yards to the left of the line occupied, had become casualties, he crossed the intervening space, which was continuously swept by heavy rifle and machine-gun fire, and, having dressed all the cases, manned the post single-handed till a relief could be sent. Private Clare then carried a seriously wounded man through intense fire to cover, and later succeeded in getting him to the dressing station. At the dressing station he was told that the enemy was using gas shells to a large extent in the valley below, and as the wind was blowing the gas towards the lines of trenches and shell-holes occupied, he started on the right of the line and personally warned every company post of the danger, the whole time under shell and rifle fire. This very gallant soldier was subsequently killed by a shell.

After his death Clare was recommended for the VC by Lt Col H.A. Cape, CO of the 5th Lancers, and the Divisional Maj Gen W.H. Greenly, Commander of the 2nd Cavalry Division. Cape wrote to Clare's parents the following letter, which was published in the *Cambridgeshire Times* (and was clearly the basis of the official citation published six weeks later). After expressing his most sincere sympathy, Cape wrote:

I am sure however, it will be a great consolation to you when I tell you that I have forwarded his name to higher authorities and recommended him for the award of the Victoria Cross for his superb gallantry.

The history of his actions is this. Your son was detailed as a stretcher bearer when a portion of his Regiment went up dismounted, to hold the first line of trenches in Bourlon Wood. During the time they were there, the Germans kept up an incessant bombardment of shells and also gas, causing I regret to say a number of casualties. Throughout the whole time your son exposed himself most fearlessly to shell, rifle and machine-gun fire, tended the wounded and carried them to a dressing station some 500 yards in the rear. At one time the whole garrison of an isolated post about 150 yards to the flank of our position were all wounded. Your son left the main trench where he was, ran across the intervening space which was swept by fire of all sorts and attended to the wounded of the small garrison. He then held the post single handed while relief could be sent to take over. On the arrival of this relief your son carried the most seriously wounded man (Lance Corporal Glascoe) to a place of safety and placed him under a fallen tree. He then went for a stretcher and ambulance. On his return he carried the non commissioned officer to the dressing station with the aid he had secured. On arriving at the dressing station he was told that the Germans were sending many gas shells over the wood, which is on the side of a hill into the valley below. As the wind was from that direction, there was great danger of the gas being blown up the hill and reaching the troops in the first line. Your son, therefore, on his return from the dressing station, went to the first line, started on the right and personally warned every single post along the whole line of their danger, thereby giving ample time for the gas masks to be put on and so saving many casualties. During the time he was passing down the line he was fully exposed the whole time, to rifle, machine and shell fire, but he succeeded in passing down the whole line without being touched. It was, alas a few hours afterwards that a shell exploded quite close to him, killing instantly.

I am sure that you will agree with me that such conduct merits the highest awards and in further support of this I am enclosing a copy of a letter I received from Major General Greenly, the General Officer Commanding the Division in which the Regiment is. I only hope that our efforts to secure the most coveted award may be successful and that you may receive it as a lasting memento of a most gallant soldier and son. In any case if we are not successful, you will know that your son's conduct is a magnificent example, not only to the whole Regiment who knew him but to all who hear of it. I am holding a parade of the whole Regiment for the purpose of reading out General Greenly's letter on that Parade.

The letter also said:

My dear Cape, I have been waiting till you got back to rest billets to write and congratulate you and your Regiment upon the splendid gallantry and devotion to duty and his comrades, displayed by Private George Clare, whom you have recommended for the Victoria Cross.

I have forwarded your recommendation and think that there is little doubt that the award will be made.

It is the first recommendation for the Victoria Cross for any member of the 2nd Cavalry Division, and whether granted or not, Private Clare's example is a magnificent one for us all. I wish also to express my deepest sympathy to you and the 5th Lancers, as well as to his relations, for the loss of such a gallant soldier, and hope you will be able to convey it to the latter.

After Clare's posthumous VC was announced in the *London Gazette*, Greenly promptly wrote again to Cape a letter of sympathy and congratulation on reading the news in *The Times*. Clare's parents were presented with the posthumous medal at Buckingham Palace by the King on 2 March. The couple lived in Plumstead, London, and Mr Clare wrote to Greenly about the investiture at the palace as soon as he got home that day:

My wife and I arrived a few minutes before the time specified (11 o'clock). We were shown into a reception room, where there were a few relatives of the deceased soldiers awaiting the different honours awarded to their respective sons and husbands.

After His Majesty had decorated a number of officers, soldiers and nurses, the time for the next-of-kin arrived, when we were taken to His Majesty in our respective order. After being announced, the King gave my wife and I a firm shake of the hand and said as follows:

'It is needless for me to say how sorry I am not being able to present this (looking at the Victoria Cross) personally to your son. I sympathise with you in your loss; but he died a brave and gallant soldier defending his country.'

He then presented me with the Victoria Cross. He again shook hands with us and we withdrew. His Majesty was quite homely, and spoke more like a friend, so that it makes one feel proud of such a King.

On the reverse side of the Cross is my son's number, name, regiment, and date of his death. Should you be this way at any time, or in London, and would like to see it, I should esteem it a pleasure in showing it to you. Hoping you may come safely through this terrible war and again thanking you for all the interest you have taken. . . .

George Clare VC is commemorated in several places, and as his body was never found his name appears on the Louverval Memorial, Panel 1. His name is listed, too, on the Chatteris War Memorial, and he is also remembered in the churches of SS Peter and Paul (where he used to be a chorister) with a memorial window in the south side of the Lady Chapel, dedicated in September 1918. The window depicts Christ rewarding a faithful soldier, and the inscription states:

This stained glass window was placed in this window by public subscription in grateful memory of George William Clare, pvt, [*sic* Private] 5th Lancers, formerly a chorister in this church. He was killed in France after rescuing wounded comrades November 1917 and was awarded the Victoria Cross for most conspicuous bravery and devotion to duty. Greater love hath no man than this.

The Chatteris Museum holds a copy of the letter to his parents telling them in great detail of their son's deed. But Clare's VC has had a chequered career and must have been sold at least four times before being acquired by the Museum of the 16th/5th Lancers at Belvoir Castle, Grantham.

❖❖❖

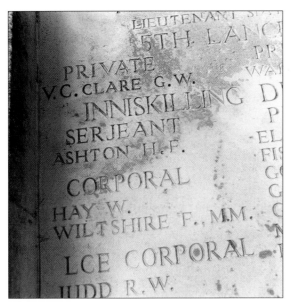

Cambrai Memorial (*Donald C. Jennings*)

George William Burdett Clare was born in St Ives, Huntingdonshire, on 18 May 1889, and later moved to Chatteris in Cambridgeshire, living at 12 Burnsfield Street. He probably left school when he was twelve or thirteen years old. There was at least one other son in the family, C.E. Clare. George worked for a brief time with a land surveyor and then became the driver of a builder's pony and cart before working for a veterinary surgeon.

Known by some as Billy, Clare had a very good singing voice and was much in demand for church services and local concerts, including Yeomanry smoking concerts. He joined the Chatteris Troop of the Bedfordshire Imperial Yeomanry, with whom he stayed for eight years. His main duties may well have been as a groom. On 29 January 1914 he registered for the National Reserve. He lived with his grandparents at a house in Anchor Street: after his death the street was renamed Clare Street.

On the outbreak of war Clare re-enlisted and was sent to a remount depot before joining the 5th (Royal Irish) Lancers.

C.E. GOURLEY

Little Priel Farm, east of Épehy, France,
30 November 1917

(*David Harvey*)

By 30 November the already weakened 55th Division was in the Épehy sector, the day when the German Army staged a massive counter-attack. It was also to be a day when seven VCs were won, exceeding the number gained on the 20th, the opening day of the battle. In many parts of the line the British were pushed back to their original front line and in some cases even beyond.

In the Épehy sector the enemy began the day with an intense barrage accompanied by aircraft that machine-gunned the exposed division. Initially the enemy broke through on the front of the 165th Brigade at a point called Eagle Quarry, where the positions were held by the 6th King's (Liverpool). However, the King's were ably assisted by a section of D Battery of 276th (West Lancashire) Brigade RFA in positions south-east of Épehy at Little Priel Farm, close to the Lempire road and the front line. The section not only supported but kept close contact with the King's, who fought on all day until they became exhausted and their ammunition ran out. Fortunately for them the enemy had by then turned their attention elsewhere, to the positions of the battalion further north.

The two-gun howitzer battery opened fire on the enemy-held Gillemont positions to the south-east at about 7.10 a.m., but after about twenty minutes their section came under heavy artillery attack from the enemy, which seriously wounded the section officer, Lt Ridealgh. The enemy barrage continued and large numbers of infantry could now be seen moving in numbers into British forward positions with the objective of breaching their lines.

By now one of the howitzers was in danger of falling into enemy hands. There was only one thing to do and that was to set the guns up to fire on the enemy at point-blank range. The detachment had become scattered, as some members had carried Lt Ridealgh away to safety while others were sheltering in dugouts in

Priel Cutting. One gun was turned and began to fire at the enemy with open sights, but after about twenty minutes the enemy retaliation made the position untenable. The guns were then put out of action and their crews returned to the dugouts of their Battery HQ.

On receiving news of the abandonment of the battery, Maj J. Hudson MC, the battery commander, gave instructions to Sgt Gourley to collect all available men and to proceed to the section and take charge and somehow keep the guns going to the last moment. It was most important for contact to be kept up between Gourley and the battery commander, and three signallers did sterling work under heavy shell fire during the operations.

Gourley then collected up all the suitable personnel he could muster and held them in readiness to man the guns. Owing to enemy artillery firing on the British front and rear between 10.30 and 11 a.m. the battery guns were unable to reply. Then the enemy guns, although still very active, moved their barrage southwards to the Lempire road. Seeking advice from the King's as to which was the best target, Gourley then operated a slow rate of fire, using one gun at a time, on a position known as the Birdcage. At noon Gourley was warned that the enemy were moving down to the north from Holts Bank and Cottesmore Road, and was asked for battery assistance. Meanwhile, one gun had been put out of action and the second one was pulled out of the pit and fired on the enemy, who by that time were in full view. About twenty rounds were fired with open sights, and all the time the battery was harassed by aircraft flying very low, shooting at the guns with machine-gun fire. Fire was also coming from the left flank. The enemy aircraft almost certainly reported the gun position to their artillery, which put over about a hundred rounds. After a short while Sgt Gourley, together with Gunner Hartley, fired about another eight rounds before being driven off.

Back at Battery HQ, Lt Biggart, a replacement officer, had arrived and was sent to take charge of the section. He arrived at about 2 p.m., and seeing more of the enemy appearing on Holts Bank and in front of it, collected five men, including Gourley and Hartley, to once more man the guns. Working as a team, with Biggart as loader, the group managed to fire twenty more rounds while the enemy were firing with machine-gun and rifle fire. When machine-gun fire was nearing their left flank they were forced to take cover in a pit. Even then one of the bombardiers successfully fired the odd round on his own initiative. But it was decided that little more could be done, and the party crawled back to Battalion HQ one by one.

By 4 p.m. the enemy were seen moving over Villers Ridge to the north. An attack through Priel Cutting was expected and a barricade was duly set up. By now it was dark and orders were given for the guns to be manhandled along the Lempire road, where they would be met by limbers. Although this operation was successful, the enemy counter-attack on the 30th had resulted in a large number of British guns being either lost or overrun. The official history notes that Little Priel Farm had been lost at one point but was reoccupied in the morning, and that by evening the enemy had got no closer than Holts Bank.

Deservedly the D/276 gun team received awards for its gallantry, and No. 681886 Sergeant Cyril Edward Gourley's recommendation was as follows:

> He took charge of the section for four hours with complete competence and unlimited courage. In addition to what is told in the preceding narrative, his behaviour in keeping his detachments together was heroic. Whenever the guns had to be left, he would not take cover himself until he was sure all his men were safe. On one occasion when the detachments were driven away and he could not find Sergeant Thornley, he walked across in the open and searched all dugouts and all possible places with absolute disregard of machine-gun bullets all around him, until he found him in a detached dugout some distance from the others. Also, he voluntarily with Gunner Hartley alone kept one gun in action at a most dangerous period.

Already the holder of the MM, Gourley had his VC published in the *London Gazette* of 13 February 1918:

> Cyril Edward Gourley, Sergeant, Royal Field Artillery (Territorial Force). For most conspicuous bravery when in command of a section of howitzers. Though the enemy advanced in force, getting within four hundred yards in front, between three hundred and four hundred yards to one flank, and with snipers in rear, Sergeant Gourley managed to keep one gun in action practically throughout the day. Though frequently driven off he always returned, carrying ammunition, laying and firing the gun himself, taking first one and then another of the detachment to assist him. When the enemy advanced he pulled his gun out of the pit and engaged a machine-gun at five hundred yards, knocking it out with a direct hit. All day he held the enemy in check, firing with open sights on enemy parties in full view at three hundred to eight hundred yards, and thereby saved his guns, which were withdrawn at nightfall.

Gourley's brother in the next brigade wrote home: 'Cyril has done something very great this time; much better than last but you will hear about it later.' Two months later Sgt Gourley was given a commission as a second lieutenant in the RFA, and remained as an officer with the 55th Division until it was disbanded in Brussels in the spring of 1919. He was decorated at Buckingham Palace with his VC by the King on 16 March 1918, and wore his sergeant's uniform, which he

Grange Cemetery, West Kirby (*Donald C. Jennings*)

also wore when he returned home to attend a civic reception and presentation. During his visit he was welcomed back to Liverpool University, where 'he had an attack of nerves' when faced with a group of lively and noisy students and failed to give a speech of reply.

On 19 May he was promoted to acting captain, and returned home to be demobilised the following month.

Cyril Edward Gourley was born at 6 Victoria Park, Wavertree, Liverpool, Lancashire, on 19 January 1893. He was the second of at least four sons of a merchant, Galbraith Gourley (Gourley Bros Ltd), wholesale grocery and provision dealers, and his wife Martha (née Ashcroft). When Cyril Gourley was six years old the family crossed the Mersey and moved to the Wirral, living at 23 North Road, West Kirby, in 1899. Two years later the family moved again, to 39 Westbourne Road, West Kirby. Cyril was educated at Calday Grange Grammar School, where he won a scholarship, and Liverpool University, where he graduated with the degree of Bachelor of Commercial Science; but for the interruption of mobilisation orders he would probably have sat for the MSc degree. With these qualifications he would have been well qualified for a career in commerce, and before being called up he had already entered the offices of Messrs Alfred Holt & Co., of the Blue Funnel Line, a Liverpool shipping firm.

Gourley joined the Territorial Army as a private in the 4th West Lancashire Howitzer Brigade, of the RFA TF on 19 May 1914, and on 4 August was mobilised. Their HQ was at a house called The Grange, where the 7th and 8th Batteries were situated. Gourley's reason for joining the RFA was that 'he was fond of horses'. After early training, beginning in the Sevenoaks and Canterbury areas in Kent, the brigade, sailing in two ships, left for France on 28 September 1915.

At the beginning of the war his Territorial unit was brought into the Regular Army and attached to the 55th Division, and its initial service was spent in the Kemmel area to the south of Ypres. It was only involved occasionally in action, and in January 1916 it moved to Pont-Remy. It was here that the batteries were reorganised, with the Howitzer Brigade ceasing to exist. Now there was just the one Howitzer Battery, together with three 18-pounder batteries to each group. Thus the former Seventh and Eight Batteries were now renamed D/276 and D/275. Shortly before these changes were made the two batteries moved into new positions six miles south-west of Arras in the Crinchon Valley. In the third week of July the batteries were transferred to the Somme and were sent to the Guillemont area, and for just over two months were involved in continuous action. On 28 September they returned to the Ypres area, where they also saw frequent action and were often subjected to enemy barrages. On 1 June they contributed to the week-long bombardment against the enemy-held Messines Ridge, which was subsequently captured.

Gourley was awarded his MM in July 1917 near Ypres, when he acted very promptly in extinguishing a blaze that threatened an ammunition dump. The fire was the result of enemy shelling. In November the batteries moved southwards to take part in the Battle of Cambrai, where he won his VC on 30 November. After the war, on 19 May 1919, Gourley, by now an acting captain, proceeded home for demobilisation with the cadre of the 276th Brigade, RFA.

Gourley attended the King's Garden Party for VC holders in June 1920, and in November attended the ceremonies at the Cenotaph and for the Unknown Warrior. In 1919 he joined Lever Brothers, with whom he worked for most of his life in the export department, then known as the Marketing Advisory Service, and spent many years in the Balkans and then in Central and South America opening up Lever Brothers' trade.

On the morning of 19 July 1924 King George V and Queen Mary visited Liverpool for the consecration of the new cathedral. During the afternoon the King reviewed the 55th West Lancashire Territorial Division at the Wavertree playground, and Cyril Gourley was one of the VC holders present who were presented to Their Majesties; Arthur Procter was another.

In 1925 the Gourley family moved again, this time to Hill Close, School Lane, off Column Road, Grange, West Kirby. The house was later renamed Gourley's Grange, Gourley's Lane, in honour of Cyril Gourley VC, MM. In the Second World War Gourley became a 'fire-watcher', dealing with many of the air raids on Liverpool. In 1952 he moved south to Grayswood House, Grayswood, Haslemere, where he lived with his mother, brother and sister. In June 1956 he attended the VC centenary review in Hyde Park. At a reception prior to his retirement on 28 March he was presented with a silver salver and two decanters by Mr Morrell, a Director of Unilever, who spoke of Gourley's 'quiet, gentle courteousness and his readiness to do all he could for other people. In fact he was a jolly good man to have beside you when you were in trouble. I ask you all to drink his health.'

Gourley was by all accounts a modest, kindly and courteous gentleman who remained a bachelor, lived out his twenty-four years of retirement tending his garden and restoring his house, and died of natural causes at home on 31 January 1982. His body was taken back to the Wirral, where he was buried with his parents in the Grange Cemetery, West Kirby, reference F-17.

He is commemorated in several ways. In September 1919 a trust was formed which set up a scholarship in his name for pupils from his old school at Calday Grange, Wirral, destined for Liverpool University. A plaque in the RA Chapel in Woolwich, a photographic collage at Grayswood School, Surrey, and a memorial collage (unveiled in April 1983) of local heroes at West Kirby by the Mayor of Wirral also bear witness to his memory. His medals are owned by the Royal Artillery.

S.T.D. WALLACE

Gonnelieu, France, 30 November 1917

(David Harvey)

By the evening of 29 November the British front line to the south of the Bonavis–Péronne road had been pushed back to a line which ran in a south-westerly direction between the villages of Banteux and Gonnelieu. Its southern point was Twenty-Two Ravine, a continuation of Banteux Ravine. The immediate threat from the enemy – whose plan was to attack with the intention of reaching the village of Metz-en-Couture – was to the villages of Gonnelieu and Villers Guislain. It was felt that the enemy would attack from the south-east, making full use of Banteux Ravine.

Gonnelieu, situated on the Quentin Ridge, was the responsibility of the British 12th Division, and the HQ of its 36th Brigade was housed east of the cemetery to the north of the village. Five batteries of howitzers and field guns were established to the north-west of the village. They included 377th and 379th (169th Army Brigade, RFA), C/63 Battery (12th Division Artillery), the 25th Heavy Battery and the 354th Siege Battery. Gen Snow, commander of VII Corps, predicted the direction of the German advance and felt that Gonnelieu and Villers-Guislain to the south were particularly vulnerable. He therefore ordered thirteen extra Vickers guns to cover the southern slopes of the valley and the ravine.

From 6.45 a.m. on 30 November enemy howitzer shells began to fall on the village, and soon communication was broken. There were many casualties and some men simply ran for their lives. The 12th Division HQ had ordered Brig Gen Owen (36th Brigade) to organise the defence of the village, and although troops could not be sent to the eastern side of the village a field company was ordered to occupy a communication called Gin Avenue, which ran in an east–west direction to the north of the village before it turned south-west and became Green Switch.

The enemy moved into the village soon after 9 a.m. when the 36th Brigade HQ retired to Farm Ravine to the north-west, leaving the defenders of the village in Gin Avenue and the gunners who were in positions to the north and south of the main road. Later Brigade HQ had to move to Villers-Plouich, and was followed by 37th Brigade HQ.

The 377th and 379th Batteries were established on either side of Gin Reserve, and C/63 Battery behind them to the west. The remaining two batteries were north of the road. 377th and 379th Batteries began to fire on groups of the enemy in the village at very close range until their ammunition was exhausted, and at this point they withdrew their guns by hand and their remaining crews then joined the defenders in the village. By their efforts they had stopped the enemy from making further progress towards Villers-Plouich. Similarly C/63 to the west also 'displayed the same spirit'.

The war diary of the 12th Division CO RA takes up the story:

Below them in the valley was C/63 now threatened by the enemy infantry on both flanks and from the crest in front. Until now the Battery had escaped any serious attention from the enemy's artillery but now shellfire was coming in from all sides. Men were falling. The Battery Commander who had done magnificent work all the long morning was mortally wounded. (A/Major Raymond Belcher DSO, MC) and in spite of his protests was carried back to the CAMBRAI road. Lieutenant WALLACE assumed command. His detachment was getting weaker every minute from casualties while the enemy fire was continually increasing. Enemy aeroplanes now circled overhead and added their fire to the hail of bullets which was pouring into the sorely tried detachment. The Battery was reduced to Lieutenant WALLACE and five men . . . but still continued to work their guns – running from one gun to another and still firing in three directions. They had been engaged from 5 a.m. but they kept their guns in action until 1 p.m. and only retired then, when they had fired all their ammunition, collected their wounded and removed the breech blocks of their guns. The range at which they were firing varied from 300 to 600 yds; they effectively protected the infantry in Green Switch and they made it impossible for the enemy to cross the Cambrai road to gain the high ground to the North.

The official history also describes what happened:

Two guns of C/63 were run out of their pits and swung to cover the front and both flanks. They were kept in action even when only Lieutenant S.T.D. Wallace and five men of the battery were left. Under heavy fire these survivors served each gun alternately, running from one to the other, until, about 10.30 a.m. when the fight had lasted two hours the German infantry closed in. But British infantry were now arriving from the north and the task of the battery was done: Lieutenant Wallace and his men stripped the guns of sights and breech-blocks and then withdrew, taking their wounded with them.

Although Gonnelieu was lost, a later British counter-attack allowed the British front line to be re-established on the outskirts of the village. It could have been a great deal worse. The five surviving gunners were awarded the DCM and Lt Wallace the VC, which was published in the *London Gazette* of 13 February 1918:

Samuel Thomas Dickson Wallace, Temporary Lieutenant, Royal Field Artillery. For most conspicuous bravery and devoted services in action in command of a section. When the personnel of the battery was reduced to five by the fire of the artillery, machine-guns, infantry and aeroplanes; had lost its Commander and five of its sergeants, and was surrounded by enemy infantry on the front right flank, and finally in the rear he maintained the fire of the guns by swinging the trails round close together, the men running and loading from gun to gun. He thereby not only covered other battery positions, but also materially assisted some small infantry detachments to maintain a position against great odds. He was in action for eight hours, firing the whole time, and inflicting severe casualties on the enemy. Then, owing to the exhausted state of his personnel, he withdrew when infantry supports arrived, taking with him the essential gun parts and all wounded men. His guns were eventually recovered.

In fact the guns, remaining in No Man's Land, were recovered about a week later when they were brought in by the infantry of the 9th Division.

When his VC was gazetted, Wallace's former school was given a day off. A month later when he was home on leave he and his parents visited his old school. He passed through a guard of honour made up from members of the Academy's Cadet Corps, and a troop of Boy Scouts and Girl Guides was also on parade: he inspected them all and congratulated them on their smart turn-out. At a gathering of pupils in the main hall his entrance was greeted by the strains of 'See the Conquering Hero Comes' played by a small orchestra. He was presented by one of the Girl Guides 'with a fitted suitcase by the pupils, teachers and managers as a token of the admiration of the honour that he had brought to the school'. There were loud cheers and the singing of 'He's a jolly good fellow'. Captain Wallace gave a speech in which he thanked them for all the kindness shown to him. One of the pupils then gave a rendering of 'There's a Land', and the pupils later sang 'Rule Britannia', followed by a final vote of thanks to the Rector of the School.

Four months later, on 17 July 1918, Wallace was presented with his VC at an investiture in the quadrangle of Buckingham Palace.

Samuel Thomas Dickson Wallace was born, at Holmhill, Thornhill, Dumfries, Scotland, on 7 March 1892, eldest son of J.W. Wallace and Mrs Wallace, of Ford. He was educated at Dumfries Academy between 1903 and 1910, continuing his education at the East of Scotland Agricultural College and later Edinburgh University. He was a member of the University OTC from 1911 to 1914 and graduated with a BSc in Agriculture in March 1914. He had a 'distinguished college career', being medallist in 'structural and field geology and also in agricultural chemistry and gaining first-class certificates in these subjects as well as in veterinary science and forestry. His college training was just completed when war broke out. He immediately offered his services to his country', and joined the Army on 13 October as a temporary lieutenant with the RFA. He became a member of C Battery 63rd Brigade RFA, 12th Division.

Moffat Cemetery (*Donald C. Jennings*)

Wallace served in France from May 1915 and was promoted to captain in August. He served in every engagement that the 63rd Brigade RFA of the 12th Division took part in until the end of the war. In February 1919 he was appointed deputy director of agriculture, in Central Province, India. Retaining the rank of captain, he supervised the training of the Nagpur Volunteer Rifles and 'with them took an active part in suppressing civil disturbances'. In 1925 he married Margaret Noel Edenborough of Woking, and in 1932 returned home to Moffat, Dumfries. From 1940 to 1943 he served as a flight lieutenant in the RAF Volunteer Reserve and become an expert in small-arms training. He was stationed at Langham Camp, North Norfolk, and remained with the RAF Regiment until he was invalided out on 19 December 1943. He was then given an appointment by the Ministry of Agriculture in Lincolnshire for three years before returning to Moffat.

In his mid-fifties he spent much of his retirement following shooting and other country pursuits in the Moffat area. In June 1956 he attended the VC centenary celebrations held in London.

Wallace died at his home at Grey Ghyll, Moffat, on 2 February 1968 after a few days' illness, and was survived by his wife and daughter. He was buried in Moffat Cemetery on the right side of the main gate. He was the last of the First World War VCs who were former students of Edinburgh University. Together with Sgt Cyril Gourley, he is one of the VCs commemorated in the RA Chapel in Woolwich, South London, and both VCs are in the Regimental Collection.

N.B. ELLIOTT-COOPER

East of La Vacquerie, France, 30 November 1917

(*David Harvey*)

The ground gained by the Allies in the first ten days of the Battle of Cambrai had created a distinct salient in the enemy lines, and towards the end of November it became increasingly clear that the Germans were determined to regain the lost ground and to hang on to the all-important Bourlon Ridge in particular. Their plan was to concentrate on breaking through to the north and south parts of the battlefield.

On 30 November, in the southern part of the battlefield, the 8th and 9th Royal Fusiliers (36th Brigade, 12th Division) were to feel the full brunt of the German counter-attack. The 9th had one company south of the Cambrai–Gouzeaucourt road in the south-western part of Pelican Trench. This position was held until the enemy broke through the 7th Norfolk lines to the right. A counter-attack was successful and a withdrawal was made to the front system of the Hindeburg Line. This allowed contact to be kept with the 60th Brigade and parts of 35th Brigade in front of the village of La Vacquerie.

At the same time the 8th Battalion's C and D companies were occupying perilous positions in another section of Pelican Trench across the road. The positions were to the north-east of Bleak House and close to a track which led to Pam Pam Farm. The official history tells what happened:

The two forward companies were crushed by heavy attacks from the front and the right flank, whilst a third company, coming forward over the Cambrai road to reinforce, was caught by the concentrated fire of light machine-guns. The commanding officer, Lieut-Colonel N.B. Elliott-Cooper, called upon his headquarters personnel and the remaining company and led a counter-attack which drove the Germans back over the crest of the Bonavis Ridge; but hostile machine-gun fire then checked this effort and the colonel fell, severely wounded, whilst well in advance of his men. He was captured, after ordering withdrawal. This counter-attack enabled the remnants of the battalion to rally in the reserve line south-east of La Vacquerie.

The enemy had reached within fifty yards of the Royal Fusiliers' line when in a counter-attack Elliot-Cooper charged them back over the Cambrai road, where the line came under heavy machine-gun fire, which knocked out Elliot-Cooper and the officers with him. By the end of the day the enemy advance was checked in this section and the 8th Battalion was in touch with the 9th Royal Fusiliers on the right and the 37th Brigade on the left and a new line established. The 8th Battalion had lost 10 officers and 247 men and the 9th 13 officers and 208 men. Cooper himself was seriously wounded and taken prisoner. He was Mentioned in Despatches on 18 December 1917. According to his file, Elliott-Cooper died at 11 p.m. on 11 February 1918 in the hospital of No. 1 (Reserve) POW Camp Lazaret, Hanover, from wounds in his right thigh, as well as cardiac weakness. He was buried in Hamburg Cemetery, Hanover, Plot V, Row A, Grave 16.

His VC citation was published in the *London Gazette* of 13 February 1918, two days after he died as a prisoner of war:

> For most conspicuous bravery and devotion to duty. Hearing that the enemy had broken through our outpost line, he rushed out of his dug-out, and, on seeing them advancing across the open, he mounted the parapet and dashed forward, calling upon the Reserve Company and details of Battalion Headquarters to follow. Absolutely unarmed, he made straight for the advancing enemy, and under his direction our men forced them back 600 yards. While still some forty yards in front he was severely wounded. Realizing that his men were greatly outnumbered, and suffering heavy casualties, he signalled to them to withdraw, regardless of the fact that he himself must be taken prisoner. By his prompt and gallant leading he gained time for the reserves to move up and occupy the line of defence.

News of his death came via the British Red Cross Society in Copenhagen, and his effects were later forwarded from Hanover in April 1918. His parents were presented with his posthumous VC at Buckingham Palace on 25 May 1918. A month after his death a service was held in his memory at St Paul's, Knightsbridge, on 15 March 1918, which was attended by his relations and friends, and a detachment of Royal Fusiliers which lined the aisle during the service. Various tributes were made in his memory, and the following is an extract from a letter received from his tutor at Eton: 'He has been the very best, and has won the best thing in life here, and if he did not know it on earth, at least he knows it now. He has been most happy in life, and he has laid down his life, crowded with every earthly honour for his country.' And a fellow officer noted: 'His life will always be a shining example to all who knew him. Absolutely fearless, he never for one moment considered his own safety. Always happy and cheerful, his spirit was never daunted by hardship or danger. He was universally loved and admired, and his influence was enormous on those serving with him.'

Elliott-Cooper's name was commemorated in several permanent locations, including Eton College and St Mary's, Bentworth, Hampshire, and the south aisle of Ripon Cathedral (his great-grandfather used to live at Elliott House in Ripon). He is also remembered on a Royal Fusiliers memorial, together with the name of his brother, Gilbert D'Arcy, who died in 1922 as a result of wounds received in August 1915.

Elliott-Cooper's VC, DSO and MC, as well as his bronze memorial plaque, were presented to the Royal Fusiliers Museum in 1973 by his family. His remaining medals are in private hands.

Neville Bowes Elliott-Cooper, the youngest son of Sir Robert Elliott-Cooper KCB, a civil engineer and builder of railways, and Lady Fanny Elliott-Cooper (née Leetham) was born in London on 22 January 1889 at 81 Lancaster Gate.

He was educated at Eton (1901–7), where he became a member of the Eton College Volunteers, and Sandhurst. On 9 October 1908, aged nineteen, he joined the Army as a second lieutenant in the Royal Fusiliers, and saw service in South Africa, Mauritius and India. On the outbreak of war he was already a member of the Regular Army, and rose to become commander of the 8th Royal Fusiliers (City of London Regiment); he went on to win the MC and DSO, as well as the VC.

He won the MC at the beginning of March 1916 for his work with the 8th and 9th Battalions in operations

Hamburg Cemetery (*Donald C. Jennings*)

against the Chord at the Hohenzollern Redoubt, which was in enemy hands and which joined Big Willie with Little Willie. Seven mines had been exploded but they had only partially damaged about a third of its length. Immediately after the mine explosions the companies drawn from the two battalions rushed to seize the section of the Chord which had been allocated to them. Elliott-Cooper was in command of C Coy of the 9th Royal Fusiliers, and after rushing three craters the company seized a crater in the Triangle that linked with Big Willie. The operations, although expensive in casualties, were considered a success. Cooper was one of three officers to be awarded the MC and was made a captain (*London Gazette*, 14 May 1916), and both battalions were mentioned in Sir Douglas Haig's despatch of 12 May. On 3 April he was one of those decorated with ribbons at Sailly La Bourse by the commander of 1st Army, Gen Sir Charles Monro KCB.

It was when he had been made temporary lieutenant-colonel that his DSO was published in the *London Gazette* of 18 July 1917 'for rallying his battalion when it became temporally disorganized, and for leading forward a patrol of 20 men under very heavy fire and returning to his Brigadier with 20 prisoners and very valuable information'.

He was also given a special mention in Haig's Despatch of 7 November 1917.

R. GEE

Masnières and Les Rues Vertes, 30 November 1917

(*David Harvey*)

On 30 November the 29th Division had two brigades in positions in the front line at Masnières on the north side of the St Quentin Canal. The 86th Brigade occupied trenches covering the village and the 16th Middlesex held posts to the south-east at the lock bridge opposite Mon Plaisir Farm and at the farm itself. A flanking battalion was on the left, close up to the main road to Cambrai. In addition, two companies of the 2nd Royal Fusiliers were in support on the east side of the village at a sugar factory among the houses where four machine-guns were set up. The 87th Brigade occupied a front stretching from the Masnières–Cambrai road on the right to Château Talma north of Marcoing. The 1st Royal Guernsey Battalion was the reserve battalion, and Brigade HQ was also in the village close to the main bridge over the canal. The St Quentin canal divided Masnières from the adjacent suburb of Les Rues Vertes (to the south), which on 30 November was without a garrison. The village was also split by a divisional boundary and its defence was the responsibilty of the 20th as well as the 29th Division. The eastern part of the village was marshy and defence relied on machine-guns rather than infantry.

In Masnières the 86th Brigade HQ was in a building 200 yards north of the bridge on the left side of the main street. Rear Brigade HQ was immediately south of the canal, and the brigade dump for bombs and small-arm ammunition was also south of the canal, housed in a building in the Les Rues Vertes–La Vacquerie road. The brigade was expecting a possible enemy attack as there had been artillery activity through the night, and the brigade commander warned his battalions to be on the alert and for the 1st Royal Guernsey Battalion sheltering in some catacombs to 'stand to'.

As predicted, the enemy duly opened artillery fire on Masnières and the brigade trenches, and the barrage lasted for about three quarters of an hour between 7 and 8 a.m. on what turned out to be a misty morning. Just before

9 a.m. the German 107th Division began a frontal attack from the direction of Crèvecoeur to the east, which was preceded by low-flying aeroplanes. The brigade defence positions managed to keep the enemy at bay and suffered heavy casualties, but the Germans were able to secure the brigade posts at Mon Plaisir Farm, which then had to be withdrawn. British artillery response was weak, and, unbeknown to 86th Brigade, the enemy were successfully moving against the left flank of the 20th Division to the south of Les Rues Vertes and were able to enter the village from the south without much opposition.

Much of the following account of Gee winning his VC has been based on the article compiled by Major A.F. Becke published in *The Journal of the Royal Artillery*. Capt Robert Gee, a staff officer, was in command at 86th Brigade rear headquarters in Les Rues Vertes. He was also responsible for the brigade dump of bombs and small-arm ammunition that was in the village. At 8 a.m. he received a telephone call from brigade informing him of the retirement of the 20th Division and giving him instructions to immediately establish a defensive flank in the village. At the same time a messenger was sent to warn 88th Brigade, which was reserve in Marcoing, and Gee also informed the Royal Engineers who were in the southern half of Les Rues Vertes. In fact the 497th (Kent) Field Company RE was quickly captured, as it was taken by surprise. Shortly after the above telephone call, the phone wires at 86th Brigade HQ were cut by shell-fire, and heavy fighting in Les Rues Vertes could be heard.

The 86th Brigade commander ordered two companies of the Royal Guernsey Light Infantry to cross the canal and assist in pushing the enemy out of Les Rues Vertes.

At Brigade HQ Capt Gee had with him a dozen signallers and orderlies and one officer, Capt Loseby of the 1st Lancashire Fusiliers. Loseby was sent to make contact with the 16th Middlesex Battalion at the lock bridge with six of his men, and they would then act as the left flank of Gee's defence, as the 29th Division was becoming hemmed in from three sides. Gee then set off with a small party of his remaining six men, four signallers and two orderlies, to set about the clearing of the enemy out of Les Rues Vertes itself. He was desperate to prevent the brigade dump of bombs and small-arms from falling into enemy hands. His small party rushed out of the HQ and he could see that, southwards:

German infantry in fours marching down the La Vacquerie road towards the chapel and, nearer still, more German infantry in pairs were working along each side of the street. One of the party was at once sent back to the bridge to bring up a Lewis gun, two men were sent across the street to open fire from there – one was killed getting across – and two men were sent into the nearest house to fetch material to form a barricade, whilst the Staff Captain

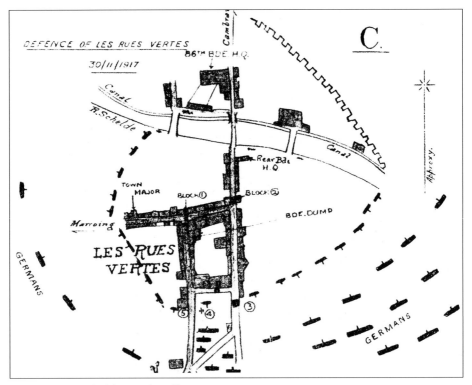

Masnières (*Journal of the Royal Artillery*)

and the other man held on where they were. The German infantry hesitated to rush three men, and thus missed the real opportunity of capturing Les Rues Vertes.

The deadly rifle-fire of the three defenders held up the German advance and gained sufficient time to make a rough barricade of furniture, including two chairs, a table-top, and a feather-bed, and Captain Gee emphasised to his men that the last-named was absolutely bullet-proof. The Barricade was then manned by the party of five rifles. Five minutes later the Lewis gun arrived, but even when placed on a chair it could not look over the mattress. To save a waste of time, Captain Gee at once ordered the Lewis gunner to blow a hole through the feather-bed, so that he could then fire along and rake the road. This was done; but it seems to have aroused no feelings of inadequacy of the bulletproof cover of that featherbed in the minds of the small party; no doubt the proximity of the Germans occupied all their attention. Directly the Lewis gun had opened fire along the road Captain

Better than the
"Perfumes of Arabia."

Captain GEE, V.C.
stands up for Beer.

Gee felt that the security of the barricade was assured, at any rate for a long enough time to enable him to climb into the back of the house (the second from the barricade on the enemy's side) where the brigade dump was located and ascertain if it was still untouched.

Captain Gee went back to the forkroads, so that he could then go up the easterly street and work through to the dump. Hearing the quick steps of a man behind him, and thinking that it must be one of the tiny garrison of the barricade running away, he turned round, hit the man over the head with his stick and felled him, but the stick broke. Gripping the part that remained at the point of balance, and it was still a formidable weapon for it was shod with a lancehead, Captain Gee climbed into the back of the house which contained the bombs. He found the two dump-men lying dead and the Quarter-Master-Sergeant missing. Just as he made this discovery the Staff Captain himself was pounced on and collared by two Germans. Captain Gee reacted very swiftly. He drove the point of his stick through the stomach of one of his opponents, who then ceased to have any further interest in the Battle of Cambrai, and then gripped the other German round the throat so as to strangle him. A long, tough struggle took place. It was terminated by a deafening explosion close to Captain Gee's ear.

The man the staff captain had recently knocked out had left the barricade with the intention of accompanying Captain Gee and assisting him should he require help when the dump was entered. After coming-to from the blow, the man followed on to the dump-house and there found Captain Gee struggling with the German soldier who was gasping for breath. Pushing his rifle over Captain Gee's shoulder, he inserted the muzzle in the German's wide-open mouth, and pulled the trigger. The struggle was at an end; and for the moment the precious dump was secured. Leaving the two dead enemy in the dump, Captain Gee (accompanied by the man) went back to direct operations for clearing Les Rues Vertes of Germans and to secure the rear of the two brigades of the 29th Division which were holding the front line on the north bank of the canal. While climbing out of the dump-house under a hot rifle fire the soldier was shot and killed.

When Captain Gee got back to the road he saw at once there was no time to be lost, and fortunately at this juncture thirty or forty men arrived to assist him. Some of these men were sent to reinforce Captain Loseby's party, some were set to work on building No. 2 barricade, and Captain Gee took six men. With his party he entered the bomb store and, loading up with bombs, his party bombed the Germans out of all the houses along the east side of East Street, and then turning back they cleared the enemy out of all the houses on the west side of that street.

The former brewery, Masnières (*Peter Batchelor*)

Two companies of the 1/Roy Guernsey L.I., sent by Brigade Headquarters, now reported to the staff captain. Some of these men were then placed along a sunken lane which ran just in front of the orchard at the south end of Les Rues Vertes, thus joining up with Captain Loseby's defence; whilst others were detailed to safeguard the canal bridges, and some were used to build and hold a barricade (No. 3) across the south end of East Street.

From the remainder a bombing party was organised to clear the houses along the Marcoing Road. In this quarter, however, the Germans put up no fight, but bolted from house to house as the bombs were thrown, and this street was secured. Another bombing party was then organised by the staff captain, and the Germans were steadily cleared out of all the houses along the east side of West Street (which leads to La Vacquerie, and in which No. 1 barricade had been constructed earlier in the day). These houses were cleared as far as the brewery; then the party turned back, cleared all the houses on the west side of this street, and to safeguard the now-cleared south-west corner of the village a party under a young subaltern was posted just north of the brewery.

The staff captain's next task was to send a supply of SAA (Small Arms Ammunition) and bombs up to his brigade headquarters in Masnières (north of the canal), and to ensure that a supply of SAA and bombs was also available at the main roadbridge over the canal. When this was accomplished, Captain Gee determined to clear the Germans out of the brewery, their last foothold in Les Rues Vertes. For this he organised a special party, each man carrying six bombs, three in each pocket, and with these men he moved up to the orchard on the east side of the brewery. A plank was found, and with that, assisted by some bombs, a hole was blown in the brewery wall. Captain Gee then jumped in and found part of one of the divisional field ambulances (89th) still there, the doctors quietly smoking German cigars. The staff captain was informed that the Germans had left only just before, taking with them as prisoners, about a hundred of the 497th Field Company (3/Kent), who had been quartered in the building. Captain Gee at once ran out to ascertain if the young officer and his party at the south-west end of the village (north of the brewery) had accounted for these Germans. On arrival at the place where he himself had posted this party he discovered that the young officer, on his own responsibility, had withdrawn his men. Even so the officer had seen the Germans withdrawing from the brewery, but he had not fired because the Germans and their prisoners (3/Kents) were all mixed up together. Captain Gee at once re-posted the party to secure the south-west corner of the village and the brewery. The staff captain then reconnoitred the situation to the south of the brewery, and saw German infantry entrenching about a hundred yards south of the village, with a machine-gun on the La Vacquerie road at the west end of the line. When the officer in command of this sector of the defensive front was taxed with allowing the enemy to dig in at this close range, he replied that many of his men (Guernsey L.I.) had no ammunition; they had arrived from the base without any, to find themselves pitched-forked head-first into a vital fight.

Captain Gee promptly sent back for a Stokes gun, so as to neutralise the German machine-gun during the onslaught of a bombing party. Then working out to a flank with his one remaining orderly (four others had already been killed beside him) Captain Gee waited for the Stokes gun. As it fired its first round (a wild one) Captain Gee and the orderly rushed the machine-gun, and, although the orderly was shot, Captain Gee with two revolvers accounted for the German detachment of eight men. As more of his own men arrived the machine-gun was turned on the enemy line; by its fire and the simultaneous onslaught of a bombing party, the German infantry were driven from the hastily constructed trench and the position was then occupied and consolidated. Fortunately German machine-gun ammunition was plentiful, for a large dump had been left behind by the defenders of Masnières when the 29th Division captured the village on 20th November. This German machine-gun proved to be a splendid acquisition for Captain Gee's slender force, since later in the fight it did deadly work when the German infantry to the westward were retiring before the counter-attack of the 88th Brigade from Marcoing.

A German machine-gun which now opened fire from a house near the Crucifix on the La Vacquerie road was promptly silenced by the Stokes gun. Feeling that this south-western angle of his defensive perimeter had at last been secured, Captain Gee walked along the brewery wall to establish contact with the parties holding the left of his line. He then learned that a good deal of trouble was being given by a machine-gun and snipers. The staff captain went forward to make his own reconnaissance, and saw that the snipers were quite numerous and that a machine-gun was placed in a house near the crossroads. He decided at once that it was necessary for a Stokes gun to come up and put the machine-gun out of action before it was quite dark. To arrange for this plan to be effected as soon as possible, he started to work back to the line of posts; but, unfortunately, just as he reached the barricade at the southern end of Les Rues Vertes, a sniper's bullet hit him in the knee as he was jumping from the bank to the barricade.

When the brigade commander heard that the staff captain had been wounded, he insisted that Captain Gee should be relieved and come back to brigade headquarters, and an officer was sent to take over command of the defence of Les Rues Vertes. When he arrived, Captain Gee took him round the defensive line which had been established outside the village and formally handed over the defence; then the staff captain went back to brigade headquarters in Masnières, made a full report of the situation to his brigade commander, had his wound dressed, and remained on duty until it was finally decided that the position must be evacuated. The brigadier then ordered Captain Gee back to Marcoing. Even now his adventures were not over, for, as he went along the canal bank towards Marcoing, he was suddenly challenged (not in English) and to evade capture he jumped into the canal, swam across and got safely away.

The successful defence of Les Rues Vertes did far more than merely save the rear of the 29th Division on that 30th November; undoubtedly, it was the principal cause on this day of the slowing up of the drive and speed of the right flank of the main German counter-attack through Gouzeaucourt, and the vigorous defence of Les Rues Vertes compelled the enemy to use up more and more troops as the day wore on . . . .

His (Gee's) Brigade Commander's appreciation of his Staff Captain's unconquerable determination was officially recorded in these words: 'By his heroic conduct, his energy, his fine leadership, and utter neglect of himself, Captain Gee certainly saved the 86th Brigade.'

The 29th Division began to evacuate its untenable positions at Masnières and Les Rues Vertes the following day, and brigade headquarters was set on fire before it left. The two villages were virtually destroyed in the fighting and shelling and left in ruins. After Marcoing had also been vacated the new British line became the former Hindenburg support line.

Capt Gee was recommended for the award of a VC by Brig Gen G.R.H. Cheape of the 86th Brigade in a report dated 9 December, which was submitted to the commander of III Corps, Lt Gen Sir William Pulteney. He was Mentioned in Despatches a second time on 11 December for work carried out prior to the Battle of Cambrai, and returned to duty after less than three weeks at the dressing station. His VC was approved and the citation was published in the *London Gazette* on 11 January 1918. Ten days before, at Brandhoek B Camp, a brigade ceremonial parade took place when he was presented with his VC ribbon by the commander of 29th Division. 86th Brigade also held a ceremonial parade to mark the VCs awarded to Capt Gee, Col Sherwood-Kelly and Sgt Spackman on 12 January at Wizernes.

The citation was as follows:

Robert Gee, M.C., Lieut (Temporary Capt.) 2nd Battalion. Royal Fusiliers. For most conspicuous bravery, initiative and determination when an attack by a strong enemy force pierced our line and captured a brigade headquarters and ammunition dump. Capt. Gee, finding himself a prisoner, killed one of the enemy with his spiked stick, and succeeded in escaping. He then organized a party of the brigade staff, with which he attacked the enemy fiercely, closely followed and supported by two companies of infantry. By his own personal bravery and prompt action he, aided by his orderlies, cleared the locality. Capt. Gee established a defensive flank on the outskirts of the village, then finding that an enemy machine-gun was still in action, with a revolver in each hand, and followed by one man, he rushed and captured the gun, killing eight of the crew. At this time he was wounded, but refused to have the wound dressed until he was satisfied that the defence was organized.

In the New Year Robert Gee was Mentioned in Despatches a third time and, accompanied by his 12-year-old daughter Amy, he was presented with his VC by the King at Buckingham Palace on 23 February (as were Arthur Borton and Charles Spackman). He later returned to France, but on his arrival there he became unwell and was readmitted to a divisional rest station of the 89th Field Ambulance on 5 April. He was invalided home three days later.

Robert Gee, son of Robert and Amy Gee, was born at 29 Metcalf Street, Leicester, on 7 May 1876. His father was employed as a framework knitter and died at the early age of forty-five, a few months before his son was born. Gee's mother only lived until the age of forty-eight, which left young Robert an orphan at the age of nine. In July 1887 he was taken into the care of Leicester Union Workhouse, and a few weeks later transferred to Countesthorpe Cottage Homes, where he was educated. He was discharged in 1890 and was then apprenticed to Robert Austin, an elderly shoemaker. The two did not hit it off particularly well and Gee was readmitted to the workhouse in March 1892. Two months later he became an apprentice to Mr Joseph Shaw, who ran a firm of ornamental and metal iron works in Aylestone Park, Leicester.

Before Gee completed his apprenticeship the firm closed down, and when still not quite 17 years old he decided to join the 4th Queen's Own Hussars, which he did in April 1893. Having given a false age and name, he deserted on 18 October and enlisted in the Royal Fusiliers the following day. He was posted to their 2nd Battalion when they were serving in Guernsey. His misdeeds eventually caught up with him and he was imprisoned for six weeks for fraudulent enlistment and forfeited his then service of 256 days with the Royal Fusiliers.

He later served with the 1st Battalion in the East Indies from 25 November 1896 to 14 March 1900. He became a lance-corporal on 1 January 1896, and while in India, a corporal on 20 August 1898. He returned to England in March 1900 and was posted to the recently formed 4th Battalion. He was promoted to sergeant on 1 August and was stationed at Shorncliffe Barracks, Dover. It was during this period that he met his future wife, Elizabeth Dixon of Huntingdon, and the couple were married in Folkestone in March 1902. They were to have two daughters; the first, named Edith, was born at 103 Samuel Street, Woolwich, and the second, Amy, named after his mother, was born in Dublin in May 1905. Gee was stationed in the Portobello Barracks.

On 4 March 1904 Gee was made a colour sergeant. On 30 June 1907 he was initiated into the Freemasons at a lodge in Hounslow at a time when he was stationed in the Regimental Depot, also in Hounslow.

During 1908 Gee was ill with heart trouble, and on 8 November was made quartermaster sergeant, assuming the duties of orderly room sergeant. He was promoted to regimental quartermaster sergeant on 1 January 1911, and in the following year was awarded the Long Service and Good Conduct Medal. He had taken a keen interest in military history and used to give lectures on the subject, one of very few NCOs qualified to do so. While at Hounslow, the depot was also home to a cavalry regiment, and he took the opportunity of working with horses, learning to ride and carrying out mucking-out.

On the outbreak of war he was posted to the 6th Reserve Battalion of the Royal Fusiliers stationed at Dover. On 29 January 1915 he was promoted to WO, Class II (QMS), and after being in the Army for nearly twenty-two years he was discharged on 20 May 1915 on appointment to a commission in the Royal Fusiliers on the following day. He was posted to the 2nd Battalion, his parent unit, which was now part of the 86th Brigade (29th Division). He sailed for Egypt in March 1915, arriving in Alexandria on 29 March, and served in Gallipoli from August as a company commander. He later held the rank of acting captain from 27 September, and on 26 November was involved in a terrible action when a violent storm flooded their trenches in Suvla Bay, leaving several men drowned and some of the others scrambling to safety in now freezing conditions, only to be shot down by Turkish snipers. Gee was one of very few survivors.

Gee later left Gallipoli in early January and served for a time in Egypt, having disembarked in Alexandria on 8 January 1916. He was made acting staff captain attached to 86th Brigade in Suez on 2 February, and on 13 March was made staff captain at brigade headquarters. Later in the year the Division moved to France. Technically still only a second lieutenant, he was promoted to lieutenant on 21 March. Retaining his staff captaincy, he was also with the 2nd Battalion serving in the front line in time for the beginning of the Battle of the Somme. On the opening day, 1 July, Gee won the MC and was seriously wounded during the fighting at Beaumont Hamel. He was invalided home on 4 July.

The award of his MC was announced in the *London Gazette* of 22 September 1916, and the citation read:

> Second Lieutenant (temporary Captain) Robert Gee, (Royal Fusiliers). He encouraged his men during the attack by fearlessly exposing himself and cheering them on. When wounded he refused to retire and urged his men on till, after being blown in the air by a shell, he was carried in half-unconscious.

He was also Mentioned in Despatches in September for his part in an earlier action. He remained on sick leave until 19 October and partly used the time learning French and continuing his association with Freemasonry. He returned to France in February 1917, when he served as a staff captain with the 29th Division until he was transferred to the staff of 86th Brigade on 25 June. He took part in the Ypres battles and was wounded a second time on 13 August. He received treatment at 88th Field Ambulance, returning to his brigade on 31 August.

The 86th Brigade was continuously in action in the Ypres Salient, and when it was relieved in Elverdighe on 11 October Capt Gee was ordered by his brigade commander to prepare a hot meal at headquarters for the exhausted men. He produced an appetising stew from the carcasses of dead mules killed by shellfire. A few days later, during the third Battle of Ypres, in which both sides were literally bogged down, Gee was on leave and suffering from neurasthenia as a result of his experiences at Beaumont Hamel. On being invalided home in April 1918 he never returned to the Western Front. When he was well enough, and accompanied by his wife and elder daughter Edith, he was given a great reception in Leicester, his home town, on 11 July 1918, where he was presented with a gold watch and chain by the Mayor. Mrs Gee was not forgotten, as she was presented with a gold brooch.

Still in the Army, he was appointed temporary staff captain with the Tees Garrison, Middlesbrough, on 12 September, and continued with his lecturing in military history, which included visiting public schools. He also took part in various patriotic events in the summer in Nottingham, Hartlepool and Middlesbrough. He continued his active involvement with Freemasonry and was installed as Master of the Roll Call Lodge on 10 October.

Gee was a good speaker and a man of strong opinions, and decided that he would leave the Army and try his hand at politics or the law. He began to read for the Bar in the autumn, but as he still suffered from his head wounds he was unable to continue his studies. He therefore decided to switch to politics, and his first foray was to stand as Coalition Candidate for the Consett Division of Durham during what was known as the 'Coupon Election' held on 14 December 1918. He was defeated, and failed again at Bishop Auckland and Newcastle East.

Gee was promoted to staff captain on 7 February 1919 and transferred to the Royal West Kent Regiment. In the same year he had a medical board, which noted that he was suffering from a duodenal ulcer. The following year he retired from active duty and left the Army on 8 March, when his name was placed on the reserve list of officers. After the war he was never a well man, his ill health being attributed to his active service; as a result he was awarded a gratuity. Gee attended the VC garden party in the grounds of Buckingham Palace in June 1920 and the Cenotaph and Westminster Abbey services for the Unknown Warrior in London in November.

Trying for Parliament again, on 2 March 1921 Gee won a by-election (by a margin of 600 votes) as a Coalition Candidate against Ramsay MacDonald, a former chairman of the Parliamentary Labour Party. In the following year the House of Commons formed its own branch of the British Legion and Captain Gee was elected its treasurer. Sadly, he lost his Woolwich seat soon afterwards. He tried for Parliament twice more in the North-East without success, but was back in the House in October 1924, when elected (by 358 votes) Conservative and Unionist MP for the Bosworth Division. In the following year he was made an Honorary Freeman of Leicester.

As Gee was just entering his early forties, he seems to have made up his mind to leave England and start afresh elsewhere. The reasons for this can only be surmised, but, as mentioned, he was not a well man, and his ulcer, together with war wounds, might have influenced his decision. He was encouraged by the possibility of a new life in Australia, as free passages were being offered to 'men and women of good character'. He failed to put his parliamentary affairs in order and left his constituency without a representative in the House of Commons – and so it remained until 1927, when the seat was declared vacant and a by-election called. However, Gee did make time for resigning from the Freemasons. Thirty years later he explained why he had left: he said that the main reason was that his war wounds were troubling him. He also said that although he had intended to return to England from Australia, once he had taken up farming his health improved and he decided to stay.

On the voyage to Australia he became seriously ill and was put ashore at Fremantle, Western Australia. When he recovered he planned to become a farmer. Setting aside all his available money, including what remained of his gratuity, he applied to the authorities with a view to purchasing 2,000 acres of land in Mullewa, north-east of Perth in Western Australia. Together with a former Army friend, he began work on the virgin land on 13 September 1926. He named the farm after the French town of Cambrai. The farm was successful for a short time and Gee's health improved considerably.

However, an economic slump created a depression that hit small farms particularly severely. Gee became virtually bankrupt and in 1934 had to turn his back on the whole venture. But although the scheme failed he had gained a new lease of life, and his next move was to find accommodation in a small cottage 20 miles to the east of Perth. For about three years he was without any financial security, until he managed to get a temporary job in the despatch department of Boans Limited, a well-known store in Perth.

On the outbreak of war in 1939 Gee falsified his age by ten years in order to join the Volunteer Defence Corps, but was later discharged on medical grounds. In 1940 he was offered a newly created position of welfare officer in Boans. He retired in 1951 at the age of seventy-five, and two years later was appointed Commissioner of Declarations, Western Australia.

In 1956, as part of the Australian contingent of VC holders, he was able to return once more to England in order to take part in the VC centenary celebrations. All travel expenses were paid for by the Australian government. While in his home town he was received by the Lord Mayor and was generally given a very warm welcome wherever he went. He was also made an honorary life vice-president of the Leicester Branch of the Association of Jewish Ex-Servicemen.

Gee was based in London for most of his visit to England, and stayed in the Regent Palace Hotel in Oxford Street. He was able to meet up with many of his former friends and colleagues from his days with the Royal Fusiliers. These included former Pte Cattermole, who took part in Gee's VC action, covering him with Lewis gun fire at Les Rues Vertes, Masnières. Another meeting was with his former batman, Pte Herbert (Harry) Niblett from Eltham in south-east London. Seemingly short of cash, Gee wrote to the authorities seeking extra financial assistance. He was given a small compensation when a scheme for a small annual pension (£10) to holders of the VC was begun in August 1959.

In the late 1950s Gee's health began to fail and he became a patient in the 'Home of Peace', Thomas Street, Subiaco, a suburb of Perth, from the end of January 1960 until his death six months later, on 2 August, at the age of eighty-four. His last request was that on his death he should be dressed in his uniform. He was cremated at Karrakatta Crematorium and his ashes were scattered in the rose garden. His last home address had been Dunmuvin, Orange Road, in the small town of Darlington, where he had lived quietly in retirement surrounded by books.

As requested by her father, Gee's elder daughter Edith presented his medals to the Royal Fusiliers Museum, in May 1960. The medals included the VC, MC, 1914/15 Star, BWM, VM, Coronation Medals for King Edward VII, King George VI and Queen Elizabeth II, and lastly the Long Service and Good Conduct Medal. She also gave them the copy of the illuminated address from the City of Leicester. His medals were later displayed at the Regimental Museum.

Gee was also commemorated by the directors and staff of Boans, who contributed to the cost of a memorial fountain in the grounds of the war veterans' home in Perth. The inscription is as follows:

This Fountain of Memory was erected by the staff and executives of Boan's Ltd. in proud and honoured memory of Captain Robert Gee VC, MC who became the firm's first Welfare Officer (1940–51). He died on 2nd August 1960 at the age of 84 years, renowned for his courage and tenacity of purpose.

In 1967 Edith presented her father's revolver (the one he had used when killing eight Germans when he won his VC at Les Rues Vertes, Masnières, on 30 November 1917) to the Regimental Museum. On reading about the revolver, a Mr Frank R. Caulton wrote to the Regimental Association stating that in November 1917, when he was Captain Gee's scout, he 'took possession' of two revolvers belonging to two sleeping Germans at Ribecourt. The Luger marked L was given to his captain, and when Gee was shooting eight Germans ten days later he was using two revolvers. An account published in *The Times* of 3 August 1960 stated: 'With a revolver in each hand he silenced an enemy machine-gun, killing eight of its crew, and although wounded, he refused medical attention until he was satisfied that the defence was organized.'

In 1986, shortly before she died, Edith encouraged her son Robert Harrison to present to the Royal Fusiliers the casket given to his grandfather when receiving the Freedom of Leicester in 1925, together with his Sam Browne belt.

Even by the standards of many holders of the VC, the name of Robert Gee stands out, especially considering the handicap of his early start in life as an orphan who had only a very basic education. Never one to shirk a new challenge or the chance of self-improvement, his life appears to have been one continuous adventure.

J. THOMAS

Fontaine-Notre-Dame, France, 30 November 1917

(David Harvey)

At 5.30 p.m. on 28 November the 176th Infantry Brigade of the 59th Division was ordered to move forward to relieve the 2nd Guards Brigade close to the village of Fontaine-Notre-Dame to the west of Cambrai, and the 2/5th North Staffordshires relieved the 1st Grenadier Guards, who were the centre front battalion to the right of the Cambrai–Bapaume road. The relief was completed by 9.45 p.m., and the line consisted of a series of detached posts. During the night two companies of the battalion were mainly employed in working and carrying parties.

On 30 November the 2/5th North Staffordshires were still holding part of the 59th Divisional line to the south of Bourlon Wood, and between 11 a.m. and midday they successfully beat off a German counter-attack. During this time and in broad daylight, in view of the enemy Cpl John Thomas had reconnoitred the southern edge of the copse at F 21 a.4 and an isolated house at F21.a.30.85 and factory at F 15c 38.05 on the western edge of Fontaine. He returned with very useful information, which was of particular assistance to snipers. A second enemy counter-attack took place about half an hour after the first, at 12.30 p.m., which once again was repulsed. By the end of the day battalion casualties were fifty-eight officers and men.

In describing the facts of Corporal Thomas's actions later, the published battalion history is more detailed than the war diary:

. . . Corporal Thomas jumped out of his trench, ran forward 200 yards, and then dropped down and crawled through some trees and out at the other side. He then crawled further forward for another 150 yards. From here he could see a large German dug-out, and watched 200 men come out in threes and fours, who passed within 20 yards of him. He allowed them to go about 200 yards, and then fired at them in the back. He went out at 11 a.m. and came back at 3.30.

Cpl Thomas was awarded the VC for his reconnaissance work, which was published in the *London Gazette* of 13 February 1918 as follows:

> John Thomas, Private, No. 50842, L.-Corpl., North Staffordshire Regiment. (East Manchester). For most conspicuous bravery and initiative in action. He saw the enemy making preparations for a counter-attack, and with a comrade, on his own initiative, decided to make a close reconnaissance. These two went out in broad daylight in full view of the enemy and under heavy machine-gun fire. His comrade was hit within a few yards of the trench, but, undeterred, L.-Corpl. Thomas went on alone. Working round a small copse, he shot three snipers, and then pushed on to a building used by the enemy as a night post. From here he saw whence the enemy were bringing up their troops and where they were congregating. He stayed in this position for an hour, sniping the enemy the whole time and doing great execution. He returned to our lines, after being away three hours, with information of utmost value, which enabled definite plans to be made and artillery fire to be brought on the enemy's concentration, so that when the attack took place it was broken up.

According to an account published in Creagh and Humphris, Cpl Thomas later described the incident as follows:

> I wish to mention how I got so close to the enemy was by crawling on my stomach for about 800 yards of open country. I was sniped by the enemy snipers, but I bluffed them by pretending that they had hit me but I again crawled on and gained the village of Fontaine, which was then in German occupation, and worked my way from house to house, so that I got valuable information as regards his movements, and that is how I spent the three hours away from our lines.

A few months later he wrote home: 'I am working very hard for a living. I suffer from the effects of shell concussion, through being blown up at Bullecourt, March, 1918.' Thomas was in fact blown up and concussed at Bullecourt in March 1918, the same month he received his VC from the King at Buckingham Palace. After arriving home at 7 Gorton Lane, Lower Openshaw, Thomas was given a civic reception and the Mayor presented him with several gifts, including a gold watch and an illuminated address. He was promoted to corporal just before the Armistice on 10 November 1918 and to sergeant on 21 March 1919. Meanwhile he had married Amelia Wood from Hulme, Manchester. The ceremony took place on the Isle of Man at the parish church of St Matthew's, Douglas. The couple went to live in Stockport, and they were to have two sons, who both served in the SAS in the Second World War.

John Thomas, son of Edward Thomas, a boot and shoemaker, and his wife Elizabeth, who was a nurse, was born in Openshaw, Manchester, on 10 May 1886. He and his two sisters were brought up by relatives after their parents both died early. Thomas was educated at St Barnabas, Openshaw. At the age of twenty-three on 7 June 1909 he enlisted in the Regular Army as a private in the 2/5th North Staffs (TA). In 1912 he became a Reservist and joined the Merchant Navy with the Cunard Line.

Thomas was described 'as a small cheery man' and attended the VC garden party in June 1920. During the dedication and unveiling of the war memorial in St Peter's Square, Manchester, in 1924 he was one of a group of five holders of the VC introduced to Lord Derby. Thomas was the only one in the group wearing a flat cap! He later attended the House of Lords' Dinner in November 1929 and the Victory parade and dinner in London on 8 June 1946. His health was permanently affected by the First World War, however, and by November 1947, at the age of sixty-one, he could only walk a few steps at a time and had become unemployable. This notwithstanding, on 30 January 1952 he was one of the welcoming committee at Altrincham Town Hall to greet Pte Speakman, who had won his VC in Korea the previous year. Thomas was also able to attend the Coronation parade in 1953.

Having been ill for eight years, John Thomas died at his home at 33 Lowfield Road, Stockport, on 28 February 1954. On 4 March, the day of his funeral, the Salvation Army conducted a service at his home, and later the coffin, draped in a Union Flag, was borne on a gun carriage to Stockport Borough Cemetery for burial (LB/550). Members of the North Staffordshire Regiment escorted the gun carriage and eight of them acted as bearers. The regiment also supplied a bugler who played the 'Last Post'.

Thomas's name is featured on a plaque in the Garrison Church, Lichfield. His medals, apart from the VC, which is not publicly held, were the 1914–15 Star, BWM, VM and Coronation Medal.

W.N. STONE

Cambrai Sector, France, 30 November 1917

(*David Harvey*)

Two hours after the enemy had made a massive counter-attack in the southern half of the Cambrai battlefield on 30 November, the German Army began an equally strong attack against the Bourlon Ridge area. They were determined to retake the ground lost between 20 and 28 November. In terms of scale it was to be a struggle between four fresh German divisions assisted by massive artillery support and three British, the 56th, 2nd and 47th. From high ground in the British positions it was all too easy to see the enemy swarming towards their lines.

The 2nd Division was responsible for the section between the village of Moeuvres and Bourlon Wood to the east. Its front line consisted of the 1st Royal Berkshires to the right, the 1st KRRC to the left and the 17th Royal Fusiliers, with whom we are directly concerned, in the centre.

At 9 a.m. a heavy German bombardment fell on the whole of the 2nd Division lines, much of it in the area of the Bapaume–Cambrai road, and an enemy mass attack quickly followed. To begin with the 17th Royal Fusiliers were in possession of a sap-head known as the Rat's Tail which ran 'almost at right angles from the main British line, 1,000 yards to a point overlooking the enemy's position'. B Coy, under the command of Capt Walter Stone, occupied the section that was closest to the enemy front line. His phone line to HQ was intact, and half an hour after the bombardment began he was ordered to withdraw his company to the main divisional line, leaving a rearguard to cover the retirement, as the position was far too exposed. Using his local knowledge of the situation and seeing the enemy moving along the front from Bourlon Wood to Moeuvres, Stone decided to send back three platoons and kept one back as rearguard under the control of Lt Benzecry.

For the next hour Stone's actions were truly inspirational, as his platoon managed somehow to delay the enemy advance with machine-gun, bayonet, bullet and bomb until the main battalion positions had been reorganised. The enemy were not only overwhelming in numbers but also had the advantage of speed, as they had the protection of dead ground in their advance on the northern side of the Bourlon–Moeuvres road, 800–1,000 yards north of the Rat's Tail. Throughout a tremendous bombardment and storm of bullets, Stone stood on the parapet, with phone in hand, observing the enemy and sending back valuable information, which helped to save the whole line from disaster. He led his gallant group by example of tremendous courage. Eventually the enemy closed in on the small group, and Stone, fighting to the last, was shot through the head. Lt Benzecry was also wounded in the head and fought to the last. By 10.30 a.m. 300 yards of the northern end of the Rat's Tail had fallen to the enemy. At 1 p.m. the 17th Royal Fusiliers reorganised their line, and two advanced companies were withdrawn from the Rat's Tail, but one company remained. By the end of the day the battalion had suffered eleven officer casualties, and 167 other ranks.

The citation for Capt Stone's posthumous VC was published on 13 February 1918:

Cambrai Sector:
Walter Napleton Stone, Lieutenant (Acting Capt.) 3rd, attached 17th (Service), Battalion. Royal Fusiliers. For most conspicuous bravery when in command of a company in an isolated position 1,000 yards in front of the main line, and overlooking the enemy's position. He observed the enemy massing for an attack, and afforded valuable information to battalion headquarters. He was ordered to withdraw his company, leaving a rearguard to cover the withdrawal. The attack developing with unexpected speed, Capt. Stone sent three platoons back and remained with the rearguard himself. He stood on the parapet with the telephone under a tremendous bombardment, observing the enemy, and continued to send back valuable information until the wire was cut by his orders. The rearguard was eventually surrounded and cut to pieces, and Capt. Stone was seen fighting to the last, till he was shot through the head. The extraordinary coolness of this officer and the accuracy of his information enabled dispositions to be made just in time to save the line and avert disaster.

Three days later the battalion commander received a letter of congratulation on the announcement of Capt Stone's VC from Maj Gen C.E. Pereira, commander of the 2nd Division.

Stone's parents received the medal on 2 March 1918. In the same year his father, Edward Stone, died and one of his brothers, Arthur, was killed in action on 2 October when serving as a temporary lieutenant-colonel attached to the 16th Lancashire Fusiliers. He held the DSO. He formerly played football for Cambridge and Kent and was a well-known rifle shot.

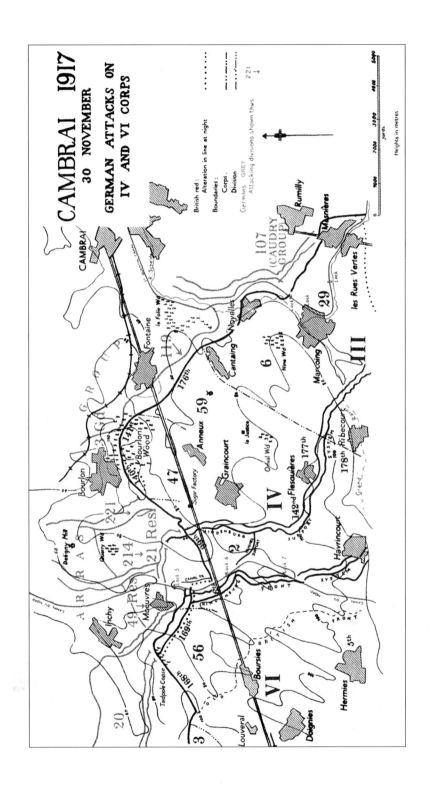

Walter Stone was subsequently commemorated on the Cambrai Memorial, Panels 3 and 4, and in the South Transept of St Mary's, Shrewsbury, possibly the church where his mother used to worship. His name is also included on the Shropshire County Roll of Honour and appears on the stone wall of Greenwich Cemetery, Well Hall Road, London SE.

Reginald, a third brother, served as a naval commander, and like Arthur also held the DSO.

Walter's BWM and VM medals were issued to his family on 30 September 1922. His VC is not publicly held.

Walter Napleton Stone, youngest son of Edward Stone FSA and Emily Frances Stone, was born at Lansdowne Place, Blackheath, on 7 December 1891. Two older brothers were Arthur and Reginald. Walter was educated at Harrow and went up to Pembroke College, Cambridge, in 1910. In 1914 the family moved to 21 Vanbrugh Park in Shrewsbury. Edward Stone, a solicitor,

Moeuvres British Cemetery (*Peter Batchelor*)

Cambrai Memorial (*Donald C. Jennings*)

died in 1918, and his widow remained at Vanburgh Park until 1936, dying in 1943.

Like so many young men at the time, Walter decided to emigrate to Canada and in 1913 met Mabel Maud Jukes from Ontario, who had a son by him, Reginald Merville, in Toronto on 21 May 1914. Walter's address was 66 Bloor Street East. His son became an American citizen in 1982. Walter Stone returned to England on the announcement of war and joined the Inns of Court OTC on 9 November 1914 and entered Sandhurst on 29 December 1914. He was commissioned into the 3rd Royal Fusiliers on 12 May 1915 and attached to the 17th Battalion, which arrived in France on 5 January 1916.

A.M.C. MCREADY DIARMID

*Moeuvres Sector, France, 30 November/
1 December 1917*

(*David Harvey*)

On 30 November the 17th (S) Battalion Middlesex Regiment (6th Brigade) 2nd Division was in support positions on the west side of the still unfinished Canal du Nord, just south of the Bapaume–Cambrai road, and at 8.30 a.m. the enemy bombardment began to fall on its lines. The battalion had been relieved the night before by the 1st King's, and two companies. A and C were in dugouts just south of the Cambrai road in K.2.b. D Coy was to its rear, also in dugouts, and B was in reserve in dugouts close to Lock 6.

At 9 a.m. companies were instructed to 'stand to', and D Coy moved forward to take the place of A, and B Coy took D's place south of the road, when two enemy *Flammenwerfer* were seen in action to the north-east of Lock 5. They were quickly knocked out by Lewis-gun fire. A short time later C Coy moved up to the 1st King's HQ after it had been heavily attacked by the enemy, who emerged from the shattered houses of Moeuvres and left the left company of the 1st King's in disarray.

By then the enemy, moving down trenches, had almost reached the Cambrai–Bapaume road from 15.c. and d. At this point Capt McReady Diarmid, leading a spirited attack, drove the enemy back and by 2 p.m. was in a position about 500 yards to the south-west of Lock 5, or G.20.d.4.2. However, owing to a shortage of bombs further advance was not possible. Progress over the open would have also been prevented by the presence of masses of wire.

By nightfall on the 30th the enemy had gained a few hundred yards of trenches along the front of the 6th Brigade, but at a considerable cost in casualties. They continued to bomb their way down the Hindenburg Line trenches and down both sides of the Canal du Nord, but their attempts were repulsed.

At about 8 a.m. the next morning the enemy made a series of strong bombing attacks, one being made down Edda Weg, but part of C Coy of the 17th (S)

Middlesex was able to beat them back without losing any ground. The enemy tried again, and this time made some progress and endeavoured to capture the 1st King's Battalion HQ, despite the heroic efforts of B Coy of the Middlesex to stop them. All officers of this company were later reported as missing.

It was at this point, when the men were 'tired and shaken', that Capt McReady Diarmid of D Coy called for volunteers from his company. Equipped with a plentiful supply of bombs, he rushed forward to attack the enemy which single-handedly he managed to push back up the trench. The official report said: 'By throwing all the bombs himself this officer killed and otherwise disposed of 94 of the enemy – 67 dead and 27 wounded were actually counted after the recapture of the trench, a feat which can hardly, if ever, have been equalled in the past.' Sadly, he did not live very long himself, as he was killed by an enemy bomb. At nightfall six platoons of the 2nd HLI relieved the now totally exhausted B and D Companies, and on the night of 3/4 December the battalion was relieved and moved back to camp at Hermies. During the operations from 26 November to 3 December the battalion had seven officer casualties and 180 other ranks, and against this the bodies of 150 of the enemy were found dead in the trenches.

McReady Diarmid was awarded a posthumous VC for his remarkable deed, together with his leadership on the previous day, the citation being published in the *London Gazette* of 15 March 1918:

T/Lieutenant Acting Captain Allastair Malcolm Cluny McReady (formerly Arthur Malcolm McReady-Drew), Temporary Lieutenant (Acting Capt.), late 17th (Service) Battalion. Middlesex Regiment. For most conspicuous bravery and brilliant leadership. When the enemy penetrated some distance into our position and the situation was extremely critical, Capt. McReady-Diarmid at once led his company forward through a heavy barrage. He immediately engaged the enemy, with such success that he drove them back at least 300 yards, causing numerous casualties and capturing 27 prisoners. The following day the enemy again attacked and drove back another company which had lost all of its officers. This gallant officer at once called for volunteers and attacked. He drove them back again for 300 yards, with heavy casualties. Throughout this attack, Capt. McReady-Diarmid led the way himself, and it was absolutely and entirely due to his marvellous throwing of bombs that this ground was regained. His absolute disregard for danger, his cheerfulness and coolness at a trying time inspired all who saw him. This most gallant officer was eventually killed by bomb when the enemy had been driven right back to their original starting-point.

Back at home his deeds were written up in the press as a 'bomb-throwing display'.

Relief panel on the Louverval Memorial (also known as the Cambrai Memorial and the Tank Memorial), designed by the sculptor Charles Sargeant Jagger (*Peter Batchelor*)

Since his body was not recovered, his name is listed on the Louverval Memorial, Panel 9. His widow was presented with the posthumous medal by the King at Windsor Castle on 20 April 1918. After the war Diarmid's name was included on the Dursley War Memorial and he was also commemorated at the Victoria College, Jersey. In 1929 his eleven-year-old daughter Alison, wearing her late father's VC, assisted Earl Jellicoe in laying a wreath at the base of the

Cenotaph on 11 November 1929. In 1973 her 83-year-old mother presented her late husband's medals to the Middlesex Regiment, and they were later acquired by the National Army Museum.

Arthur Malcolm Cluny McReady Diarmid was born in Southgate, London, on 21 March 1888 and educated at Queen Elizabeth's, Barnet, Ealing Grammar and Victoria College, Jersey. His parents' address in Acton was at 71 Goldsmith Avenue, where he had lived for a number of years.

Cambrai Memorial (*Donald C. Jennings*)

Diarmid made his home in Dursley, Gloucestershire, and joined the London University OTC on the outbreak of war, when he was twenty-six years of age. He was commissioned on 10 March 1915 and served with the 4th Middlesex Battalion until November 1916, when he was placed on loan to the 14th (Reserve) Battalion He was promoted to lieutenant on 1 July 1917, and later returned to the 4th Battalion. In February 1917 he was serving with the 17th (S) Middlesex Regiment (1st Football), which had been raised in mid-December 1914 by the Rt. Hon. W. Joynson Hicks MP. He was promoted to acting captain on 26 October 1917.

At some point Diarmid was wounded and was invalided home, where he recuperated in Dursley. It was possible that at this time he met Hilda, who lived locally and was a nurse. The couple married in September 1915 and later had one daughter, Alison. Their home address was Springfield, Dursley. Hilda might have later lived in the Hastings area of Sussex.

Diarmid's original surname was in fact Drew: according to his National Archives file he was asked by his colonel to change it, as there were too many men with the name of Drew in the regiment and he thought that a name change would obviate confusion. So on 10 September 1915 Drew's name was changed by deed poll from Arthur Malcolm McReady Drew to Allastair Malcolm Cluny McReady Diarmid.

G.H.T. PATON

Gonnelieu, France, 1 December 1917

(David Harvey)

The 2nd Guards Brigade of the Guards Division took part in an ill-conceived attack against the undemolished village of Fontaine-Notre-Dame and Bourlon Wood on 27 November 1917 during attempts to capture the Bourlon Ridge to the west of Cambrai. Four days later the Guards were once again actively involved, this time in the southern half of the Cambrai battlefield. The enemy had managed to capture the village of Gonnelieu to the south of the Bonavis–Péronne road on 30 November, and the 3rd Guards Brigade was ordered to retake it on 1 December. Troops set off for Metz-en-Couture to the north-west and in the afternoon left for the village of Gouzeaucourt to the south-east. They were then ordered to change direction slightly and move northwards over the Gouzeaucourt–Trescault road, where they halted to the north-west of Gouzeaucourt.

At a meeting at the HQ of the Guards the GOC of 16th Brigade, Gen Walker informed Viscount Gort that his brigade was intending to make a night attack against the Quentin Ridge and Gonnelieu that evening. If the brigade succeeded, the 3rd Guards Brigade would be called upon as relief and would continue the assault. But the hastily arranged plan for a night attack did not meet with Gort's approval, and his suspicions were quickly verified, as the attack of the 16th Brigade was a total failure. This was partly because of confusion in the darkness and the unfamiliar ground and a massive enemy machine-gun barrage. Gort feared that the Guards' attempts to take the village during the day would meet with the same results. There was to be no artillery preparation and thirty-seven promised tanks failed to appear; indeed there was very little tank assistance at all.

At 6.20 a.m. the 4th Grenadier Guards and 1st Welsh Guards on the right moved from the railway line that ran down a valley to the east of Gouzeaucourt and moved up the Quentin Ridge to the south-west of Gonnelieu. With no cover the Welsh Guards on the right were the hardest hit. To the left No. 3 Coy of the

Grenadier Guards fought its way through to the outskirts of Gonnelieu but were unable to progress further without tank or artillery support. A Lewis gun was established at the cemetery in the north-west of the village, which briefly assisted the progress of No. 2 and 4 Companies, but the enemy quickly dealt with this threat and the attackers were forced to retreat.

However, some platoons of No. 3 Coy did actually manage to reach the main street of Gonnelieu, but were later forced to withdraw. Capt Paton in command of No. 4 Coy, realising that No. 3 Coy on his left was now having to withdraw and that there was no sign of the Welsh Guards on his right, was faced with a very difficult decision. He decided to stay put but realised that on his left were a mixed medley of men without their officers and decided that they had to be reorganised. Leaping from his trench he ran across the open ground through a rain of machine-gun bullets and somehow managed to go from trench to trench in order to encourage the men from groups from various regiments – all the time in full view of German machine-gunners. In his efforts to save the left flank he had led a charmed life, but his luck eventually ran out and he fell mortally wounded. The battalion did manage to link up with the Welsh Guards and the brigade line when the line became more secure, but no further advance was possible. Later the adjutant, Capt Gerard, came up to gather information for Viscount Gort, who himself was badly wounded in the same action. Gonnelieu was not recaptured, and the British front line at the end of the Battle of Cambrai a few days later ran to the west of it.

The commanding officer of the Grenadier Guards, Col Sir Henry Streatfield, wrote to Paton's parents:

> Amongst all who have laid down their lives upon the field of Honour, there is no one that I regret the loss of more than your son. He was a born soldier and leader of men, beloved by his brother officers and esteemed and respected by his men, and his loss to the regiment is a great one. We, his old comrades, will long remember him with affection.

Viscount Gort wrote on 14 December:

> His loss was a great personal grief to me, as he was extremely popular with everybody, both officers and men; always cheerful in difficulties, and above all, an officer who had a wonderful aptitude for soldiering which I am confident would have carried him a long way had he been spared to develop it. I only write because I feel I should like to express to you my feelings of gratitude and admiration for the loyal and unselfish way your son carried out his duty, which was in every way worthy of the best traditions of the regiment.

Paton was buried at Metz-en-Couture Communal Cemetery, British Extension, Plot II, E, 24, and his headstone carries the inscrption 'Bright is their glory now boundless their joy above.' At the beginning of the same row is the grave of Lt Cdr Patrick Shaw Stewart. After his death *The Sphere* published a picture of Paton wearing a kilt (which an officer in the Grenadier Guards would never have worn when on active service).

Gort wrote again to Paton's parents after the announcement of his posthumous VC was published in the *London Gazette* on 13 February 1918: 'I need hardly tell you how proud I am about it, as he is the first Grenadier officer to gain the V.C. this war, or, indeed, since the Crimea.' The citation was as follows:

George Henry Tatham Paton, M.C., Lieutenant (Acting Capt.) Grenadier Guards. For most conspicuous bravery and self-sacrifice. When a unit on his left was driven back, thus leaving his flank in the air and his company practically surrounded, he fearlessly exposed himself to readjust the line, walking up and down within fifty yards of the enemy under a withering fire. He personally removed some wounded men and was the last to leave the village. Later, he again readjusted the line, exposing himself regardless of all danger the whole time, and when the enemy four times counter-attacked he sprang each time upon the parapet, deliberately risking his life, and being eventually mortally wounded, in order to stimulate his command. After the enemy had broken through on his left, he again mounted the parapet, and with a few men – who were inspired by his great example – forced them once more to withdraw, thereby undoubtedly saving the left flank.

Paton's parents were presented with their son's medal at Buckingham Palace on 2 March. Later George Paton's name was commemorated in the book of remembrance at St Mary's Church, Bow, where there is a plaque to his regiment. He is also remembered at Dunoon, Strathclyde, where his name is listed on the war memorial on the Promenade.

His father had served on the Argyllshire County Council for Innellan and Toward for several years, and had been President of the Caledonian Society of London since 1913. Both father and son had been associated with the Royal Scottish Corporation, and both men took a keen interest in Scottish charities. The family had a home at Woolviston House, Whyteleaf, Surrey, and Sir George, as he had become, died in 1934 when on his way back from holiday in the south of France. He was buried at Putney Vale Cemetery in the family plot, and the cemetery also has a path called Paton's Path. Lady Paton lived on at Portley, Caterham-on-the-Hill, Surrey. Her son's VC is with the Grenadier Guards in London.

George Paton (*Anon*)

❖❖❖

Metz-en-Couture (*Donald C. Jennings*)

George Henry Tatham Paton was born in Innellan, Argyllshire, Scotland, on 3 October 1895, the only son of George William Paton of Messrs Ross, Corbett & Co., of Greenock, and Etta Tatham, who came from Edinburgh. The couple were married in 1886 and also had one daughter. George senior later became chairman of Bryant & May and of the British Match Corporation. He was knighted in 1930.

Young George was educated at Rottingdean School and Clifton College. He entered the Army in September 1914 when he was nearly nineteen years old. He was gazetted second lieutenant on 1 October and joined the 17th City of London Regiment, being made full lieutenant on 3 October 1915. In January 1916 he was transferred to the Grenadier Guards and joined the 4th Battalion on 23 July as a member of No. 2 Coy. He took part in the Somme fighting in September and became an acting captain on 4 June 1917, being placed in charge of No. 4 Coy. On the first day of Third Ypres he took part in an attack near Boesinghe and in August won the MC: 'For most conspicuous bravery and self-sacrifice during August 1917.' Four months later he won a posthumous VC at Gonnelieu on 1 December.

GOBIND SINGH

East of Peizière, France, 1 December 1917

(*David Harvey*)

Before 20 November 1917, the opening day of the Battle of Cambrai, the British front line in the Épehy sector, north-west of St Quentin, bent round to the south-west of Gonnelieu and Villers-Guislain and then bypassed Little Priel Farm, Le Tombois Farm and Gillemont Farm.

After the initial Allied success on the 20th, the enemy, heavily supported with fresh troops, began an equally successful counter-attack ten days later. Thus by 1 December many of the earlier British gains had been wiped out and the British front positions were often back where they had been on 20 November. The new British line had been pushed back even beyond their original start line and was now established to the west side of Gonnelieu and to the south close to Peizière and Épehy.

In the previous August two men had already won the VC in this sector, one close to a strongpoint known as the Knoll, south-west of Vendhuille, and the other to the east of the village of Lempire. Now, in the last stages of the Battle of Cambrai, a third was to be gained, by Lance-Dafadar Gobind Singh of the 28th Light Cavalry, attached 2nd Lancers (Gardner's Horse) (4th Cavalry Division). He gained the coveted award in a most extraordinary set of circumstances when three times he volunteered and successfully carried crucial messages over a distance of one and a half miles between battalion and Brigade HQ.

On 30 November, in a move to try and retake some of the ground captured by the recent successful enemy counter-attacks, two Indian cavalry divisions, the 4th and 5th, were to be thrown into a gap in the infantry line. At 4.15 a.m. on the following morning orders were received that the Mhow Brigade (4th Cavalry Division) was to take part in a mounted attack towards the village of Villers-Guislain, south of Gonnelieu, which was being desperately fought for by both sides. Their specific task was to 'gallop' Pigeon, Quail and Targelle ravines to the south of Villers-Guislain and then form a defensive flank to the south-east.

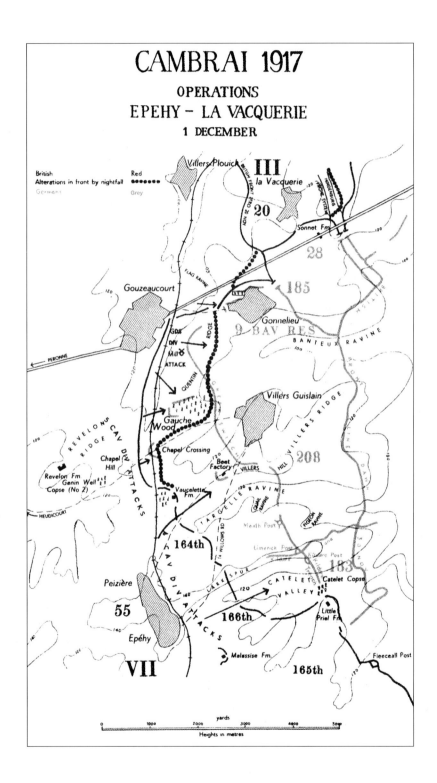

At 5.30 a.m. the brigade (consisting of the 2nd Lancers, 6th Inniskilling Dragoons and 38th Central India Horse) concentrated to the west of Peizière, and, moving through the village, formed up behind a railway cutting on the other side of the village in a position of readiness. Owing to a sudden barrage of high explosives the regiment was ordered to move back several hundred yards to safer positions in the north of the village. The 2nd Lancers were delayed at the rendezvous as their lances had been left behind and had to be brought up by cart.

At 8.30 a.m. the three battalions, accompanied by a section of 11th Machine Gun Squadron, moved off beyond the railway bank in order to attack the German-held trenches. The 2nd Lancers moved through Peizière into Épehy, where they turned to leave the village via the level crossing east of the cemetery. They began to pass through British infantry lines and the road then forked at a crucifix. The road to the left ran over the ridge in an east-north-east direction and into their objective, Targelle Ravine. The road to the right led down the side of the valley to Catelet Copse to the west of Le Priel Farm. Because of better cover Maj Knowles in charge of C Squadron chose the route to the right, and he would then turn northward, gaining Targelle Ravine from the east. The four squadrons 'advanced in open column of troop columns extended'.

The squadrons moved across the shallow valley, which was about four hundred yards wide and was 'covered with rank, dead grass, and pitted here and there with fresh shell holes'. To the left was a bare slope which climbed the road from the crucifix. About a mile away was a clump of four elm trees known as 'Limerick Post', which had been captured by the enemy the day before.

C Squadron had barely begun its charge down the valley before a tremendous burst of machine-gun fire burst out from both sides, as well as from Kildare Trench, which barred the way to the front. However, the charge continued, with the squadron increasing its pace to a gallop as the landscape suddenly became full of fleeing grey figures. Despite their vulnerability to machine-gun fire, the squadron did not waver, and having travelled about a mile they were pulled up short by a line of wire which stretched across Kildare Lane, a fortified sunken road. Some horses quickly jumped the wire before two gaps were found in it, and they then moved through them down to the road. D Squadron used the same gaps and entered the road to the right of C Squadron. Some of the enemy fled for their lives as the squadron set to with lance and sword.

At about this time Col Turner was killed by machine-gun fire as he passed through one of the gaps in the wire, and Maj Knowles assumed command. The cavalry, being fired on by machine-guns from the front and flank, were now unable to proceed, and a garrison was set up at Kildare Trench and Kildare Post on the slope of Lark Spur. As the day continued the dismounted Lancers strongly defended their front-line positions, and some even tried to reach Pigeon Ravine by foot.

Catelet Copse was about a hundred yards to the right, and the low ground beyond it was under a continuous barrage of enemy small-arms and machine-gun fire. Little Priel Farm was about 1,200 yards away to the south-east on rising ground. The enemy was to the 'right rear', 1,200 yards away to the south side of the valley. On the left flank rising ground gave a short field of fire and to the left rear about 1,000 yards away was Limerick Post, which was manned by German machine-guns that were causing casualties to the Inniskilling Dragoons.

At about 10 a.m. the right flank made contact with infantry positions of 165th Brigade holding ground around Little Priel Farm. Soon the enemy attacked from the 'right rear' and were driven back by members of B Squadron, and at 11 a.m. an attack to the left died away. Parties of the enemy advancing from Limerick Post were pushed back by bombing parties of the Inniskillings. As it appeared to Brigade HQ that the 2nd Lancers might well have been 'swallowed up' within the German lines, three dismounted squadrons of the 38th Central India Horse were sent forward in support, but they made little progress against enemy machine-gun fire, in particular from Limerick Post.

Volunteers were called at this point to take a message giving the Lancers' positions at Kildare Trench to Brigade HQ in the north-eastern outskirts of Peizière. Of those who came forward, Sowar Jot Ram and Lance-Dafadar Gobind Singh were selected and given identical messages. They started off at a gallop. Jot Ram took a right-hand course and was shot down as he passed Limerick Post, Gobind Singh took the lower ground to the south and had travelled half a mile before his horse was killed by machine-gun fire. Playing possum he waited until he considered that he was no longer being watched and then got up, rolling over and over as dead before getting up again and running. Although he was shot at by the enemy he continuously pretended to be hit, but all the time was moving closer to Brigade HQ, which he eventually reached at about 10.50 a.m.

Having delivered his message he was then given a reply and a fresh horse. He took the higher ground to the south of the valley until he reached close to the German post. Having covered two-thirds of the way, his new horse was then shot and he finally made his way into the sunken road and his regiment.

An hour later another message had to be taken to Brigade HQ, and once more Gobind Singh stepped forward. He was told that he had already done his share, but he reasoned that it would be sensible if he took the message as he knew the ground better than anyone else. Taking a different route this time from the direction of Catelet Copse, he rode on right through the barrage, and when he was half-way through Épehy his horse was cut in half by a direct hit. He then ran on, trying all the time to keep out of enemy sight, and eventually reached Brigade

HQ at Peizière just before noon. He offered to return with a new message, but this time was not allowed to.

An order to retire was later received by the adjutant, and the garrison at Kildare Lane began to leave at 5 p.m., taking with them the body of Col Turner, their wounded, and their unwounded horses. Moving behind British infantry lines, they moved up the southern road to Lempire. From there they moved back in the dark to Épehy and 'joined the remains of the led horse party half a mile to the west of the village'.

Regimental casualties were just over a hundred, but the villages of Épehy and Peizière, which had been shelled by the enemy all day and which were only protected by a small infantry force, were saved and possibly a major enemy breakthrough prevented. The following day the regiment moved south to the outskirts of Ste-Emilie, and on the 3rd the brigade marched back to billets to rest and reorganise. The British lines at the end of the Cambrai battle were a thousand yards to the east of Épehy.

For his outstanding gallantry Gobind Singh was awarded a very well-deserved VC, which was published in the *London Gazette* of 11 January 1918:

> (No. 2008), Gobind Singh, Lance-Dafadar, Indian Cavalry. For most conspicuous bravery and devotion to duty in thrice volunteering to carry messages between the regiment and Brigade Headquarters, a distance of one and a half miles over open ground, which was under observation and heavy fire of the enemy. He succeeded each time in delivering his message, although on each occasion his horse was shot and he was compelled to finish his journey on foot.

Gobind Singh attended an investiture at Buckingham Palace on 6 February. On the same day as he received his medal from the King, he was given a reception, together with two Indian cavalry officers who were visiting London as guests of the nation. He was presented with a piece of silver plate, together with a gold watch. Those present at this reception included Gen Sir O'Moore Creagh, VC, late Commander-in-Chief India, and Lt Gen Sir Pertab Singhji, a distinguished soldier who had fought in a great many campaigns, including a number in the First World War.

Born in Damoe Village, Jodhpur, India, on 7 December 1887, Gobind Singh was a member of the same tribe to which the Maharajah Sir Pertab Singhji belonged. He joined the Jodhpur Lancers of the Indian Army and throughout the war he

Pigeon Ravine Cemetery (*Peter Batchelor*)

served with the 28th Light Cavalry, with whom he left India for France as part of the Indian Expeditionary Force. He served as lance-dafadar attached to the 2nd Lancers (Gardner's Horse) Indian Cavalry.

After the war he was made a jemadar in the 28th Cavalry and remained in the Army, and was still serving in 1934. He died two days after his 55th birthday at Nagaur, Rajputana, on 9 December 1942, and his body was cremated. His medals included the 1914–15 Star and the Order of British India 2nd Class (Bahadur). His VC is not held publicly.

A.M. LASCELLES

Marcoing, France, 3 December 1917

(David Harvey)

During the morning of 30 November the 14th Durham Light Infantry (S) Battalion (18th Brigade) 6th Division was sent to occupy a section of the Hindenburg Line on Highland Ridge just to the north of the village of Villers-Plouich. On its arrival patrols were sent out making contact with troops on its front and the right. The battalion remained in this position until 2 December, when it received orders to relieve the 1st Royal Inniskilling Fusiliers, a unit of the 29th Division, in trenches east of the St Quentin Canal at Marcoing. The Durhams, moving up in darkness, took over the front line before dawn. The right flank of the battalion was 'thrown back along the canal in touch with troops of the 29th Division to the south; the left joined the 1st King's Shropshire Light Infantry.'

The Durhams had three companies in the front line and one in support at a bend in the canal. There was no wire in front of the sector, and soon after 10 a.m. an enemy barrage came down on the whole line, which was followed by an enemy advance against the troops south of the canal, as well as on A Coy of the Durhams, which was occupying a poor and shallow trench. A Coy commander, Capt Arthur Lascelles (attached from the 3rd Battalion), asked for artillery support as his company was unable to stand the enemy onslaught. Although wounded, Lascelles, together with L/Sgt Wilson, quickly gathered twelve men together and began a counter-attack. Although the odds must have been at least five to one they were able to somehow drive the enemy from the trench.

Communication had been severed by the bombardment, and the enemy launched a second attack after another heavy barrage. This time Lascelles' company was driven back and he was taken prisoner, and the enemy were then able to set up a machine-gun position in the house by the lock. A reserve company then came up and drove the enemy out of the trench, and taking advantage of the resulting confusion Lascelles managed to escape from the clutches of the enemy.

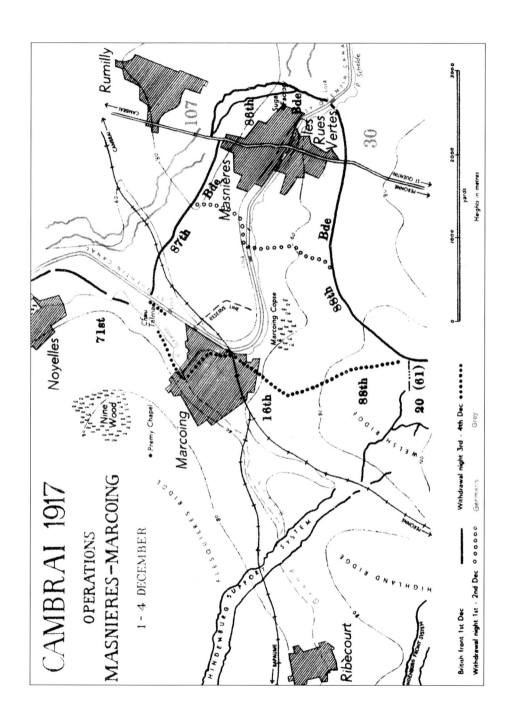

223

A counter-attack by a reserve company of the Durhams drove the enemy out again, causing them heavy casualties, but in turn the Durhams suffered badly from the machine-guns in the lock house.

At about 12.15 p.m. a third enemy attack was launched, and although the right front trench was lost once more, a barricade was set up to safeguard the flank. However, by now there were no bombs left to defend it with. The enemy continued to press all along the line, and the Durhams, as well as the Shropshires to the left, were beginning to give ground, while from Masnières a column of German infantry could be seen advancing. In the circumstances it was decided that the position was untenable and that the best thing would be to evacuate the rest of the battalion over the railway bridge at Marcoing. This was achieved without enemy observation. From a sunken road about 650 yards west of Marcoing troops were organised to assist troops of the 29th Division on the right, and a line was occupied on a ridge to the south-west of Marcoing Copse from which a counter-attack was launched, which prevented the enemy from moving down the north side of the canal towards the crossing.

At 4 p.m., with the help of a company of the 8th Bedfords, the Durhams advanced to the attack. The canal had been bridged by a barge that the Durhams used to cross by, and they were then involved in fierce fighting on the railway line. A second company from the Bedfords arrived in support, and the companies, together with the Durhams, were able to push on and to cover the railway bridge as well as the barge bridge. Despite fierce enemy resistance and a decline in bomb supply, the attackers were able to hold on until 10.15 p.m., when they were ordered to withdraw. Once this was done sappers were instructed to blow up both bridges. The battalion war diary noted: 'There was some trouble about the barge bridge, as the barge had become stuck in the mud owing to the water in the canal going down.' It was probably destroyed by shellfire or fire. The survivors from the Durhams went back to a position to the north-east of Ribecourt in the Hindenburg Support line by morning. Of the 450 men who took part in the operations, 276 had become casualties; and for his work as A Coy commander Lascelles was awarded the VC.

Reporting on the operation, Lt Col J.B. Rosher wrote in the war diary:

Officers and men fought splendidly throughout the day. Had it not been for the manner in which they stood the bombardment with its little cover, and the readiness with which they responded to all calls for counter-attack, the whole force North of the Canal must have been captured, as the enemy forces used against us were very heavy, and had he once penetrated to the BRIDGE nothing more could have been done.

Canal at Marcoing (*Peter Batchelor*)

The citation for Lascelles' VC was published in the *London Gazette* of 11 January 1918 as follows:

Arthur Moore Lascelles, Capt., 3rd Durham Light Infantry. For most conspicuous bravery, initiative and devotion to duty when in command of his company in a very exposed position. After a very heavy bombardment, during which Capt. Lascelles was wounded, the enemy attacked in strong force, but was driven off, success being due in a great degree to the fine example set by this officer, who, refusing to allow his wound to be dressed, continued to encourage his men and organize the defence. Shortly afterwards the enemy again attacked and captured the trench, taking several of his men prisoners. Capt. Lascelles at once jumped on to the parapet, and followed by the remainder of his company, 12 men only, rushed across under very heavy machine-gun fire and drove over 60 of the enemy back, thereby saving a most critical situation. He was untiring in reorganizing the position, but shortly afterwards the enemy again attacked and captured the trench and Capt.

Lascelles who escaped later. The remarkable determination and gallantry of this officer in the course of operations, during which he received two further wounds, afforded an inspiring example to all.

In the process of winning his VC, Lascelles was severely wounded by gunshot wounds to his head and right elbow, and was admitted to No. 48 CCS on the same day. He subsequently lost the use of his right arm and was invalided home, arriving at Folkestone on the 12th. The *Western Mail* of 14 January quoted an account given to a reporter by Captain Lascelles when in hospital:

. . . today he related to me the story of how a body of miners only about 60 strong withstood the attack of an overwhelmingly stronger force of the enemy. His company was in a very exposed position, when, about ten o'clock at night, the Germans opened a heavy bombardment with trench mortars and aerial darts. Early on Capt. Lascelles was wounded, and in a matter of 25 minutes or so his company sustained heavy casualties, but he declined to allow his wounds to be dressed. Preferring to continue to encourage his men by a fine example which so encouraged these miners that he was able to organize his defence successfully. 'My company,' remarked Capt. Lascelles, 'was on the right of my battalion, and the position had become so precarious that had my company given way it would have meant that the whole of the battalion would have been enfiladed and the Bosches enabled to get round to the rear. That would have resulted in seriously jeopardizing the position, and near by was a Welsh Regiment, who, let me add, have done notable work in that particular part of the front. Shortly afterwards the enemy renewed the attack, and there ensued a period of bitter fighting. There was no question of retiring – it could not be done. Very soon the Bosche smashed my right bombing post, which enabled him to enfilade the whole of the trench occupied by my company. Two machine-guns were in action, and at eleven o'clock, after an hour's fighting, the trench for a distance on the right of 250 yards was non-existent. The trench, of a depth of only about three feet, which forced us to keep our heads under the parapet, was soon reached, and several of my men were captured. By this time there were only about a dozen of us left. So it meant neck or nothing. About 50 yards to my rear I saw a number of Germans approaching. I sent a corporal and three men to try and hold them, or otherwise the company on my left would have been attacked in the rear. Meanwhile, what now remained of my company had a go at the Bosches. I at once jumped up on the parapet, and followed by only 12 men, rushed across under heavy machine-gun fire and drove about 60 of the enemy back. I was, unfortunately, wounded again, being hit in the elbow just as I went over the top; but I was able to reorganize the defence. Soon afterwards the enemy again attacked and captured the trench and myself. I was in their hands for a couple of hours, and when I recovered consciousness, after exhaustion, a big Hun took possession of my glasses and all I had, struck me with his fist, and kicked me. I escaped later as a result of a counter-attack by the rear, but it was due to the untiring devotion of a body of miners, mostly from the North, with a number from the South, that we were able to hold the ground. A more heroic company of men no officer would wish to command.'

Lascelles was presented with his VC by the King at Buckingham Palace on 23 March 1918, and returned home to Olton, where he slowly regained his strength. However, he probably began to be increasingly restive at being out of action, and despite still having a useless right arm he volunteered once more for active service and returned to the Army base at Etaples on 14 October. This time he was attached to the 15th Battalion, part of the 64th Brigade of the 21st Division, and he had returned to service in the field at Inchy on 27 October. Nine days later, in the final operations of the war, the battalion advanced through Mormal Forest without encountering any opposition, and soon moved towards the Sambre river to the south-west of Mauberge and then moved eastwards.

The HQ of 21st Division was based at Berlaimont, where at 7 a.m. on 7 November the 110th Brigade of the 21st Division began an advance, experiencing no opposition. The 64th Brigade with the 15th Battalion set off later and passed through the lines of 110th Brigade, and was held up by heavy machine-gun fire from Limont-Fontaine. Later in the afternoon the brigade made progress and captured not only Limont-Fontaine but also Eclaibes, together with one hundred prisoners. It was probably during the fighting in the afternoon that Capt Lascelles was killed, one of three officers and over a hundred other ranks to become casualties. His file at the National Archives states that in 1919 his body was exhumed from an isolated grave on the southern outskirts of Limont-Fontaine. It was re-buried 3 miles to the south at Doullers Communal Cemetery Extension, II, G, 24. The remains of forty-five men were brought in from Limont-Fontaine Cemetery German Extension. The inscription on his headstone is 'Utterly regardless of fear he died for God King and Country.'

At the time of Lascelles' death, his home address was 9 Richmond Road, Olton, Warwickshire, but his widow later lived at 110 New Avenue, Acocks Green, Birmingham, before moving to Merionethshire. His name was commemorated in several places, including the regimental book of remembrance kept in the regimental chapel in Durham Cathedral. Other commemorations were on the family grave at Pennal Cemetery, in the church there and on the war memorial. Others were at Tywyn Memorial, Gwynedd, Edinburgh University War Memorial and the University College of North Wales War Memorial.

In 1983 his medals were purchased for £18,500 by the regiment. Apart from the VC and MC, they included the 1914–15 Star (South African Issue), BWM, and VM.

Lascelles' son Reginald also had an Army career and became a lieutenant-colonel, dying in 1984.

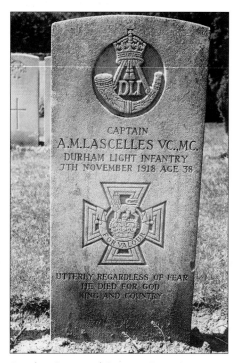

Dourlers Communal Cemetery Extension, France (*Donald C. Jennings*)

Arthur Moore Lascelles came from a Welsh family of military and naval stock, son of John and Mary Elizabeth (née Cotton) Lascelles. He was born at Wilby Lodge, Nightingale Lane, Streatham, London, on 12 October 1880, and his home address was Penmaen, Pennal, Machynlleth, Merionethshire, North Wales. His father's occupation was given as 'gentleman'.

Lascelles was educated at Malvern School and Uppingham School (May 1895–December 1898), Bangor College, later University College of North Wales (1899), and he then studied medicine at Edinburgh University (1899–1902). In his twenty-second year he decided to leave the country and emigrate to South Africa to begin a career as a professional soldier, joining the Cape Mounted Rifles as a trooper on 11 August just after the Boer War. He possibly came across John Sherwood-Kelly, another future holder of the VC at this time, as he also served in the same regiment. On 8 December 1907, when he was twenty-five, Lascelles married Sophie Hardiman at Idutywa, Transkei, South Africa.

The Cape Mounted Rifles became the 1st South African Mounted Rifles. Lascelles served in the De Wet Rebellion and also in the successful campaigns in German South-West Africa from 1914 to 1915. By October 1915 he had reached the rank of quartermaster sergeant, and after serving in South Africa for thirteen years decided that he wished to return to Europe. He subsequently obtained his

228

discharge on 10 October and left for England, with his wife and son, arriving in November. By 28 December 1915 he had obtained a commission in the Durham Light Infantry (SR) as a second lieutenant in the 3rd Battalion. He attended an officers' training course in Cambridge from 1 January to 3 February, which was later followed by a sniping course at Rugby in July.

Lascelles served in France and Flanders when attached to the 14th Battalion from July 1916, arriving in France on the 16th. He was wounded on the Somme by shrapnel on 18 September and was invalided to England four days later suffering from gunshot wounds. On 6 February 1917 he was posted to the 11th Battalion and joined them on the 18th. He was posted again to the 14th Battalion on 14 May, joining them on the 29th. On 15 June he won the MC when taking part in a daylight raid in the Bis Sector near Loos. The citation (1 January 1918) was as follows:

> In the Bis action, near Loos, on 15 June 1917, he showed great courage, endurance and initiative in a very successful daylight raid. He commanded a party of forty other ranks. He led them with great gallantry, capturing all his objectives, taking five prisoners and killing twenty Germans. He conducted operations throughout with great coolness and it was largely due to his fine work that the withdrawal of the whole raid was carried out without a casualty. He was last to leave the trench. The success of the raid was largely due to the valuable reconnaissance carried out by this officer before the raid. This officer has many times been brought to notice for his gallantry in action and he commanded his company very well.

On 22 July 1917 he was admitted to No. 42 CCS with a dislocated knee and returned to England for ten days' leave from 3 to 13 August. He was made lieutenant on 1 July 1917, acting captain on 20 July to 18 August and then temporary captain.

During the war his wife worked in a canteen for workers in a munitions factory in the Midlands. The couple had a young son, born in 1909, who was named Reginald after a younger brother of Lascelles, who had drowned in India in 1904 when also serving with the Army.

J.S. EMERSON

Hindenburg Line, North of La Vacquerie, France,
6 December 1917

(*David Harvey*)

The strongly defended and subsequently much-fought-over village of La Vacquerie in the south-east corner of Welsh Ridge was captured from the Germans in the morning of the first day of the Battle of Cambrai on 20 November. Ten days later the enemy penetrated the British positions both at La Vacquerie and at Gouzeaucourt to the south-west. Later on in the same day a British counter-attack managed to retake the village. Two days later the enemy tried to recover the high ground overlooking the village and on the following day the British withdrew from the village altogether.

By 4 December the fighting had died down in the Cambrai battlefield, except at Welsh Ridge, where the enemy were still trying to improve their forward positions. This was the ground held by the British 61st Division, whose 182nd Brigade lines stretched along the slopes of the Ridge as far as Ostrich Avenue, which was still in British hands.

At 10 a.m. on the 5th, and after a fierce German bombardment, the enemy made several very strong attempts to capture Ostrich Avenue and to move up the front system of the Hindenburg Line. By now Ostrich Avenue had been virtually destroyed by shell-fire. However, the 182nd Brigade stood firm, and then at 3 p.m. the enemy made an even stronger attempt to take the trench line. They advanced eastwards along Ostrich Avenue as well as approaching it from the north. This time they were successful, although they suffered many casualties. The enemy then continued a series of bombing attacks along the Hindenburg front system. The 2/7th Royal Warwickshires were being pushed hard in defence, but were ably assisted by the 9th Royal Inniskillings from 109th Brigade of the 36th (Ulster) Division. The Ulster Division was due to relieve the 61st Division that night.

On the 6th the enemy were still trying to improve their forward positions. The section of front that the 9th Inniskillings had taken over included part of the front of the Hindenburg Line on the right reaching as far as the remains of Ostrich Avenue on the left. In addition, remnants of two companies belonging to the 2/7th Royal Warwickshires had been retained to assist them in trying to regain the ground lost the day before.

At 6.30 a.m., No. 2 Coy (under 2/Lt J.S. Emerson) and No. 4 Coy (under Capt Douglas) tried to recapture lost positions by bombing their way back along 200 yards of trench. They killed a number of the enemy and took six prisoners. The enemy attacked in force at 10 a.m. and one of the battalion outposts was forced to retire. Repeated enemy attacks were then made between 10 a.m. and 2 p.m. but without making progress. During the fighting, which continued for most of the day, the gallant leadership of 2/Lt J.S. Emerson was outstanding. Though badly wounded in the head he led frequent attempts to repel the German bombers until he fell mortally wounded. The 11th Inniskillings relieved the two companies at 8 p.m. and the latter then proceeded to Couillet Wood 1,200 yards north-east of Villers-Plouich, where the battalion remained for the night. The higher slopes of Welsh Ridge were still in British hands.

The 36th (Ulster) Divisional History carries an eye-witness account of the fighting at this time by Lt Densmore Walker of the 109th Machine-Gun Company, who was in the line having heard that his guns had been lost:

> We went up the main front Hindenburg Line. This really was a filthy place. Corpses were touching, laid along the fire-step, all men of the 61st Division . . . . On and on we went and then cut to the left, where we found an officer called Emerson of the 9th Inniskillings. Emerson said we couldn't get further as the Hun was thirty yards away bombing down the trench. Poor fellow, he thought his whole company was wiped out, and he had been hit on the head by a bomb. There was a hole in the top of his tin hat . . . . He was right about the Huns. Moore said we were still one hundred and fifty yards from the machine-gun positions. . . .

The divisional history mentioned that casualties that day had been very high as a result of the desperate fighting, in particular in the ranks of officers. Of Emerson's heroism it stated:

> This heroic young officer, who had led his company in the original attack that morning and captured four hundred yards of trench, had as Captain [*sic*] remarks, been severely wounded in the head. For three hours he had rallied the remnants of his company to withstand the German bombers. He had made

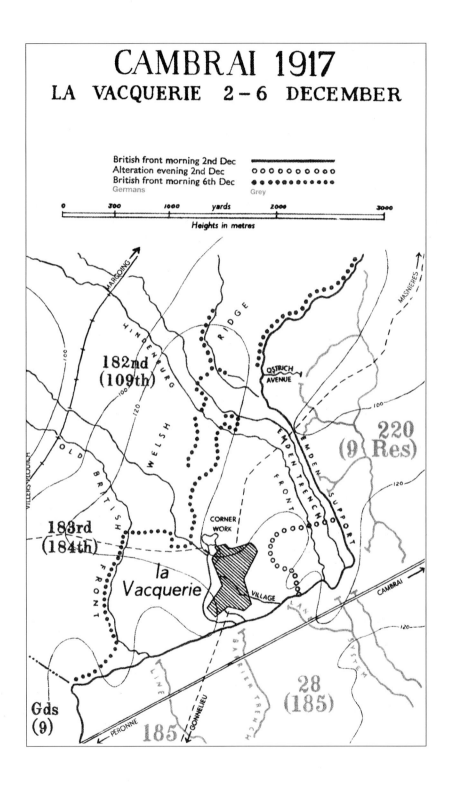

a previous attack over the open and captured six prisoners. On this last occasion of which Captain Walker speaks, having driven back the Germans at least a hundred yards, he fell, mortally wounded. He was awarded the posthumous honour of the Victoria Cross . . . .

Emerson's VC was published in the *London Gazette* of 13 February 1918:

James Samuel Emerson, Temporary Second Lieutenant, late 9th Battalion. Royal Inniskilling Fusiliers. For repeated acts of most conspicuous bravery. He led his company in an attack and cleared 400 yards of trench. Though wounded when the enemy attacked in superior numbers, he sprang out of the trench with eight men and met the attack in the open, killing many and taking six prisoners. For three hours after this, all other officers having become casualties, he remained with his company, and repeatedly repelled bombing attacks. Later, when the enemy again attacked in superior numbers, he led his men to repel the attack, and was mortally wounded.

In a letter to his mother, Lt Col Peacocke, his commanding officer wrote:

He was one of the most gallant officers I have ever seen, and his death was one of the biggest blows I have had since I have been out here. He was shot through the body when defending a most vital spot in the line – had he lost it a most critical situation would have arisen. He led his men for twenty-four hours in the hardest fighting I have yet seen, and he was calm, cool and collected the whole time. I cannot possibly say too much for his behaviour – he was quite wonderful. I saw him a very few minutes after being hit, and he was suffering no pain, and he died about fifteen minutes afterwards. My very deepest sympathy in your great loss, and I can't tell you how much I shall miss him as one of the best officers I have ever had.

A medical officer, Capt T.W.G. Johnson, also wrote to Emerson's mother:

He had had his steel helmet torn with a bullet and been hit in the hand, but refused to leave his men. An enemy sniper eventually shot him, and before he passed away he asked me to write to you and let you know that he did his duty. We all miss him very much, and his place will never be filled in the battalion, as far as I am personally concerned. His death was very quiet, and he suffered very little pain and the padre and myself were with him in his last moments. We lost a lot of fine officers the same day, and, believe me, my heart is torn for every one of their parents.

In the possibility of his death Emerson had willed any property which might have been found on his body to No. 14434 W.G. Abraham of the 2nd Royal Irish Rifles 2nd Machine-Gun Section 'to do with as he already knows'. The two men's service numbers were only four apart, and they probably joined up as privates on the same day in Dublin in September 1915. Emerson's body was never found, and his name is commemorated on Panels 5 and 6 of the Louverval Memorial.

His posthumous VC was presented to his mother at a distinguished gathering at Whitworth Hall, Drogheda, on 3 April 1918 by Brig Gen W. Hackett-Payne CB. The Mayor of Drogheda presided over the ceremonies, and apart from Emerson's mother three brothers attended, as well as L.R. Mercer, an uncle. Members of the Northumberland Fusiliers 'lined up on both sides of the hall and presented arms when the presentation was made'.

In July 1919 Emerson's Mountjoy School issued a special number of its school magazine with a list of military honours won by former pupils. Emerson's name headed the list. Emerson's family were also sent the 1914–15 Star, BWM and VM. Emerson's name is commemorated on several other memorials apart from Louverval, including the war memorial in Mary Street, Drogheda, and the cenotaph in front of Collon Church. His name is also included on the family headstone at the Church of Ireland Churchyard, Collon, and there is also a plaque at Mount Temple School, Dublin. Emerson's name is featured, too, at the Ulster Tower in Thiepval, and on the regimental memorial at St Anne's Cathedral, Belfast. His VC is not publicly held.

James Samuel Emerson was the youngest son of John Emerson and his wife and was born at Seven Oaks in Collon, six miles from Drogheda, Co. Louth, Ireland, on 3 August 1895 (or 1896 according to his National Archives file). The address that Emerson gave for his father on his attestation papers was the Estate Office, Collon, Drogheda. James attended the local school and later the Mountjoy Secondary School in Dublin. On leaving school he became a clerk.

His eighteenth or nineteenth birthday fell on the day before war was declared, and he enlisted as a private in the 3rd Royal Irish Rifles, a Reserve battalion, in Dublin on 16 September 1914. At his medical his teeth were found to be in a very poor state and a note in the file indicated that something should be done about them. Emerson carried out his military training in Ireland. His regiment was stationed at Kinnegar Camp, Hoywood, County Down, but later moved nearer to Dublin, where it was first at Wellington Barracks and secondly at

Villers–Plouich (*Peter Batchelor*)

Cambrai Memorial (*Donald C. Jennings*)

Portobello Barracks. Towards the end of his training period on 6 February 1915 his father died.

Emerson sailed to France as a member of the Expeditionary Force on 16 April 1915 and served as a machine-gunner. He was later promoted to lance-corporal and then corporal. He was badly wounded at Hooge on 29 September with gunshot wounds to his right wrist and right foot, and spent eight months in hospital in the United Kingdom. After his convalescence finished on 24 January 1916 he returned to the 3rd Battalion, which was still in Dublin, and he was in time to take part in the Easter Rising in April 1916. He acted as a member of the guard on the Bank of Ireland. On 28 June 1916 he was posted as an acting corporal. A few weeks after the failure of the Rebellion he left for France again, and was a member of the 9th Battalion, which was part of the 107th Brigade of the 36th (Ulster) Division, and took part in the July 1916 Somme fighting. Singled out as a potential officer, he was returned for officer cadet training on 7 February 1917 and on 7 April he was accepted for admission to an officer cadet battalion at Lichfield. At Finner Camp as a second lieutenant on 1 August 1917 he was posted to the 9th Royal Inniskilling Fusiliers of the 109th Brigade of the 36th (Ulster) Division.

H.J. NICHOLAS

Polderhoek Château, Belgium, 3 December 1917

(David Harvey)

Sometimes the information on the original circumstances of how a man won his VC is fairly sketchy, but in Henry Nicholas's case additional light has been shone upon the gallant deed by a Mr Hugh Johnston, who owned some of his father's field service books, in one of which was found a carbon copy of the original recommendation that was to bring Henry Nicholas his VC. They were used for the basis of an article published in the *Review* in March 1959.

The report is of an operation carried out by the 12th Nelson Coy 1st Canterbury Infantry Regiment, against Polderhoek Château in Belgium at noon on 3 December 1917. After the opening of an erratic barrage, the first wave of men from No. 12 Platoon moved forward only to be caught by a machine-gun on the right that was firing across the River Scherriabeek. Its fire was returned by a Lewis gun and by continuous sniping, which inflicted heavy enemy casualties. No. 11 Platoon destroyed another machine-gun position. No. 9, with Nicholas as a member of its Lewis gun section, took on an enemy position to the front in a system of trenches, captured the machine-gun and killed eleven, capturing four more.

More information on the whole operation appears in the battalion diary entitled 'Report of Operations, Polderhoek Château 1 December to 5 December 1917 1st Battalion – Canterbury Regiment.' It notes that after orders to take part in operations against the château had been received, reconnoitring parties from the battalion were sent up to the sector west of the château, as well as a position known as the Butte, in order to check the ground over which the battalion was due to advance. On Sunday 25 November the battalion moved to Walker Camp and the men to take part were selected the following day – those left out returned to the brigade school. Practice for the attack was carried out over the next four days and the practice of the 30th was witnessed by the GOC of the 2nd Anzac Corps and the GOC of the New Zealand Division.

Enemy defences were bombarded by artillery for two days, and patrols from the 2nd Canterbury Battalion went out to cut the wire and to try and ascertain the strength of the enemy. This battalion also dug out assembly trenches and brought up ammunition, bombs, water and other supplies. On the night of 1/2 December platoons from the 1st and 12th Coys left Walker Camp at 2.30 p.m. and entrained for Dickebusch, and then moved to Birr Cross Roads in preparation for their march to the front line. A relief of the 2nd Canterbury Battalion was carried out efficiently, and the next day was quiet with no casualties reported. During the afternoon of the 2nd the remaining men due to take part in the attack left Walker Camp at 3 p.m. and also travelled to Birr Cross Roads, moving up to the front line.

The 3rd dawned fine and bright with a fairly strong westerly wind, and at zero hour (12 noon) the 12th Coy on the right joined with the 1st Coy on the left, which in turn linked with the 1st Otago Battalion. The assault began after the opening of a barrage that was both erratic and ragged. However, it later improved, except on the left where it fell short on its own troops. The Otago Battalion also suffered from the same source. As the attackers reached a ridge they came under heavy machine-gun fire, but a pillbox was captured, and an enemy dugout, machine-gun and eight prisoners taken. The 12th Coy on the right of the line facing Gheluvelt was managing very well and a Lewis gun took out an enemy machine-gun that it had located. To quote from the diary:

> Another piece of good work was done by another section; the section commander had been put out of action but a private named Nicholas took charge and alone took a strong point which had been holding up the advance. He shot the officer from the parapet and then rushed the remainder of the garrison with the bayonet killing ten of the garrison and taking four wounded prisoners and capturing a machine-gun.

All this time the Otago Battalion at the château was suffering heavy casualties, and the whole attack was severely held up over the next two hours owing to the toll being taken by enemy machine-gunners. However, a German counter-attack during this time was unsuccessful. As lines were cut communication had become very difficult, and at 5.40 p.m. orders came from brigade instructing the attackers to consolidate on the ground taken. Later a plan was hatched for the château to be taken during hours of darkness, but the men in the line considered this scheme an impracticable one and it was later abandoned. The main success of the day had been to the right, where 'very good observation of the whole of the Scherriabeek Valley was obtained'.

On the following day, the battalion conferred with brigade. The day was fairly quiet and at dusk the Otago front-line troops were relieved, as were later the 1st and 12th Companies. Positions were consolidated and a communication on the right deepened and improved. The enemy threatened a counter-attack from the direction of the château, which did not materialise, but their artillery caused casualties throughout the day. Finally the New Zealanders were relieved from their exposed positions by the 2nd Bedfordshire Regiment and returned to Birr Cross Roads, and from there entrained to Howe Camp, arriving there at about 1.30 a.m. Just over seven weeks later it was announced in the *London Gazette* of 11 January that Private Nicholas had been awarded the VC for his work at Polderhoek.

> Henry James Nicholas, No. 24213 Private. 1st Battalion. New Zealand Infantry (Canterbury Regiment). For most conspicuous bravery and devotion to duty in attack. Private Nicholas, who was one of a Lewis gun section, had orders to form a defensive flank to the right of the advance, which was subsequently checked by heavy machine-gun and rifle fire from an enemy strong point. Whereupon, followed by the remainder of his section at an interval of about twenty-five yards, Private Nicholas rushed forward alone, shot the officer in command of the strong point, and overcame the remainder of the garrison of sixteen by means of bombs and bayonets, capturing four wounded prisoners and a machine-gun. He captured this strong point practically single-handed, and thereby saved many casualties. Subsequently, when the advance had reached its limit, Private Nicholas collected ammunition under heavy machine-gun and rifle fire. His exceptional valour and coolness throughout the operations afforded an inspiring example to all.

Six days after the announcement of his VC the citation was published as a Special Divisional Routine Order by Brig Gen G.N. Johnston DSO, RA, commander of the New Zealand Division.

Nicholas was immediately promoted to corporal and six days later given a fortnight's leave in England, rejoining his battalion on Boxing Day. In the New Year he was attached to brigade school for training on 7 January. He rejoined his battalion on 28 January.

Nicholas's files show that he made a will in favour of his mother dated 24 March 1918. On 21 May he was promoted to lance-sergeant, and to full sergeant on 18 June, arriving back in England on leave from 28 June. The leave might in part have been sick leave, and he was readmitted as a patient to the New Zealand Hospital at Walton-on-Thames. During this period he was presented with his medal at Buckingham Palace by the King, at the same ceremony as Percy Storkey. On 7 August he was detached to APM London HQ and handed his VC over to the New Zealand Record Office 'to be held in safe custody'. He was then attached to a position at New Zealand HQ in London on 22 August 1918 and on 2 September returned to his battalion and rejoined it in the field.

He won a Military Medal on 14 October 'for acts of gallantry in the field' and was killed nine days later, just short of three weeks before the Armistice, when demanding the surrender of a group of German soldiers at the Escaillon Bridgehead close to Beaudignies Le-Quesnoy Road. A note in his file refers to a report by Revd G.T. Robson, attached to the 1st Canterbury Infantry Regiment, dated 29 October 1918. A few days back he had sent in a burial return for Nicholas as buried in Beaudignies Cemetery. Later, and acting under orders from his CO, he had Nicholas's body exhumed and reburied with full military honours on 29 October in the churchyard of Vertigneul, a hamlet in the commune of Romeries, north of Solesmes, Grave 15. Eighteen other casualties from New Zealand units are buried there.

Nicholas's MM was announced after his death, and, as we have seen, his VC had been left in safe-keeping in England in July/August 1918 at the New Zealand Record Office after he had returned to France. His mother received her son's VC medal in Christchurch on 30 April 1919. His commemorative scroll was dispatched on 27 June 1921, and his remaining medals on 19 October 1921. His plaque was despatched on 3 February 1922 and his certificate on 6 October.

In 1932 his mother, Mrs Hannah Nicholas, presented the VC and MM to the Canterbury Museum. His other medals, including the BWM and VM, were presented to the museum in July 2002, together with some items of memorabilia. Surviving items include Nicholas's identity disc, an aluminium ring possibly made from a water bottle, his VC citation, a regimental medal for boxing (1918), his pay book, a commemorative scroll and plaque, a soldier's diary with very few entries and four photographs, one of which is included in this book. His father, Richard Nicholas, received a letter of sympathy dated 14 November 1918 from the Governor-General, Lord Liverpool, addressed to his home at 35 Berry Street, St Albans, Christchurch. Henry James Nicholas was later commemorated at the Returned Soldiers Association HQ in Dunedin.

Henry James Nicholas was born in Lincoln, New Zealand, on 11 June 1891, son of Richard and Hannah, and had at least two brothers who served in the Army, Ernest and Frederick, and two sisters. In his enlistment papers he gave his

Burial of Sgt H.J. Nicholas, VC MM, NZ Canterbury Regiment, Vertingeul Cemetery (*Unknown photographer, Nicholas Collection, Canterbury Museum, Ref 2002.106.2*)

religion as spiritualist and his occupation as a carpenter, and his last employer was Baker Brothers of Loburn.

Nicholas tried to enlist in Australia in 1915 but was rejected on medical grounds, owing to his having loose teeth. This was possibly due to his being a good boxer! Growing increasingly frustrated, he decided to return to New Zealand to try his luck there. His decision paid off and his application in January 1916 for enlistment in the New Zealand Army was accepted, and he enlisted on 8 February, becoming a member of the NZEF. He was taken on the strength of C Coy 13th as a private.

On 13 May he was docked one day's pay for overstaying his leave at Trentham. Soon after he sailed to England he became ill during the voyage, and became a patient in the ship's hospital for five days in early July. He disembarked at Devonport on the 26th, and was posted to a reserve company of the 1st Canterbury Infantry Regiment two days later, and then to the battalion on 23 August. He joined the 12th Coy and on 24 September was attached for machine-gun training at Rouen, returning to the battalion on 27 October.

Vertigneul Churchyard (*Donald C. Jennings*)

On 4 May 1917 Nicholas was admitted to hospital in St Omer with a slight attack of mumps, and on the 13th he was transferred to Base Depot. A week later he was fined 7s 6d (37½p) for damaging government property when he cut off the legs of his trousers, thus turning them into shorts! A week later he absented himself from billets and was given five days' field punishment No. 20. A short time later he was admitted to the 2nd New Zealand Hospital at Walton-on-Thames in Surrey with tonsillitis, where he was a patient from 8 July until 7 August.

On 7 September he was detached to 2nd Army Rest Camp in Rouen, and rejoined his battalion on the 20th. He was back in the field from 25 October and won his VC nearly six weeks later.

W. MILLS

Givenchy, France, 10/11 December 1917

(David Harvey)

On 1 December 1917 the 1/10th Manchester Regiment (126th Brigade) 42nd Division was billeted at Beuvry after a long march. It had just arrived in the Bethune Sector, which was to be its 'home' for the next three months, and its positions were close to La Bassée Canal. On the 9th its officers were sent forward to reconnoitre the line. After its brigade relieved the 125th Infantry Brigade on 10 December, the 10th Battalion was ordered up to forward positions at the Red Dragon Crater, Givenchy, to relieve the 6th Lancashire Fusiliers. They were the left battalion and the 1/9th Manchesters the right, and the relief was completed by 10.30 a.m.

As Pte Walter Mills of the 1/10th Manchesters went up the line for what was to be the last time, he met his brother James, a private with the Lancashire Fusiliers, coming back. The two brothers were able to exchange a brief word and to shake hands. A few days later James was to place a floral tribute on his late brother's grave at Gorre.

Knowing that a relief had recently taken place, the enemy bombarded the Manchesters with gas-drums prior to making an attack, and the war diary noted that 'it was the first occasion that gas has been projected by the enemy on the British front'. The gas had come as a surprise, and it was not long before almost every man in Red Dragon Crater, which was occupied by C Coy was affected by poison gas, so that most men were out of action when the enemy attacked. However, despite being blinded and choking, the Oldham men somehow managed to put up a heroic stand, using bombs, rifles and Lewis guns. But one by one they slipped back into the trench to die from the effects of the poisonous gas.

One man in particular, Pte Walter Mills, knowing the danger of the position being lost, and yet suffering acutely from the effects of the gas, 'fought magnificently to save the situation'. Remaining in position on the trench fire-step, he continued to throw bomb after bomb, which caused the German advance to falter. Although the fight only lasted about half an hour, both sides had suffered casualties, including fifteen men from C Coy. Of five men awarded medals, 'Spud' Mills was chosen to be the recipient of a posthumous VC and the other four men were presented with the MM. Next day men from the 6th Manchesters dug the graves for the dead Oldham men at Gorre British Cemetery, which, although only a short distance from the front line, did not prevent the burials of these brave men from being conducted with full military honours. The inscription that Mrs Mills selected for her husband's grave was 'Death does not part the love that formed the link between us'.

An account written by Capt A.G. Wynne published in a local newspaper of 31 May 1919 described the event as follows:

> Trusting to the presence of new troops in the line, and anticipating success, the enemy advanced boldly. But the 10th were not to be caught napping. Forgetful of gas masks, forgetful of anything but the security of the line, and disdaining death, the brave lads, choking and blinded stood up to the foe, and with bombs, rifles, and Lewis guns drove them back to their own trenches. This was one of the many occasions on which every man was a hero, and every man deserved special recognition. But as this was impossible a selection was made. To Private Mills ('Spud') was awarded the much coveted V.C. This gallant lad stood on the parapet and bombed the enemy until he fell back – dead. Four other men were awarded the Military Medal, and the company, which was commanded by Captain P. Stott, was specially commended by the G.O.C. the 42nd Division. The next day twenty of these heroes were laid to rest in the village of Gorre.

Only a few hours before his death, Mills wrote home telling his family the good news that he would be leaving for home on the 13th for a long Christmas leave. He had only been home once during the war up to then.

The citation for Mills's VC was published in the *London Gazette* of 13 February 1918, and his VC ribbon arrived at 42nd Division in May, having been sent to Lt Col W.R. Peel DSO.

> W. Mills, (No. 375499) Private, 1/10th Battalion. Manchester Regiment. (Territorial Force). For most conspicuous bravery and self sacrifice. When, after an intense gas attack, a strong enemy patrol endeavoured to rush our posts, the garrisons of which had been overcome, and though badly gassed himself, he met the attack single-handed and continued to throw bombs until the arrival of reinforcements, and remained at his post until the enemy's attacks had been finally driven off. While being carried away he died from gas poisoning. It was solely due to his exertions, when his only chance of personal

The Prince of Wales, Mrs Mills and Ellen at Oldham Athletic Football Ground 1921 (*Oldham Local Studies Archives*)

safety lay in remaining motionless, that the enemy was defeated and the line retained intact.

Mills died from the effects of gas and was buried at Gorre British Cemetery, Plot V, Row C, Grave 2. His wife, whose maiden name was Britt, stayed at the same address until 1923, when she remarried and lived in Fielding Street, becoming Mrs Brown.

Walter Mills was commemorated on the Roll of Honour at Eli Mills. His posthumous VC was presented to his widow by the King at a ceremony at the Orthopaedic Hospital, Beckett's Park, Leeds, on 31 May 1918. Three years later, at a function for First World War veterans held in June/July at the Oldham Athletic Football Ground, Mrs Mills and her daughter Ellen were presented to the Prince of Wales. Mrs Mills had dressed her daughter in white and she was wearing her father's VC. After they climbed the steps of the dais they curtseyed to the Prince, who shook their hands. Afterwards the Prince talked to her about her late husband and the circumstances of his winning the VC. Ellen was then held up by her mother in order to present the Prince with a small blood-red rose

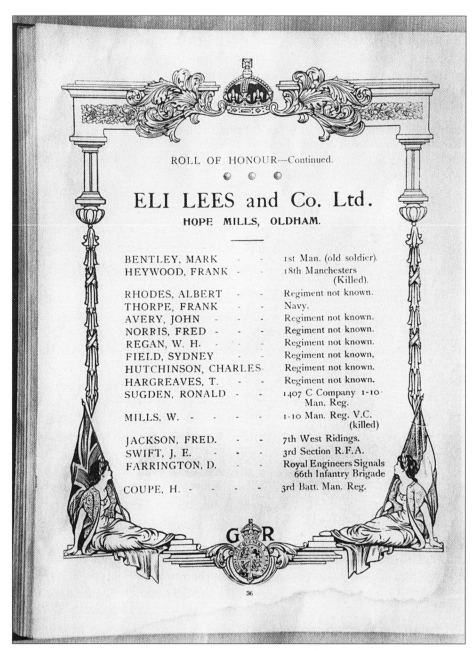

ROLL OF HONOUR—Continued.

ELI LEES and Co. Ltd.
HOPE MILLS, OLDHAM.

BENTLEY, MARK	1st Man. (old soldier).
HEYWOOD, FRANK	18th Manchesters (Killed).
RHODES, ALBERT	Regiment not known.
THORPE, FRANK	Navy.
AVERY, JOHN	Regiment not known.
NORRIS, FRED	Regiment not known.
REGAN, W. H.	Regiment not known.
FIELD, SYDNEY	Regiment not known,
HUTCHINSON, CHARLES	Regiment not known.
HARGREAVES, T.	Regiment not known.
SUGDEN, RONALD	1407 C Company 1-10 Man. Reg.
MILLS, W.	1-10 Man. Reg. V.C. (killed)
JACKSON, FRED.	7th West Ridings.
SWIFT, J. E.	3rd Section R.F.A.
FARRINGTON, D.	Royal Engineers Signals 66th Infantry Brigade
COUPE, H.	3rd Batt. Man. Reg.

G R

36

Plaque at Hope Mills, Oldham (*Anon*)

on behalf of all ex-servicemen of Oldham. The Prince then bent down, patting the child's head, and with a beaming smile presented the small girl with his buttonhole and a second handshake. Needless to say this gesture brought on a huge burst of cheering as the Prince walked over to a group of disabled soldiers. The Prince's rose became a treasured family possession. As a postscript, Ellen died at the young age of 20 in October 1935 and was buried wearing her father's VC pinned to her gown at Greenacres Cemetery, Oldham. The buttonhole remained in the care of her mother.

Gorre British Cememtery (*Donald C. Jennings*)

Walter Mills, a son of James, a labourer in an ironworks, and Clara Mills (née Sidall) was born at 4 Wellesley Street, Oldham, Lancashire, on 20 June 1894. He was one of at least five brothers.

He worked firstly as a piecer and later as a labourer at Eli Mills & Co. Ltd (Hope Mills), and after he married lived with his parents-in-law at 10 Smith Street. His daughter, christened Ellen, was born a few weeks before he enlisted on 6 September with the 1/10th Manchester Battalion TF. The battalion had been formed in Oldham on the outbreak of war on the same day as the 2/10th Battalion. The 1/10th Battalion was part of the East Lancashire Brigade of the East Lancashire Division, and left Southampton for Egypt, arriving at Alexandria on 25 September 1914. Mills completed his training in Egypt before landing at Gallipoli on or around 10 May 1915.

During his time at Gallipoli, Mills was wounded in the eye and suffered from dysentry and typhoid fever. He recovered and left Egypt for France, arriving there in March 1917. His battalion was part of 126th Brigade, 42nd Division.

SOURCES

The main sources used in the preparation of this book include the archives listed below, followed by additional material from individuals, libraries, newspapers, county record offices or obituaries:

The Lummis VC files at the National Army Museum, London, cared for by the Military Historical Society
The Victoria Cross files, at the Imperial War Museum, London
The Liddle Collection 1914–1918, Leeds University Library
The National Archives, Kew, Surrey
Regimental Museums and Archives
The London Gazette 1914–1920 (HMSO)

E.A. McNair
West Sussex County Council Archives
Eastbourne Gazette, 13 September 1916
Redoubt Fortess, Military Museum of Sussex, Eastbourne
Buckman, D., *Royal Sussex Regiment Military Honours & Awards 1864–1920*, J & K.H. Publisher, 2001
NA WO95/2189 24th Division
NA WO95/2216 73rd Inf. Brigade
NA WO95/2219 9th Royal Sussex Regiment
NA WO339/24602 E.A. McNair

W.R. Cotter
Kent County Council Local Studies, Folkestone
Folkestone Herald, 30 June 1956, 21 December 1963 and 4 January 1964
Kentish Express, 1 April 1916
Kentish Messenger, 13 December 1963 and 27 July 2000
NA WO95/1823 12th Division
NA WO95/1858 37th Brigade, Appendix L
NA WO95/1860 6th East Kents
NA W0363/C1190 W.R. Cotter

E.N. Mellish
Liddle Collection (1914–1918) (Brotherton Library, University of Leeds)
The Gallant Comradeship (Unpublished Memoirs)
Sunday Graphic, 12 November 1933
NA WO95/1431 4th Royal Fusiliers
NA WO339/69554 E.N. Mellish

E.F. Baxter
Sidney Lindsay 'Merseyside Heroes' (unpublished manuscript)
NA WO95/2844 51st (Highland) Division and 2846
NA WO95/2921 164th Infantry Brigade
NA WO95/2923 1/8th King's Liverpool Regiment
NA WO374/4830 E.F. Baxter

R.B.B. Jones
Dulwich College
NA WO95/2221/2222 25th Division
NA WO95/2241 Infantry Brigade
NA WO95/2243 8th Loyal North Lancashire Regiment
NA WO339/25813 R.B.B. Jones

G.W. Chafer
Rotherham Advertiser 5 March 1966
The Sapper, May 1954
Sheffield Star, 3 March 1966
NA WO95/2161 1st East Yorkshire Battalion
NA 95363/C184 G.W. Chafer

A.H. Procter
Sidney Lindsay, 'Merseyside Heroes' (unpublished manuscript)
Captain J.M. Procter
Glendinings Catalogue, 18 September 1990
NA WO95/2899 55th (West Lancs) Division
NA WO95/2925 165th Infantry Brigade
NA WO95/2926 1/5th King's Liverpool Regiment
NA WO363/P 1527 A.H. Procter

J. Erskine
South Lanarkshire Council
The Covenanter, March 1956
NA WO95/2405 33rd Division
NA WO95/2420 19th Infantry Brigade
NA WO95/2422 5th Cameronians Battalion
NA WO633/E443 J. Erskine

W. Hackett
Doncaster Metropolitan Borough Council
Doncaster Free Press, 6 February 1997, 29 May 1997 and 7 August 1997
Doncaster Star, 3 April 1966, 6 February 1997, 1 May 1997, 23 July 1997, 31 July 1997
    and 11 November 2001
Mexborough & Swinton Times, 22 July 1916, 12 August 1916 & 19 August 1916
The Ypres Times (Ypres League), ND
NA WO363/H 10 W. Hackett

SOURCES

A.H.H. Batten-Pooll
NA WO95/1231 1st Division
NA WO95/1231 3rd Infantry Brigade
NA WO 95/1279 2nd Royal Munster Fusiliers

W. Jackson
Francis, C., *Australia's Youngest V.C. Winner*, n.p., n.d.
Bean, C.E.W., *The Official History of Australia in the War*, vol III, The A. I. F. in France
    1916 (University of Queensland Press, 1982)
Wigmore, L. (ed.), *They Dared Mightily*, Australian War Memorial, Canberra, 1963
NA WO363/J

J. Hutchinson
The Fusiliers' Museum, Lancashire
Lancashire Fusiliers' Annual (ND)
Torquay Times, January 1972
NA WO95/2899 55th Division
NA WO95/2920 164th Infantry Brigade
NA WO95/2923 2/5th Lancashire Fusiliers
NA WO363/H 2702-3 J. Hutchinson

N.V. Carter
West Sussex County Council Archives
Buckman, D., *Royal Sussex Regiment Military Honours and Awards 1864–1920*,
    J & K.H. Publisher, 2001
Eastbourne Gazette, 13 September 1916
Redoubt Fortress, Military Museum of Sussex, Eastbourne
NA WO95/2563 39th Division
NA WO95/2581 116th Infantry Brigade
NA WO95/2586 12th Royal Sussex Regiment
Leslie, K.C., *Great War*, WSCC 1989
NA WO363/C611 N.V. Carter

W.B. Butler
Leeds City Council (Dept of Leisure Services)
Leeds Mercury, 18 and 19 October 1917
'The White Rose', August 1972
Yorkshire Evening News, 18 October 1917, 22 November 1917, 3 December 1917,
    4 December 1917 & 5 December 1917
Yorkshire Evening Post, 24 November 1917 and 28 November 1917
Yorkshire Observer, 30 November 1917
Yorkshire Post, 5 December 1917
NA WO95/2469 35th Division
NA WO95/2489 106th Infantry Brigade
NA WO95/2490 17th West Yorkshire Battalion
NA WO363/C611 W.B. Butler

M.J. O'Rourke
Personal Record 428545 (National Archives of Canada)
NA WO 95/3728 1st Canadian Division
NA WO95/3765 2nd Canadian Infantry Brigade
NA WO95/3767 7th British Columbia Regiment
NA WO363/0250 M.J. O'Rourke

H. Brown
Personal Record 226353 (National Archives of Canada)
NA WO95/3728 1st Canadian Division
NA WO 95/3765 2nd Canadian Infantry Brigade
NA WO95/3770 10th Quebec Regiment (Appendix B)

F.W. Hobson
Personal Record 57113 (National Archives of Canada)
NA WO95/3786 2nd Canadian Division
NA WO95/3812 4th Infantry Brigade
NA WO95/3817 20th Canadian Battalion
NA WO 363/H1850-1 F. Hobson

O.M. Learmonth
Personal Record 22893 (National Archives of Canada)
NA WO95 3761 2nd Battalion East Ontario Regiment

R.H. Hanna
Personal Record 75361 (National Archives of Canada)
Belfast Telegraph, 9 November 1917 & 17 June 1967
NA WO95/3786 2nd Canadian Division
NA WO95/3828 6th Canadian Infantry Brigade
NA WO95/3833 29th British Columbia Regiment
NA WO363/H250 R.H. Hanna

F. Konowal
Personal Record 1444039 (National Archives of Canada)
Lubomyr Y. Luciuk and Ron Sorobey, *Konowal: A Canadian Hero*, the Kashtan Press, Kingston, 2000
NA WO95/3881 4th Canadian Division
NA WO95/3896 10th Canadian Infantry Brigade
NA WO95/3899 47th British Columbia Regiment

H.F. Parsons
The Victor, 11 July 1970
Western Daily Press, 15 April 1935
NA WO339/73298 H.F. Parsons
NA WO95/2469 35th Division
NA WO95/2486 105th Infantry Brigade
NA WO95/2488 14th Gloster Battalion
NA WO339/73298 H.F. Parsons

S.J. Day
East Anglian Daily Times, 25 July 1959
Eastern Daily Press, many references in 1917–19, 23 June 1956 & 6 August 1959
Eastern Evening News, 13 June 1956, 19 October 1962, 23 October 1971, 24 December 1970 & 17 June 1977
Peace Souvenir Norwich War Record (Jarrold & Sons Ltd n.d.)
NA WO95/2434 34th Division
NA WO95/2456 101st Infantry Brigade
NA WO95/2458 11th Suffolk Battalion
NA WO363/D625

A.E. Shepherd
Barnsley Chronicle, 23 February 1918 and 5 November 1966
NA WO95/2097 20th Division
NA WO95/2119 60th Infantry Brigade
NA WO95/2120 12th KRRC
NA WO363/S1190 A.E. Shepherd

R.W.L. Wain
The Tank Corps Journal, Vol. 4
The Tank Museum, Bovington
The Victor, 5 December 1964
NA WO95/2121 12th Rifle Brigade
NA WO95/109 1st Battalion Tank Corps
NA WO339/36624 R.W.L. Wain

R. McBeath
NA WO95/2844 and 2846 51 (Highland) Division
NA WO95/2863 152nd Infantry Brigade
NA WO95/2866 1/5th Seaforth Highlanders
NA WO363/M213 R. McBeath

C.E Spackman
Southern Evening Echo, 7 May 1969
NA WO95/2283 29th Division
NA WO95/2303 87th Infantry Brigade
NA WO95/2305 1st Border Battalion
NA WO363/S2195

J. Sherwood-Kelly
John Kelly
The African World, 22 August 1931
Uys, I., *For Valour – The History of South Africa's Victoria Cross Heroes*, Johannesburg 1973
Daily Express, 6 September 1919, 13 September 1919 & 7 October 1919
Eastern Daily Press, 8 September 1919 & 19 August 1931
Eastern Evening News, 11 November 1919
NA WO95/2283 29th Division

NA WO95/2305 1st Royal Inniskillings
NA WO95/2303 87th Infantry Brigade
NA W0339/13469 J. Sherwood

H. Strachan
Personal Record 15585 (National Archives of Canada)
Gardam, J., *Seventy Years After 1914–1984*, Canada's Wing Inc., Ottawa 1983
Johnston, W. 'Who's The Sojer in the Photie Then?'
Law, D., *Harcus Strachan V.C.*
The Edmonton Journal, 15 July 1989
Seely, J.E.B., *Adventure*, Heinemann 1930
Thirty Canadian VCs, Skeffington, Canada, 1919
NA WO339/139058

J. McAulay
A.F. Young, John McAulay V.C., D.C.M.
NA WO95/1193 Guards Division General Staff
NA WO95/1214 1st Guards Brigade
NA WO95/1214 and 1219 (1st Scots Guards)
NA WO363/M204 J. McAulay

G.W.B. Clare
Chatteris Museum, Cambridge
Letter from the Revd J.C. Hawthorn to the Revd W.M. Lummis, 11 October 1971
NA WO95/1118 2nd Cavalry Division
NA WO95/1133 3rd Cavalry Brigade
NA WO95/1134 5th Lancers
NA WO363/C593 G.W.B. Clare

C.E. Gourley
Lindsay, Sidney, B. 'Merseyside Heroes' (unpublished manuscript)
Liverpool Courier, 14 December 1918

S.T.D. Wallace
Dumfries & Galloway Standard, 16 & 20 February 1918
NA WO95/1825 12th Division
NA WO95/1832 12th Division CO RA (January–December 1917)
NA WO95/1838 63rd Brigade RFA

N.B. Elliott-Cooper
NA WO95/1825 12th Division
NA WO95/1854 36th Infantry Brigade
NA WO95/1857 8th and 9th Royal Fusilier Battalions
NA WO339/7185 N.B. Elliott-Cooper

R. Gee
Seaton, D., *A Tiger and a Fusilier – Leicester's VC Heroes*, Self Pub 2001
Becke, Major A.F., Cambrai 1917 '*The Defence of Les Rues Vertes, 30th November*'

The Journal of the Royal Artillery, Vol. LXVII No. 3
Leicester City Libraries
Leicester Mercury, 3 August 1980
Morning Post, 5 June 1926
The Times, 3 August 1960
NA WO95/2283 29th Division
NA WO95/2298 86th Infantry Brigade
NA WO339/30007 R. Gee

J. Thomas
NA WO95/3010 59th Division
NA WO95/3020 176th Brigade
NA WO95/3021 2/5th North Staffordshire Battalion
NA WO95/3021 5th North Staffordshires. The two Battalions. Combined end January 1918.

W.N. Stone
NA WO95/1298 2nd Division
NA WO95/1369 99th Infantry Brigade
NA WO95/1350 & 1363 17th Royal Fusiliers

A.M.C. McReady Diarmid
NA WO95/1361 6th Brigade
NA WO 339/38513 McReady Diarmid

G.H.T. Paton
Dunoon Herald and Cowal Advertiser, 15 February 1918

Gobind Singh
Capt W.E. Whitworth, M.C., *A History of the 2nd Lancers*
Kaushala, R.S., *Tiger Son of India*, n.d.

A.M. Lascelles
B. Durham Light Infantry Museum and Durham Art Gallery and Malcolm McGregor
NA WO95/2134 21st Division
C. NA WO95/1617 14th Durham Light Infantry
D. NA WO339/51660 A.M. Lascelles

J.S. Emerson
Francis O'N. Rodgers, 'An Irish VC: James S. Emerson (Battle Lines)', *Journal of The Somme Association*, 13
'The Sprig of Shillelagh' March 1918 (*Journal of the Old Drogheda Society* 1996)
NA WO95/2510 9th Royal Inniskillings
NA WO339/98614 J.S. Emerson

H.J. Nicholas
Curator of Manuscripts (Canterbury Museum)
'Story Behind Award of Little Known V.C.', *Review*, March 1959

Sergeant H.J. Nicholas (WW1) Personal File 24213 (New Zealand Defence Force)
NA WO95/3659 New Zealand Division
NA WO95/3695 2nd New Zealand Brigade
NA WO95/3697 1st Battalion Canterbury Regiment

W. Mills
Daily Sketch, June 1921
Oldham Evening Chronicle, 25 & 29 September 1964
The Standard, 14 February 1918 & 6 June 1921
NA WO95/2645 & 2646 42nd Division
NA WO95/2656 126th Brigade
NA WO95/2658 1/10th Manchester Battalion
NA WO363/M2130 W. Mills

BIBLIOGRAPHY

The following list of published sources used in the preparation of this book does not include the many regimental and divisional histories which were also consulted.

Bancroft, J.W., *Devotion to Duty: Tributes to a Region's VCs*, Air High Productions 1990

Butler, R. and Gilbert, D., *For Valour: Kidderminster's Four VCs*, n.d.

Canadian War Records, *Thirty Canadian VCs*, Skeffington, Canada, 1919

Cave, N., *Battlefield Europe. Arras Vimy Ridge*, Leo Cooper, 1996

Cooper, B., *The Ironclads of Cambrai*, Souvenir Press, 1967

Creagh, O'M. and Humphris, E.M., *The V.C. and D.S.O.*, 3 vols, Standard Art Company, 1924

Doherty, R. and Truesdale, D., *Irish Winners of the Victoria Cross*, Four Courts Press, 2000

Edmonds, J.E. (ed.), *Military Operations France and Belgium 1914–1918*, Macmillan/HMSO, 1922–1949

Grieve, W. Grant and Newman, B., *Tunnellers – The Story of the Tunnelling Companies, Royal Engineers, during the World War*, Herbert Jenkins, 1936

Jean-Luc Gibot-Philippe Gorczynski, *Following The Tanks–Cambrai–20th November–7th December 1917*, 1999

Harvey, D., *Monuments To Courage: Victoria Cross Headstones & Memorials*, Vol. 2, 1917–1982, David Harvey, 1999

Horsfall, J. and Cave, N., *Battleground Europe*, Cambrai Bourlon Wood, Leo Cooper, 2002

James, E.A., *British Regiments 1914–1918*, Samson Books, 1978

Johnson, J.H., *Stalemate! The Great Trench Warfare Battles of 1915–1917*, Arms & Armour Press, 1995

Kelleher, J.P. (ed.), 'Elegant Extracts', *The Royal Fusiliers Recipients of The Victoria Cross 'For Valour'*, The Royal Regiment of Fusiliers, n.d.

Lindsay, Sidney, 'Merseyside Heroes' (unpublished manuscript)

Montell, H., *A Chaplain's War – The Story of Noel Mellish VC, MC*, Serendipity, 2002

Moore, W., *A Wood Called Bourlon. The Cover-up after Cambrai, 1917*, Leo Cooper, 1988

Napier, G., *The Sapper VCs/The Story of Valour in the Royal Engineers and its Associated Corps*, Stationery Office, 1998

Nicholson, G.W.L., *Canadian Expeditionary Force 1914–1918*, Ottawa, 1962

Oldham, P., *Battleground Europe. The Hindenburg Line*, Leo Cooper, 1997

Pillinger, D. and Staunton, A., *A Victoria Cross Locator*, 2nd edn, Australia, 2000

The Register of the Victoria Cross, This England Books, 1988

Seaton, D., *A Tiger And A Fusilier, Leicestershire's VC Heroes* (Author), 2001

Shannon, Stephen D., *Beyond Praise. The Durham Light Infantrymen who were awarded the Victoria Cross*, County Durham Books, 1998

Smithers, A.J., *Cambrai The First Great Tank Battle 1917*, Leo Cooper, 1992

Smyth, J., *The Story of the Victoria Cross*, Muller 1963

Wigmore, L. (ed.), *They Dared Mightily*, Australian War Memorial, Canberra, 1963

Williams, W. Alistair, *The VCs of Wales and the Welsh Regiments*, Bridge Books, Wrexham, 1984

Woollcombe, R., *The First Tank Battle: Cambrai 1917*, Barker, 1967

INDEX

ARMS, FORMATION, UNITS

Armies
  First 181, Second ix,
    Third x, 156, 162,
    Fourth 38

Corps
  III ix, 104, IV xii, xiii, V
    xiii, XII 31, 104, XIX
    69, Tank 126

Divisions
  1st 52
  2nd 200, 201
  3rd 17, 18, 19
  6th 114, 127
  9th Div 175
  12th 114, 173, 174, 176
  17th 33
  20th 114
  21st 33, 227
  24th 2
  25th 26
  29th 136, 138, 140, 141,
    182, 183, 186, 189,
    190, 192, 222, 224
  33rd 42, 44
  34th 104, 105, 109
  35th 68, 69
  46th 31
  47th 200
  50th 33
  36th (Ulster) xii, xiii,
    230, 231
  42nd 247
  47th 162
  51st (Highland) xii, 127
  55th 22, 36, 39, 59, 60,
    167, 169, 171, 172
  56th 200

  59th 197
  61st 230
  62nd (West Riding) xii,
    xiii, xiv, 127, 156,
    162
  63rd Roy Naval 33
  64th 33

Cavalry Divisions
  5th 102

Infantry Brigades
  1st Guards Bde 210
  2nd Guards Bde 156,
    162, 197, 210
  6th 205
  9th 14
  16th 210
  35th 178
  36th 173
  37th 5, 7, 173
  60th 121, 178
  64th 227
  86th xiii, 134, 138, 182,
    183, 190, 192, 193
  87th 136, 138, 141, 182
  88th 134. 147, 183,
    189
  105th 101
  107th 236
  125th 243
  126th 247
  152nd 128
  164th 23, 60
  165th 25,
  176th 197
  182nd 230
Artillery Corps
  13th Heavy Artillery

Artillery Brigades
  4th West Lancashire
    Howitzer 171
  276th 167, 171

Batteries
  275th 171, 276th 171,
    377th 173, 174 379th
    173

Infantry Battalions
  1st Coldstream Guards 156
  Grenadier Guards 1st,
    197, 3rd 156, 4th 210,
    214
  2nd Irish Guards 156
  1st Scots Guards 158, 159
  1st Welsh Guards 210
  8th Argyll & Sutherland
    127, 128
  8th Bedfordshire 224
  1st Borders 132, 134, 136
  1st The Buffs (East Kent)
    13
  6th (S) The Buffs (East
    Kent) 5, 10, 13
  5/6th Cameronians 42,
    44, 45
  1/10 Cheshire 26, 15th Bn
    101
  7th Cyclist Bn. 126
  Durham Light Inf 3rd,
    222, 225, 229, 14th
    222, 229, 15th 227,
    19th 68
  1st East Yorkshire 32, 33,
    34
  14th (S) Gloucester 101,
    102, 103

2nd Hampshire 142, 143
Highland Light Inf 2nd
206, 18th 69
King' s Liverpool 1st 205,
206, 1/5th 36, 39, 40,
6th Bn 167, 1/ 8th 22,
23, 25, 28, 38
1st King's Own Scottish
Borderers 132, 136, 140
Kings Royal Rifle Corps
1st 200, 12th 114,119
1st King's Shropshire
Light Inf 222
Lancashire Fusiliers 1st
183, 2/5th 59, 60, 6th
243, 16th 201,18th 68
1st Leicester 127, 128
10th Lincolns 104
17th London 162
Loyal North Lancashire
1/4 60, 8th 29, 30, 31
Manchester 1/10th 243,
244, 25th 125
Middlesex 4th 209, 14th
209, 16th Middlesex
126, 182, 183, 17th
205, 206, 208, 209
Norfolk Regiment 140,
7th 178, 9th Norfolk
128, 12th 142
2/5th North Staffs 197, 198
21st Northumberland
Fusiliers 32
6th Oxford &
Buckinghamshire 116
12th Rifle Brigade 122
Royal Fusiliers 2nd 20,
182, 192, 4th 15, 19,
20, 6th 192, 8th 179,
180, 9th 178, 181,
17th 200, 201, 204
1st Royal Guernsey 182,
187, 188
Royal Inniskilling Fus 1st
133, 136, 137, 141,
222, 9th 230, 231, 233,
236, 11th 231
3rd Royal Irish Rifles 234

Royal Munster Fus 2nd
51, 53, 3rd 52
Royal Scots 15th 105,
16th 104, 17th 68
Royal Sussex 9 (S) 1, 2, 4,
10th 4, 12th 63, 64,
66, 67, 13th 63
2/7th Royal Warwickshire
230, 231
Royal Welch Fus 2nd 42,
43, 10th 15
6th Royal West Kents 7
5th Seaforth Highlanders
127, 129,130
15th Sherwood Foresters
101
3rd Somerset Light Inf
54
South Wales Bord 1st 53,
2nd 136
Suffolk 1st 111, 2nd 15,
9th 109, 11th 104,
106, 107
Tanks 1st 122
West Yorkshire 17th 68,
69, 70, 2/7th 162
2nd Wiltshire 84
3rd Worcester 28

Cavalry
2nd Cavalry Division
163, 164

Cavalry Regiments
Bedfordshire Imperial
Yeomanry 166
King Edward's Horse
140
Oxfordshire Yeo 162
4th Queen's Own Hussars
191
5th Royal Irish Lancers
54, 162, 163, 165, 166
Tunnelling Companies
170th 5, 254th 46, 50,
255th 84

Field Companies
497th 183, 188

Field Ambulances
29th Division 188, 88th
192, 89th 190
No: 142 18

Field Hospitals
2nd Canadian 39

Casualty Clearing Stations
No 6th (Canadian) 98,
No 7: 83, No: 42, 229,
No: 48, 226

Australian Army
5th Infantry Brigade 57
17th Bn. New South
Wales Bn 55, 56, 57

Canadian Army
1st Corps 72
1st Div 53. 72, 75, 81,
2nd 72, 77, 78, 89, 90,
3rd 72, 4th 73, 89,
5th 73, 10th 83, 11th
83

Cavalry Divisions
5th 147

Cavalry Regiments
19th Alberta Dragoons
154,15th Alberta Light
Horse 154, Fort Garry
Horse 147, 148, 150,
151, 7th Mounted
Rifles 153

Infantry Brigades
1st 77, 2nd 73, 77, 3rd
77, 4th 79, 6th 90, 91,
10th 91, 93

Battalions
1st 95,98
2nd 79, 86, 87
3rd 79
4th 78
5th 73, 77
7th 73, 75, 80
8th 73, 75
10th 73, 80
11th 81. 83

12th 86
13th 73
15th 73
16th 73, 98
20th 78, 79, 80, 84
24th 93
27th 89, 90
29th 89, 90, 91, 94
30th 81
44th 93
46th 91
47th 81, 91, 92, 93, 94, 97
49th 154
50th 91
52nd 90
77th 97
1st Foot Guard 89

Canadian Field Ambulance
No 4: 84
No 7 Stationery Hospital 86, 94
No 8 General Hosp 87, 154
No 12 Stationery Hosp 154

Indian
Mhow Bde 215
2nd Lancers 215, 221
28 Light Cavalry 215, 221

New Zealand
2nd Anzac Corps 237
1st Otago Battalion 238
1st Canterbury 239, 241
2nd Canterbury 238
12th Nelson 237

Hospital
2nd New Zealand 242

German Army
Divisions and Regiment
50th Reserve Div 56
54th xii
107th xii, 183
27th Inf Regt 52,

INDIVIDUALS
Abraham, W. G. 234
Ainscrow, H. M. 62

Barclay, M. E. 142
Baxter, E. F. VC pages 22–25, 38
Belcher, R. 174
Benzecry, Lt. 200
Biggart, Lt. 168
Bloy, L.H. 59
Booth, F. C. VC 152
Borton, A. VC 134, 190
Bradford, R. B VC xiv
Brooke, G. 147
Brooks, O. VC 144
Brown, H. VC 72–88
Browning, J. A. 19
Butler, W. B. VC 68–71, 96, 98
Byng, Sir J. x, 8, 156

Camden, H. 57
Campbell, D 148, 149, 151
Cape, H. A. 163
Carpenter, G. G. 15
Carter, N. V. VC 63–67
Cattermole, Pte. 195
Chafer, G. W. VC 32–35
Cheape, Brig.-Gen. G. R. H. 190
Churchill, W. S. 142, 143, 144
Clare, G. W. B. 162–166
Cooper, N. B. Elliott VC 178–181
Cotter, B 11, 12
Cotter, W. R. VC 5–13
Currie, Sir A. W. 72

Day, S VC 104–112
Dease, M. VC 19
Denikin, Gen 142
Dent, Maj 142
Devonshire, Duke of 84
Diarmid, A. M. C. McReady VC 205–209
Duncan, C. W. 122

Edwards, Brig Gen. 25
Edwards, W. VC 70, 71

Egerton, E. VC 70, 81, 95, 98
Elles, H. x, xi, xii
Ellis, Pte., 66
Emerson, J. S. VC 230–236
Erskine, J. VC 42–45

Fagan E. A. 22
Feilding, G. P. 156
Foster, E VC 120
French, Sir J. ix
Fuller, J. E. C xii, xiii

Gee, R. VC 134, 139, 182–196
Gerard, Capt. 211
Glascoe, Lance Cpl 164
Godley, S. VC 18, 20
Gort, Visc. VC 211
Gough, H. 9, 10
Gourley, C. E. VC 167–172
Greenly, W. H. 163, 164
Grigg, T. G. D. 65

Hackett, W. VC 46–50
Haig, Sir D. ix, x, xi, 38, 72
Haldane, J. A. L. 17
Hanna, R. VC 70, 81, 83, 89–100
Harper, G. M. xii, xiii
Hartley, Gunner 168
Hewitt, W. H. VC 152
Hoare, A 114, 116
Hobson, H. VC 72–88
Honey, S. L. VC 85
Horne, Sir Henry, 72
Hudson, C VC 143
Hudson, J. 168
Hutchinson, J. VC 59–62
Hutt, A. 152

Insley, E. A. 88
Ironside, Gen. 143

Jackson, W. VC 55–58
Jeudwine, H. S. 60
Joffre, Gen. 38
Johnson, T. W. G. 233
Johnston, G. N. 239
Jones, R. B. B. VC 26–31

Kelly, J. Sherwood VC 133, 134, 136–146, 190, 228
Kerr, G. F. VC 85
Kerr, J. C. VC 154
Kidd, A. 24
Kinnaird, The Hon. Arthur 158
Kinross, C. J. VC 154
Knowles, Maj. 217
Konowal, F. VC, 70, 81, 89–100

Lamarche, Nursing Sister 88
Lascelles, A. M. VC 222–229
Learmonth, O. M. 72–88
Lloyd George, D. 142
Loseby, Capt. 187, 188
Luard, Sister K. E. 9

Macintyre, A. C. 129
Mackenzie, Sir V. 159
McAulay, J. VC 156–161
McBeath, R. VC 127- 131
McNair, E. A. VC 1–4
McNair, Sir G. D. 3
Martyn, Brig.-Gen. 142
May, H.VC 160
Mellish, E.N. VC 14–21, 40
Mills, W. VC 243–247
Nelson, H. 147
Newman, Lance Cpl. 8
Nicholas, H. J. VC 237–242
Niblett, H. 195

Ockenden, J. VC 70, 81, 95, 98
O' Rourke, M. VC 70, 72–88, 95, 98, 154

Parsons, H. F. VC 101–103
Paton, G. H. T. VC 210–214
Payne, W. Hackett 234
Peacocke, Lt. Col. 233
Pereira, C. E. 201
Pitcher, E. VC 70, 81, 95, 98
Plumer, Sir H 14

Pooll, A. H. H. Batten VC 51–54
Procter, A. H. VC 21, 36–41
Pulteney, Sir W. 190

Ram Sowar Jot, 218
Rawlinson, Sir H. 143
Richards, F. 43
Ridealgh, Lt. 167
Robins, Pte 15
Robinson, H. C. T. 64, 66
Robinson, W. L. VC 124
Royal, Princess 71
Russell, J. Fox VC 124

Sanders, G VC 71
Seely, J. E. B. 147
Shaw, Captain 140
Shepherd, A. E. VC 114–120
Shildrick, L. R. 51
Singh, Gobind VC 215–221
Singhhji, Sir P. 219
Spackman, C. E. VC 132–135, 139, 190
Spencer, W. E. C. 65
Stair, Earl of 160
Stevenson, D. 43
Stewart, P. Shaw 212
Stone, W. VC 200–204
Stoney, G. B. 141
Storkey, P. V. VC 240
Strachan, H. VC 83, 96, 147–155
Streatfield, Sir H. 211

Thomas, J. VC 197–199
Thrupp, H. 66
Tombs, J. VC 38
Tuck, G. L. J. 111

Vernon, W. H. 48

Wain, R. W. L. VC 121–126
Wales, Prince of, 3, 4, 35, 82, 245, 247
Walker, Capt. 233
Wallace, S. T. D. VC 173–177
Ward, R. O. C. 7

Wedon, D. B. 92
Willis, R. B. VC 141
Wilson, L/Sgt. 222
Woollcombe, Lt Gen. 156
Wooley, G. VC 21, 40
Wynne, A. G. 244

Young, W. VC 1

PLACES

Albert 32
Alexander Trench 7
Archangel 142
Armentières ix, 55
Arras 26, 36, 171
Auguste Cité Road 90

Banteux 173
Basseux 136
Beaufort 142
Beaumetz 36
Berlaimont 227
Bethune 243
Beuvry 244
Bienvillers-au-Bois 107
Big Willie 5, 181
Bird Cage 68, 168
Birr Cross Roads 238, 239
Blairville ix, 22, 24, 26, 38, 42, 59
Bleak House 178
Boar's Head 63, 65
Boesinghe 214
Boiry-St-Martin 24
Boiry-Ste-Rictrude 24
Bois Grenier 55
Bois Hugo 73, 79
Bois Rase 73
Bonavis Ridge xii, 178
Bourlon xi, xiii, xiv, 156, 162
Bourlon Wood 156, 162, 163, 197, 201, 210
Broadmarsh Crater 31

Calonne ix
Cambrai 130, 156
Canal du Nord x, xiii, 205
Cantaing xii, 130, 158
Caporetto xi

Catelet Copse 217, 218
Chalk Quarry 75, 76, 79
Chantilly ix
Chord 5, 7, 181
Cinnabar Trench 90
Cité Calonne 51
Cité Du Grande Conde 90
Cité du Moulin 92
Cité St Auguste 75, 76
Cité St Edouard 73
Cité St Elizabeth 73
Cité St Emile 73, 89
Cité St Laurent 73
Cologne Farm Ridge 104, 105
Couillet Valley 115, 132
Couillet Wood 123, 231
Crèvecour xii, 121
Crinchon Valley 171
Delville Wood 146
Dessart Wood 132
Dickebusch 238
Duck's Bill 42, 43

Eagle Quarry 167
Eclaibes 227
Edda Weg 205
Épehy 68, 101, 102, 167, 217, 219
Escaillon 240
Escaudoeuvres 148
Etaples 227

Ficheux 22, 36, 38, 39, 42, 59
Flesquières xii, xiii, 127, 129
Fontaine-les-Croisilles 44
Fontaine-Notre-Dame xiii, 156, 158, 159, 162, 197, 198, 210

Gallipoli Peninsula 57, 247
Genoa 3
Gillemont Farm 68, 112, 167, 215
Givenchy ix, 42, 46
Gonnelieu xiv, 121, 173, 175, 210, 214, 215
Good Old Man Farm 114, 116, 122, 123, 124

Gouzeaucourt xiv, 121, 132, 136, 147, 210, 230
Graincourt xii, xiii
Grand Ravine 127
Green Crassier 93

Hargicourt 104
Havrincourt xi, xii, xiii, 118, 127, 136,
Henin Hill 44
Highland Ridge 222
Hill 70 x, 72, 73, 77, 89, 91
Hindenburg Line x, xi 44, 68, 101, 102, 104, 114, 121, 127, 130, 136, 178, 205, 222, 230, 231
Hohenzollern Redoubt ix, 5, 9, 12, 181
Holts Bank 168
Hooge ix, 1
Howe Camp 239
Huzzar Post 104

Kildare Post 218
Kildare Trench 218, 219
Knoll 101, 102, 217

La Bassée 42, 63, 243
Laffaux x
La Folie Wood 158
Lark Spur 217
La Vacquerie xiv, 114, 121, 178, 179, 187, 230
Lempire 68, 215, 219
Lens x, 51, 72, 89, 92, 95
Les Rues Vertes 147, 183, 184, 186, 187, 188, 189, 190, 195
Le Tombois Farm 215
Lievin 51
Lillers 9
Limerick Post 217, 218
Limont- Fontaine 227
Little Priel Farm 68, 167, 169, 218
Little Willie 5, 181
Loos ix, 45

Maizières 31
Malakhoff Farm 104, 105, 106, 112
Marcoing xii, xiii, 113, 114, 121, 132, 136, 182, 183, 189, 190, 222, 224
Masnières xii, 132, 134, 136, 137, 147, 148, 150, 151, 182, 188, 189, 195
Méaulte ix, 32, 34
Messines Ridge 171
Metz-en-Couture 173, 210
Monchy le Preux 44
Moeuvres xiv, 200, 205
Mon Plaisir Farm 149
Mont St Eloi 31
Mormal Forest 227
Murmansk 142

Niagara Camp 93
Nimy Bridge 19

Orchard Road 122
Omsk 142
Ostrich Avenue 230
Passchendaele 53, 160
Peizière 215, 219
Pigeon Ravine 215
Polderhoek Chateau 237
Pont- Remy 171
Priel Wood 104

Quail Ravine 215
Quentin Ridge 210

Rat's Tail 200
Red Dragon Crater 43, 46, 47, 243
Ribecourt 127, 128, 224
Richebourg l'Avoue ix, 63
Ronssoy 68
Rouen 141, 241, 242
Rumilly 148, 149, 150, 151

St Eloi ix, 14, 18
St Emilie 101
Ste Emilie 68, 219
St Martin-sur-Cojeul 44
St Omer 242
St Quentin 68, 215

St Quentin Canal xi, xiii, 101, 182, 222
Sallaumines 72
Sanctuary Wood 1
Scherriabeek Valley 237, 238
Shaftesbury Avenue Mine 46
Sorel 142

Targelle Ravine 215, 217
Tournant Farm 53
Trescault 127
Triangle Crater 5, 7
Triangle Trench 105, 106
Troitsa 142
Twenty-Two Ravine 173

Vadencourt Château 107
Valenciennes xi
Vat Cottages 53, 54
Veal Cottages 53, 54
Vendhuille xiv, 101, 215
Verdun ix, 1
Villers Faucon 68, 102
Villers Guislain 174, 215
Villers-Plouich 114, 120 124, 132, 136, 173, 174, 222
Villers Ridge 168
Vimy Ridge ix, x, 26

Wancourt 141
Welsh Ridge 114, 230, 231, 232
Wizernes 134, 139, 190
Wytschaete 14

Ypres Salient 1

**CEMETERIES/-
MEMORIALS**

Arras, 30, 44, 61
Australian War Memorial, 58

Aubigny Communal Cemetery Extension, 30

Beaudignies 240
Brookwood 145

Cambrai (Louverval) Memorial 121, 165, 203, 207, 234
Chatteris War Memorial 165
Chichester Cathedral 66
Chichester Memorial Hall 11

Doullers CCE 227
Dursley War Memorial 207
Dysart 45

Fillèvres British Cemetery 24
Flesquières Hill BC 151
Forest Lawn Burial Park 83
Glasgow New Eastern 161
Gorre British 43, 243, 244, 245

Grange Cemetery, West Kirby 172

Hamburg 179
Helen' s Tower 96
Hunslet 71

Jasper National Park 130
Karrakatta Crematorium 195

Lillers Communal 10, 12
Limont- Fontaine 228

Masonic Cemetery, Burnaby 96

Metz-en-Couture CC 212
Milton 111
Moffat 177
Mountain View Crematorium 131

New Munich Trench 45
Noeux-les-Mines CC 77, 80, 83, 88
North Vancouver Crematorium 155
Notre Dame 100

Pennal 227
Ploegsteert 49
Putney Vale Cemetery 212

Riddrie 160
Royal Irish Rifles 65, 67
Royston 120

St Anne's Cathedral, Belfast 145
St Lawrence's, Woolverton, 54
St Mary's, Great Dunmow 21
Sheffield Cathedral 41
Spring Vale Crematorium 58
Staglieno 3
Stockport Borough 200
Swaythling Crematorium 135

Tincourt New British 116
Torquay Crematorium 62

Vertigneul 240
Villers Faucon CCE 102
Vimy Memorial 84